THE LEGACY OF

DAVID FOSTER WALLACE

THE NEW AMERICAN CANON

The Iowa Series in Contemporary Literature and Culture

Samuel Cohen, series editor

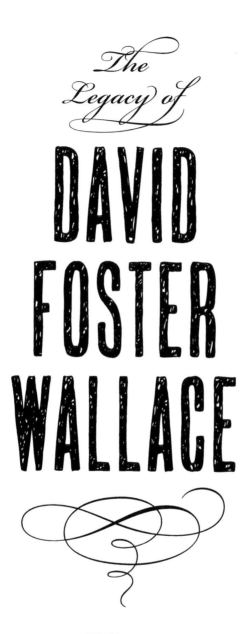

The
Legacy of

DAVID
FOSTER
WALLACE

EDITED BY

SAMUEL COHEN AND LEE KONSTANTINOU

University of Iowa Press, Iowa City

University of Iowa Press, Iowa City 52242
Copyright © 2012 by the University of Iowa Press
www.uiowapress.org
Printed in the United States of America
Design by April Leidig

The University of Iowa Press is a member of Green Press
Initiative and is committed to preserving natural resources.
Printed on acid-free paper

Library of Congress Cataloging-in-Publication Data
The legacy of David Foster Wallace /
edited by Samuel Cohen and Lee Konstantinou.
p. cm. — (The new American canon: The Iowa series
in contemporary literature and culture)
Includes bibliographical references and index.
ISBN-13: 978-1-60938-082-3, ISBN-10: 1-60938-082-7 (pbk)
ISBN-13: 978-1-60938-104-2, ISBN-10: 1-60938-104-1 (ebook)
1. Wallace, David Foster — Criticism and interpretation.
I. Cohen, Samuel S. II. Konstantinou, Lee.
PS3573.A425635Z73 2012
813'.54 — dc23 2011042542

CONTENTS

Part 2. Aesthetics

Part 3. Community

ACKNOWLEDGMENTS

THE EDITORS WOULD LIKE to thank the contributors to this volume for letting us bring together their words on Wallace's words and their words on Wallace. The intensity of their engagement with his life's work, their appreciation and love for it, drove our desire to put together a book on his legacy as much as our own wish to say what we had to say. We would like to acknowledge the invaluable help of Michael Pietsch, without whose blessing we wouldn't have wanted to move forward with the project. Joe Parsons is owed a huge thank you for his support, early and late, as are many others at Iowa — Jim McCoy, Charlotte Wright, Karen Copp, Allison Means, and everyone else who helped bring this book into the world. Sam would like to acknowledge the support of the University of Missouri and his department, and Lee extends his gratitude for the support and resources provided by the English Department and Program in Writing and Rhetoric at Stanford University, the English Department at Princeton University, and the ACLS New Faculty Fellows Program. We both want to thank our families and friends for their encouragement. The original MLA panelists and the wonderful audience at the panel contributed greatly to our thinking on Wallace, as did many others, both fans and scholars, in the wider world of Wallace appreciators. Most of all, we would like to have been able to thank Wallace himself for his work, about which we are, as *Infinite Jest*'s Don Gately says of himself, "probably mostly still clueless," but for which we are, also like Gately, grateful, both for its beauty and complexity and also for the "whiff of what's true and deep" it affords us.

SAMUEL COHEN AND LEE KONSTANTINOU

INTRODUCTION:
ZOOLOGISTS, ELEPHANTS,
AND EDITORS

EDITING A COLLECTION of academic essays is a pretty complicated thing. As an editor, you get to modify and frame the work of other writers, to mediate that work's entry into the world, to say what it all means, especially in introductions like this one. And yet, if you're a good editor, you're also, contrarily, committed to suspending your judgment in the interest of letting the essays you've gathered speak for their own excellent selves in an undistorted fashion. After all, the strength and insight of the collected essays were in part what motivated you to gather them together in the first place.[1] What could sincerely and humbly service-minded editors possibly add? As the sincerely and humbly service-minded editors of the collection of essays you're holding in your hands,[2] a collection about the still undecided literary legacy[3] of David Foster Wallace, an author universally acknowledged to be pretty obsessed with mediation in all its many paradoxical forms, we are probably even more uncomfortably conscious of how we might shape or distort or belie the rest of these essays than is usually the case. And yet it's our editorial duty to make some sort of authoritative statement, however provisional and subject to dispute, about what this book adds up to.

Let us start with a certain preponderance of key words we noticed as we were reading through these essays, presented in alphabetical order: communication, connection, difficult, human, irony, mediate, personal, sadness, suffering. That these words are overwhelmingly deployed in these analyses of Wallace's life and work may be regarded as a reinforcement of critical clichés, clichés already fully formed even in the earliest studies of Wallace — which often read his fiction in terms laid out in his essays and interviews — and yet how can critics not be acutely aware of the impassioned defense the author under scrutiny here mounted of cliché? Sometimes, despite the cheapening of the term in our Age of the Social Network, human beings do seek to connect with each other; we want to talk about how we are sad and about what it means to be human, and we sometimes want to do so through the medium of fiction. To describe Wallace as interested in connection or communication or alleviating sadness through the form of fiction may already be a cliché, but it also happens to be a true cliché, and such a description will very likely form the basis for every future analysis of Wallace's legacy, even those analyses that dispute these terms.

Which brings us to a paradox that haunts all critical writing about literature, a paradox that obliquely highlights the third obligation of editors of academic essay collections. At least since W. K. Wimsatt Jr. and M. C. Beardsley named, and in naming condemned, the "intentional fallacy"—and promoted the alternate view that "the design or intention of the author is neither available nor desirable as a standard for judging the success of a work of literary art" (468) — and since the New Critics more generally successfully stigmatized biography-based fallacies of all sorts, academic literary study has had a hard time knowing what to do with the fact of the author's existence. Our fear of committing the intentional/biographical fallacy is in part born of our related fear that if we focus our attention on all the ways in which the life and opinions of an author can be found in her creative work, we risk forgetting that literature is just as often or primarily the product of imagination and that authors don't necessarily have superior understandings of their own compositional practices or the significance of what they've produced. Many of these New Critical concerns migrated very directly into what used to be called Theory (and it is in terms of the legacy of Theory that questions of authorial intention are usually discussed today). Though proponents of Theory held a much more skeptical view of the stability of literary meaning than the New Critics did, both schools or intellectual dispositions agreed that the author has no business telling us what her texts mean. There is a lively debate that has arisen in the wake of the New Criticism and Theory around the premise, promoted with great verve by Walter Benn Michaels, that this orthodoxy is incorrect, that the intentional/biographical fallacy is no fallacy at all. Michaels provocatively maintains not only that intention *should* matter to literary study but also that intention is *the only thing* that should matter. Against Michaels's view, Wallace himself seemed to endorse the idea that when he finished with a piece of writing its subsequent interpretations were largely up to the reader.[4] And yet Wallace also insisted, across both his fiction and nonfiction, that art was a form of communication between minds. As the essays in this collection all show in one way or another, the debate over intentionality comes very directly to the heart of the interpretive challenges facing those who are interested in judging his legacy. If we insist on treating his fictions as unrelated to his goals and his life, do we risk overlooking the significant continuities (both stylistic and thematic) across his fiction and nonfiction? If we think his biography does matter, do we risk turning his stories into mere symptoms of his experience, eliding or effacing his artistry?

Without attempting to answer these questions definitively, the editors will now use their editorial bully pulpit to stipulate that since this is a book about David Foster Wallace and his writing, we feel an obligation to give you some essential facts about the person these essays discuss.[5] Here we go: Wallace was born in 1962 in Ithaca, New York, but grew up in Illinois, a state whose unique geography he often wrote about, including most recently in his posthumously published third novel, *The Pale King*, which is set at the IRS's Midwest Regional Examination Center in Peoria, Illinois. After achieving near greatness as a teenage tennis player, Wallace headed east to attend Amherst College; he entered Amherst as someone who thought of himself as a budding analytical philosopher and left as someone who saw his primary vocation as writing fiction. He published his first novel, *The Broom of the System*, in 1987, shortly after he graduated from college. On 12 September 2008, after he stopped taking the antidepressant Nardil, he hanged himself in his patio in Claremont, California. Between 1987 and 2008, the range and power of his literary output find few peers in his generation (William

Vollmann comes closest).[6] In that brief but creatively fecund time, Wallace published ten books: two nonfiction collections (*A Supposedly Fun Thing I'll Never Do Again* and *Consider the Lobster*), three short story collections (*Girl with Curious Hair*, *Brief Interviews with Hideous Men*, and *Oblivion*), two very long novels (*The Broom of the System* and *Infinite Jest*), a mathematically sophisticated book on the history of infinity, and a coauthored book about rap culture (with Mark Costello).

As D. T. Max's *New Yorker* profile makes clear, Wallace's published work is only the tip of the iceberg of what he actually wrote. His stories and essays often went through multiple drafts, and for every piece he thought worth trying to make public there are many more that never saw daylight. To complicate matters further, he published many pieces that remain uncollected.[7] At the time of this writing, *The Pale King*, Wallace's unfinished third novel, has just been released to lavish (in our view, deserved) critical praise, and there's reason to expect that his uncollected writings will shortly be collected.[8] Now that his papers are available at the University of Texas at Austin's Harry Ransom Center, we will more likely than not be learning more about the true range of his productivity during those twenty years *mirabiles*.

Understandably, much critical attention has been dedicated to *Infinite Jest*, the thousand-plus-page encyclopedic novel about terminal addiction that Wallace released into the world in 1996. This collection tries to expand the standard critical focus on *Infinite Jest* to include previously overlooked areas of Wallace's work, including especially his journalism. Still, there are significant gaps in what we're offering here. Few studies, perhaps following Wallace's own recommendation, have examined *The Broom of the System* or Wallace's engagement with philosophy and the history of mathematics. Marshall Boswell's *Understanding David Foster Wallace* provides the most comprehensive overview of the author's life and work presently available, and there is a wide range of excellent essays in *Consider David Foster Wallace: Critical Essays*, edited by David Hering, but much more work needs to be done. We have no doubt that future studies will correct our oversights and will build upon the foundation of already extensive research on Wallace and his place in literary history.

If we're not attempting to be comprehensive in this collection, what is our purpose? We can answer this question best by discussing what might be regarded as the unusual choice of soliciting and including writing by Wallace's literary colleagues and friends. Why critical *and* creative assessments? The usual M.O. in academic publishing is to analyze creative writers but not to invite them into conversations about either their own work or the work of their peers. We might recall Roman Jakobson's snarky dismissal of the idea of giving Vladimir Nabokov a job in the Modern Language Department at Harvard: "Gentlemen, even if one allows that he is an important writer, are we next to invite an elephant to be Professor of Zoology?" (quoted in Boyd 303).[9] As at least one major recent study has noted, the elephants have been sitting in on the faculty meetings of zoologists for quite a while now.[10] Beyond this brute empirical reality — critics and creative types have at times been rumored to mingle, sometimes even to inhabit the skull of a single human person — why include creative and critical voices in the same volume? One of the tacit arguments of this collection, which we will now make nontacit, is that the strict separation of creative and critical writers is problematic, for a number of reasons. First of all, both creative writers and critics participate in the process of canonization, whether or not either party is fond of that fact. The critic might claim, adopting a narratological tone or the demeanor of an old-fashioned objective critic, to bear only a scientific interest in the authors she happens to be writing about, but such a claim misunderstands the true nature of canon formation. Even the hardest of hardcore narratologists typically studies only a very narrow range of literary texts and in making her selections participates in a collective process of textual canonization, based purely on the fact that she chooses one object of study over another.[11] Moreover, even if some truly disinterested criticism were possible, and we wouldn't want to categorically deny the possibility, we would argue against such a practice, at least as a universal norm for literary study.

The other reason to pair critical and creative types is that creative writers can be pretty critical people. Indeed, Wallace was nothing if not extremely well versed in the dominant critical debates of his era, and he actively sought to contest their orthodoxies, sometimes in his essays but often (we would claim) through his fiction. Across his writings, one finds numerous engagements at various levels of depth with criticism, theory, and complex social processes of mediation that have increasingly become the defining concerns of post-WWII literary criticism. So our argument boils down to this: critics are always picking winners, sometimes against their own stated desires, and artists are, at least in the case of the highly savvy literary circles Wallace ran in, very much engaged with critics and their theories. Everyone everywhere is mediating, re-mediating, intermediating, disintermediating, and hypermediating everyone else. Our way through this Gordian knot of (please forgive us) panmediation is just to admit what we're up to: we're trying to get you to read more writing by David Foster Wallace. We think his writing is pretty great and rewards careful reading. And we think juxtaposing comments by creative and critical writers can help us figure out the precise contours of how and why his writing is so great, without, we hope, descending into uncritical fandom or hagiography. These essays bring a variety of resources to the project of examining Wallace both disinterestedly and with a deep sense of the power of his achievement. We think the creative testimonials speak for themselves, but it's conventional to give an overview of chapters in critical collections.[12] We have been very conscious of the order in which we have grouped these essays and have tried to interpolate the shorter creative pieces in ways that resonate with the critical essays that surround them. If you're interested in experiencing maximal synergistic creative-critical magic, we recommend you read the essays in order. We've grouped the critical essays into three broad thematic clusters, though other orders are obviously possible. The three broad areas are History, Aesthetics, and Community.

The first grouping (History) considers Wallace across American literary and journalistic history. Paul Giles examines where Wallace fits into the broad sweep of American writing and the project of formulating a distinctly American literary voice, noting how Wallace both invokes an American literary tradition and also pays close attention to the new digital environments we find ourselves embedded within. Discussing a range of Wallace's writing, and coordinating that writing both synchronically (in its moment) and diachronically (in relation to history), Giles argues that Wallace, sometimes reluctantly, makes use of a "hortatory idiom"— that is, he becomes almost preacherly in his style — which allows his writing to be "emotionally affective and ruthlessly abstract" at the same time. As our culture becomes more transnational and as technology dramatically reconfigures what we used to call our subjectivity, we might find ourselves looking to Wallace with increasing frequency, either for a sign of what we are becoming or for possible usable strategies to resist those powerful historical transformations. As Giles notes, Wallace was deeply invested in the possibility of human authenticity, even as he grappled with a neopragmatist and quasi-deconstructionist sense that we might be nothing more than discourse or pretense or irony,[13] all the way down. For his part, Josh Roiland takes us on an epic tour of Wallace's journalism. Roiland quite rightly focuses on how Wallace's prodigious eye for detail and massively long nonfiction pieces bespeak a commitment to seeing what most of us would prefer to ignore. Wallace's manic consciousness led him "to chronicle nearly everything he encountered" and informed his critique of contemporary American consumer culture, which he thought was designed (from television to cruise ships) to obviate thought, reflection, and awareness. Roiland provocatively suggests that what Wallace regarded as his "job"— the banishment of the oblivion we use as a means of getting through the day — Nietzsche would have regarded as pathological, an inability to let go of memories and other forms of toxic consciousness. If Wallace thought we ought to pay attention to everything (especially human pain and suffering), Nietzsche argued that forgetting or letting go was a precondition for achieving our nobler capacities, such as reflection and planning. Whether we regard Wallace's hyperattentiveness as crippling or absolutely necessary, there can be no doubt about the importance of his style to the development of U.S. literary journalism at the end of the twentieth and beginning of the twenty-first centuries. Roiland's essay is, to our knowledge, the only comprehensive assessment of that powerful legacy to date.

The second group of essays in this collection focuses on aesthetics. In particular, this group examines the relationship between what Wallace said he thought fiction should accomplish and his own aesthetic experiments. Perhaps necessarily, then, this group zeroes in on what is undoubtedly Wallace's magnum opus, his second novel, *Infinite Jest*. Samuel Cohen argues that the allegedly unresolved ending of *Infinite Jest* has been widely misread. Critics often focus on the ambiguity or lack of resolution of the novel's plotlines without acknowledging that the opening chapter of the book, which depicts Hal describing a nervous breakdown in the first person, takes place chronologically after its diegetic end. What this implies is that *Infinite Jest* is less a novel of degradation and mental breakdown than it is a story of discovering a lost self or first person. Cohen argues that this discovery of the first person might, in light of Wallace's own biography, suggest that *Infinite Jest* is a *Künstlerroman*, the story of the growth and development of an artist, where Hal is in much the same position (it is reasonable to assume) Wallace was in in the early 1990s before he wrote *Infinite Jest*. Hal's bottom — both a personal bottom and a historical bottom, as Cohen shows — can be reframed as the start of his recuperation of self. Moreover, *Infinite Jest* is less the post-postmodern end Wallace aspired to invent than part of his way of figuring out what should come next in American literary art. Also concerned with discourses of the End of History that dominated the intellectual culture of the early 1990s, Lee Konstantinou shows how Wallace participated in the larger project of creating a postironic update to metafiction (a tradition that had come to seem exhausted by the early 1990s). Wallace's commitment to imagining a form of postirony can be seen across his essays and stories as well as in *Infinite Jest*. Konstantinou argues that Wallace diagnosed disbelief or incredulity as being at the heart of the sadness and listlessness that defined the American End of History. Against this ubiquitous culture of disbelief, which traditional metafiction and postmodern fiction was supposed to help actively cultivate, Wallace wanted to plant the seeds of belief, to entreat his readers to become believers. Wallace's true aesthetic innovation, Konstantinou finally argues, came in repurposing metafiction to achieve these new ends. Heather Houser addresses the feelings of disconnection Wallace wanted his readers to overcome, but innovatively moves beyond the usual thematics that dominate criticism of *Infinite Jest*, taking us on a rare journey into Wallace's ecological imagination. Houser explores the relationships among syntactic, emotional, and environmental detachment in *Infinite Jest*, particularly as these different senses of detachment relate to the toxic waste dump the United States expels into Canada in the novel's imagined near future. Houser argues that Wallace's satirical vision of "experialism" gives us a powerful insight into how bodies and environments "cobuild" each other. Ultimately, what Houser finds is that Wallace uses the affect of disgust and the description of a range of almost Rabelaisian grotesqueries as a means (an often hilarious means) through which to break through the emotional walls of isolation, solipsism, and detachment that characterize contemporary subjects.

From here, our final quartet of essays each addresses the question of community and mediation. That is, if Wallace was incredibly concerned with how he related to his readers, Wallace criticism does well to attend to his real effects on his real readers. Ed Finn gives us a preview of his network analysis of Wallace's relationship to the marketplace, inspired by Franco Moretti's "distant reading" program and recent scholarship in literary sociology. Using large datasets drawn from Amazon reader recommendations and professional book reviews of Wallace's work, Finn gives us a rich empirical picture of how different types of readers consume Wallace's work in a variety of contexts. Finn is concerned with the "interpretive dialogue" of an author and her readers, and finds that in the case of Wallace different social networks situate the author's work very differently. When one looks at Amazon book recommendations, for example, one finds patterns of linking that are highly eccentric and different from Wallace's contemporaries at the same time that Wallace, like many canonical authors, forms a very powerful network among his own large body of works. Readers who buy Wallace books tend, perhaps unsurprisingly, to buy more Wallace. Meanwhile, collocations of professional and Amazon reviewers reveal another intriguing divergence. Whereas professional reviewers tend to link Wallace to his contemporaries (Franzen, Vollmann, Moody, Saunders) and canonical postmodernist writers (Gaddis, DeLillo, Pynchon), Amazon reviewers see him more broadly through the lens of the canon of Great Books (Cervantes, Melville, Hugo, Tolstoy, Kafka). Finn's contribution to Wallace studies, we think, comes not only from his fascinating conclusions but also from his methodology, which allows us to answer questions about our literary life we didn't even know we could ask. Studying how Wallace's fiction was discussed after his death, Kathleen Fitzpatrick looks at the *Infinite Summer* project of 2009, which gathered a community of readers together to "finally" get through a book many perhaps purchased in the late 1990s but never got around to actually reading. What begins as a study of *Infinite Summer* turns into a far more widespread investigation into different ways that readers invest emotionally in fiction. Fitzpatrick warns against "an unhealthy transformation of artist into celebrity fetish object," especially after the death of that artist, but finds that genuine communities did in fact form in the wake of Wallace's death and that these online communities, perhaps ironically, give lie to some of Wallace's own worries about the degraded and dehumanizing and community-crushing nature of new media. Whereas Wallace imagined the future of media in terms of the one-to-many centralized networks of television or George Gilder's speculative "telecomputer" system, Fitzpatrick points out how the specifically author-centered affordances of the blog brought together a wide range of readers into dialogues that inspired new writing. Rather than inspiring mere "sympathy"—brought on by readerly investment in "relatable" characters, a type of naïve reading practice typically associated with groups such as Oprah's Book Club and book clubs in general—Wallace's fiction inspires "more thoughtful forms of empathy," deeply connecting readers to each other despite the fact that the characters in *Infinite Jest* very much preserve what Dominick LaCapra might call "the otherness of the Other."

The final two essays in this section are concerned less with the empirical community of Wallace's readers than with the subtler cross-textual mediations that, though theoretically at work in all texts, were particularly visible and active in Wallace's work. Offering a magisterial overview of Wallace's use of the footnote—the stylistic tic or flourish he was probably most famous for — Ira B. Nadel argues that the footnote (or the endnote) is a "visual expression and confirmation of his nonlinear thinking." That is, "footnotes or endnotes demonstrate the active intellectual and creative energy of Wallace on and off the page while also exhibiting the double consciousness of the text." While Wallace used footnotes, endnotes, and (in his essay "Host") physically boxed asides to convey a variety of ideas, and toward many different ends, he often justified his practice as a way of creating a homology on the page of what was going on in his head. And there was a lot going on in there, as Nadel shows. In the years to come, as scholars spend more time following his footnotes, the David Foster Wallace collection at the Harry Ransom Center will become increasingly valuable. This is why we are so pleased to be able to conclude with Molly Schwartzburg's overview of the mediation process his papers went through. Schwartzburg's primary purpose is to "explain the specific ways that Wallace's materials have been mediated since their arrival at the Ransom Center, making explicit what makes possible the moment in which a researcher first encounters a Wallace artifact in our Reading and Viewing Room." And yet what emerges, as a sort of subtext to Schwartzburg's curatorial narrative, is both the tremendous excitement that the acquisition of Wallace's papers aroused in everyone who worked at the Ransom Center and the extraordinary quality of that collection. What the collection reveals — from Wallace's early drafts to his annotations on books in his personal library — is the way that footnoting and annotation were not merely stylistic devices but strategies for living.

Wallace's exegetical impulse is, these essays make clear, crucial to understanding how Wallace got through his days, how he saw his relationship to history, and how he wanted to communicate or connect with his readers and with other writers. We're sure that if Wallace were able to read this collection, he would actively respond to what he found here with his felt pen. He would mark the margins of these pages with approval, with disagreement, with questions, and with purely private notes. We invite you to do the same.

Notes

1. This collection originated as a December 2009 MLA roundtable called "The Legacy of David Foster Wallace." The present editors organized this special session, but some roundtable participants didn't contribute to the collection, and some nonparticipants ended up submitting essays to this volume.

2. We recognize you may have elected to place this book on a table, but this choice doesn't negate the strong likelihood that your hands are proximate to the pages of this book, especially since (we hope) you've just made an effort to turn to these endnotes. As a rule, or if a rule is too strict let's say as a courtesy (we don't want to be scolds), please do follow these numerological superscripts when you happen upon them, since after all the writers in this collection usually put them there for a reason, and if Wallace teaches us anything it's that you should be the sort of person who not only obligingly follows footnotes and endnotes but finds great value in doing so.

3. For the lexicographically minded, we note that the *OED* defines "legacy" in a number of ways, as a "legateship" or mission, as a postdemise bequest or monetary inheritance, and as "anything handed down by an ancestor or predecessor." All of these senses speak to our interest in Wallace's legacy. Rather than further expound upon the nuances of this frankly pretty loaded word, we'll let it stand relatively uncommented upon.

4. In an interview with Larry McCaffery, Wallace said, "This is the way Barthian and Derridean post-structuralism's helped me the most as a fiction writer: once I'm done with the thing, I'm basically dead, and probably the text's dead; it becomes simply language, and language lives not just in but 'through' the reader. The reader becomes God, for all textual purposes" (141). Of course, to cite Wallace's opinion on the question of the importance of avoiding the intentional/biographical fallacy — and the question of deadness of the author — might trap us in the Liar's Paradox–like situation of citing the author's assertion that we disregard his views as a warrant for the claim that we ought to disregard his views, which seems to defeat the purpose of the advice in the first place. The situation gets slightly more complicated depending on the precise formulation of the statement Wallace is making. If Wallace is saying, "No author is an authority on her writing," he has given us a version of the Cretan Paradox, which is resolvable; if the statement is false, some authors may be authorities on their writing, but Wallace would not be one of them. Paradox solved. If Wallace is saying, "I am not an authority on my own statements," we may be in trouble, unless we entertain the notion that one can have *some* authority with regard to one's statements but also make mistakes. There is also a possible conflation in our analysis in this footnote, and in Wallace's

original statement, of the *logical* status of intention as it relates to meaning and the *normative* practice of how we should interpret poetic sentences. We warned you, this stuff gets pretty complicated pretty quickly, which is why we're just going to avoid the whole subject from here on out.

5. Many of these facts are culled from D. T. Max's fantastic *New Yorker* article published shortly after Wallace's death. Max is writing a biography of Wallace, which will be published in 2012 by Viking.

6. Here please imagine a long and heated discussion between the editors over the relative merits of William Vollmann and Jonathan Lethem and a few other wonderful writers, which discussion we will spare you the details of and instead, in the interests of collegiality and with a recognition that pretty much nobody ever wins these kinds of arguments, move on.

7. The most complete bibliography of Wallace's writing has been put together by Ryan Niman on his Web site, *The Know(e)*. Niman scanned many previously uncollected works by Wallace, both fiction and nonfiction, and made them available as PDFs, before taking many of them down at the request of Wallace's agent, Bonnie Nadell (no known relation to Ira Nadel).

8. Wallace's senior philosophy thesis was published by Columbia University Press as *Fate, Time, and Language: An Essay on Free Will*, edited by Steven M. Cahn and Maureen Eckert. Several of his works have been republished in various contexts, including his essay on John McCain's 2000 presidential primary campaign and his 2005 Kenyon commencement address, which was posthumously republished as *This Is Water: Some Thoughts, Delivered on a Significant Occasion, about Living a Compassionate Life.*

9. Another version of the story reports Jakobson as saying, "What's next? Shall we appoint elephants to teach zoology?" and yet another has him saying, "I do respect very much the elephant, but would you give him the chair of Zoology?" Boyd offers the authoritative account, but you get the idea.

10. We speak of course of Mark McGurl, *The Program Era: Postwar Fiction and the Rise of Creative Writing*. One might also read D. G. Myers's appropriately titled *The Elephants Teach: Creative Writing since 1880.*

11. This fact no doubt is part of what inspired Franco Moretti to launch his "distant reading" research program. For a fascinating study suggesting that initial selections in a marketplace can shape the process of canonization, see Salganik, Dodds, and Watts's 2006 article, "Experimental Study of Inequality and Unpredictability in an Artificial Cultural Market." For a general discussion of debates about canonization within literary study you would not go wrong to read John Guillory, *Cultural Capital: The Problem of Literary Canon Formation*, or James F. English, *The Economy of Prestige: Prizes, Awards, and the Circulation of Cultural Value.* For discussions of the book market in par-

ticular, check out Gordon Hutner, *What America Read: Taste, Class, and the Novel, 1920–1960*, and Evan Brier, *A Novel Marketplace: Mass Culture, the Book Trade, and Postwar American Fiction*.

12. And, in spite of our flip tone in this introduction, which tone we affect out of a self-conscious and — let's be honest — probably misguided desire to express our affection for DFW's own by turns casual and erudite style, we are respectful of conventions such as these with respect to academic discourse, thank you very much.

13. (but not turtles)

Works Cited

Boswell, Marshall. *Understanding David Foster Wallace*. Columbia: University of South Carolina Press, 2003. Print.

Boyd, Brian. *Vladimir Nabokov: The American Years*. Princeton, NJ: Princeton University Press, 1993. Print.

Brier, Evan. *A Novel Marketplace: Mass Culture, the Book Trade, and Postwar American Fiction*. Philadelphia: University of Pennsylvania Press, 2009. Print.

English, James F. *The Economy of Prestige: Prizes, Awards, and the Circulation of Cultural Value*. Cambridge, MA: Harvard University Press, 2005. Print.

Guillory, John. *Cultural Capital: The Problem of Literary Canon Formation*. Chicago: University of Chicago Press, 1995. Print.

Hering, David, ed. *Consider David Foster Wallace: Critical Essays*. Universal City, CA: SSMG Press, 2010. Print.

Hutner, Gordon. *What America Read: Taste, Class, and the Novel, 1920–1960*. Chapel Hill: University of North Carolina Press, 2009. Print.

Max, D. T. "The Unfinished." *New Yorker* 9 March 2009. Web.

McCaffery, Larry. "An Interview with David Foster Wallace." *Review of Contemporary Fiction* 13.2 (Summer 1993): 127–50. Print.

McGurl, Mark. *The Program Era: Postwar Fiction and the Rise of Creative Writing*. Cambridge, MA: Harvard University Press, 2009. Print.

Michaels, Walter Benn. *The Shape of the Signifier: 1967 to the End of History*. Princeton, NJ: Princeton University Press, 2004. Print.

Moretti, Franco. "Conjectures on World Literature." *New Left Review* 1 (2000): 54–68. Print.

———. *Graphs, Maps, Trees: Abstract Models for Literary History*. London: Verso, 2007. Print.

Myers, D. G. *The Elephants Teach: Creative Writing since 1880*. Chicago: University of Chicago Press, 2006. Print.

Niman, Ryan. *The Know(e):dfw*. Web.

Salganik, Matthew J., Peter Sheridan Dodds, and Duncan J. Watts. "Experimental Study of Inequality and Unpredictability in an Artificial Cultural Market." *Science* 311.5762 (10 February 2006): 854–6. Print.

Wallace, David Foster. *Fate, Time, and Language: An Essay on Free Will*. Ed. Steven M. Cahn and Maureen Eckert. New York: Columbia University Press, 2010. Print.

———. *This Is Water: Some Thoughts, Delivered on a Significant Occasion, about Living a Compassionate Life*. New York: Little, Brown and Company, 2009. Print.

Wimsatt, W. K., Jr., and M. C. Beardsley. "The Intentional Fallacy." *Sewanee Review* 54.3 (July–September 1946): 468–88. Print.

PART ONE

HISTORY

PAUL GILES

ALL SWALLOWED UP:
DAVID FOSTER WALLACE AND
AMERICAN LITERATURE

THE IDEA OF "American Literature" as an area of professional expertise has had a checkered history. When this academic field was first mooted in the late nineteenth century, as Gerald Graff has observed, it tended to be regarded condescendingly by the Ivy League establishment as something suitable only for more populist forms of education in women's colleges or remote state universities (211); indeed, it was not until the 1920s, in the work of Norman Foerster and others, that the subject began properly to take on nationalistic contours rather than being identified simply with local color and other sectional interests. Writing under the shadow of World War I, when patriotic sentiment had been heightened within the scholarly as well as the political community, Foerster argued that American literature should seek to identify key nationalist tropes — "the Puritan tradition" (27), "the frontier spirit" (27), "romanticism" (32), and "realism" (34)— in the same way that Harvard professor Frederick Jackson Turner had recently invoked the significance of the frontier as crucial to the constitution of American history. The scholarly journal *American Literature*, founded in 1929, helped consolidate this process of institutionalization, and it was not until the last twenty years of the twentieth century that the nomenclature "American" came to be understood as problematic, since the increasing visibility of transnational flows across national boundaries exposed the ambiguity whereby the term could refer to either a country or a continent; indeed, more recently the category "U.S. Literature" has enjoyed increasing prominence. My argument here, though, is that the work of David Foster Wallace meditates self-consciously on what it means to be an "American" writer at the turn of the twenty-first century. Wallace's writing, I will suggest, emerges out of an intellectual heritage invested in quite traditional Americanist values, as adumbrated by Foerster: Transcendentalism, community spirit, self-reliance, and so on. At the same time, Wallace's acute responsiveness to new digital environments, within which liberal individualism has become a shadow of its former self, creates in his narratives an inherently ironic framework, one that explores the mythic romance of America even while recognizing how such assumptions are coming to appear increasingly strange and unfamiliar. This ultimately coalesced with Wallace's more philosophical interests in the limits of subjectivity and in how electronic grids of shared experience operated in the age of mass media; his writing sought effectively to remodel the idea of a romantic subject across an extended communal domain, one bearing a residual attachment to traditional American values, even within a globalized world where such partitioned conceptions of identity had seemingly been rendered moot. In this sense, despite Wallace's own intense sense of self-protective privacy, he was paradoxically committed as an author to the idea of his work as expressing the concerns of a public intellectual.

Aware of Wallace's projection of himself as a public intellectual *malgré lui*, I myself had an exchange of e-mails with the author early in 2007, after I had invited him to Oxford University's Rothermere American Institute, of which I was then director, to deliver our annual Esmond Harmsworth Lecture in American Arts and Letters. He first responded on 5 May 2007, saying, "I've been thinking about the Harmsworth thing, with no small trepidation. I really do not know how to deliver a 'lecture.' The one thing remotely like this I've done has been a commencement address at a college here in the States, and that took me weeks to write." However, Wallace also asked if we possessed transcripts or recordings of previous lectures, suggesting that "if I agreed to try to give a lecture on 15 May 2008, would you be willing to supply me with two or three transcripts/videotapes of such previous H.L.s so that I could get a concrete idea of what a Harmsworth Lecture actually looks or sounds like?" I replied that we had a general policy at the RAI of not recording anything, since we found this gave speakers — politicians, as well as writers — more freedom to share their ideas openly, without the intrusion of any legal or copyright issues. But I also indicated that we would be interested in something less formal than a regular academic lecture, perhaps a discussion of the kinds of things that interested him as a writer. After thinking this over for a few days, Wallace came back to me on 15 May, saying that he had "finally, and after much noodling, decided to pass on your very flattering invitation. I simply do not know how to 'lecture,' and Oxford is (to me) too hallowed and frightening a place to try doing something like this for the first time. What I will say is: If you are still interested in four or five years, perhaps you will invite me again. By that time, I hope I'll have educated myself about public lecturing and perhaps even given a couple lectures at small venues, and will have some degree of confidence that I could do a decent job for you." My response this time was to thank him anyway for considering the offer and to suggest that sometime in the future he might like to consider doing a lecture series around a particular theme, which could subsequently be published as a short book, an arrangement that we had recently been discussing in general terms with Princeton University Press. My specific suggestions involved the aesthetics of television or of sport, thinking such a framework might interestingly extend the format of Wallace's history of infinity into another conceptual area. He replied in his last e-mail to me, on 18 May: "I think I would say 'maybe' about the interlinked talks — though it sounds more like just writing a short book and then reading it aloud in chunks. But maybe. I invite you to contact me in a couple years. Pomona College will always know how best to reach me."

Part of my motivation in inviting Wallace to give the Harmsworth Lecture sprang simply from my own sense that he was the most significant writer of his generation. I came to his work relatively late, but after reading *Brief Interviews with Hideous Men* in 2001 it seemed clear not only that Wallace could do things with literary language other writers could not, but, more important, that his stylistic contortions spoke in a bizarre but entirely compelling way to the overloaded situation of the information age. It was a traditional critical acknowledgment not only of how a particular writer had managed to update rhetorical conventions to represent an altered state of affairs but also of how he had consolidated this new vision by entering implicitly into intertextual dialogue with significant literary and cultural precursors. Edmund Wilson entitled his 1943 book on American literature *The Shock of Recognition*, drawing his epigraph from Herman Melville's observation, in his discussion of Nathaniel Hawthorne's indebtedness to Shakespeare, of how "genius, all over the world, stands hand in hand, and one shock of recognition runs the whole circle round" ("Hawthorne" 249); and it is arguable that Wallace's invocation of digital America similarly gains in aesthetic power from its self-conscious negotiations with earlier American narratives. But another rationale for this invitation to Oxford stemmed from my notion of Wallace as at some level a moralist and pedagogue, a propensity that can be inferred from the concern with ethical issues that runs through his fiction and journalism, as well the author's own intense capacity for self-interrogation about what it means to be an "American" writer at the beginning of the twenty-first century.

The most overt expression of Wallace's hortatory idiom comes in the commencement address he gave at Kenyon College, Ohio, in 2005, which was subsequently published as *This Is Water: Some Thoughts, Delivered on a Significant Occasion, about Living a Compassionate Life*. There is, as is usual with Wallace, a persistently reflexive aspect to this address, with the lecturer remarking ironically upon the "standard requirement of US commencement speeches, the deployment of didactic little parable-ish stories" (5), even as he proceeds to deliver them. He continues by acknowledging to the graduating class how "the main requirement of speeches like this is that I'm supposed to talk about your liberal arts education's meaning, to try to explain why the degree you're about to receive has actual human value instead of just a material payoff" (11) before going on to suggest that the real value of higher education lies not so much in what is taught but in "how to think, how to pay attention" (92), a process that enables people "to consciously decide what has meaning and what doesn't" (95). In itself, of course, this message would appear unexceptionable: it stresses traditional American virtues of intellectual flexibility and pragmatism, while at the same time derogating "arrogance, bland certainty" and "closed-mindedness" (32). What is unusual about *This Is Water*, though, is how deliberately and systematically it critiques the idea of "natural, basic self-centeredness" (37), the assumption that "there is no experience you've had that you were not at the absolute center of" (39). This becomes a more extended meditation on the problem of solipsism, the ways in which failure to connect with a wider community can take on pathological overtones. Commenting on the "natural default setting of being uniquely, completely, imperially alone, day in and day out" (60), Wallace — somewhat oddly, within the bland, conventional context of a commencement address — raises the question of suicide as a response to the problem of isolation, proclaiming that the burden of his public wisdom is "about making it to thirty, or maybe even fifty, without wanting to shoot yourself in the head" (130).

The resolution to this conundrum, in Wallace's eyes, lies in the intellectual adroitness that would grant college graduates the imaginative capacity throughout their lives to transform the most banal material routines into emblems of a more elusive transcendent "unity": "It will actually be within your power to experience a crowded, hot, slow, consumer-hell-type situation as not only meaningful, but sacred, on fire with the same force that lit the stars — compassion, love, the subsurface unity of all things" (93). This enables him to conclude that "the real value of a real education" is linked to "simple awareness — awareness of what is so real and essential, so hidden in plain sight all around us" (131). Such alignment of the quotidian and the "sacred," along with the insistence that "real" and "essential" value is located immanently within proximate circumstances, is reminiscent of Ralph Waldo Emerson's 1844 essay "The Poet," which seeks similarly to metamorphose apparently "dull" situations into landscapes of "wonder":

> We have yet had no genius in America, with tyrannous eye, which knew the value of our incomparable materials, and saw, in the barbarism and materialism of the times, another carnival of the same gods whose picture he so much admires in Homer; then in the middle age; then in Calvinism. Banks and tariffs, the newspaper

and caucus, methodism and unitarianism, are flat and dull to dull people, but rest on the same foundations of wonder as the town of Troy, and the temple of Delphos, and are as swiftly passing away. (21–2)

Throughout Wallace's writings, indeed, there are several connections, both thematic and stylistic, to the legacy of Emerson. In his celebrated essay on television, "E Unibus Pluram: Television and U.S. Fiction" (1993), Wallace cites Emerson directly to exemplify the skill that television actors embody through their ability to act apparently naturally even before "the gaze of millions" (25). Wallace's point is that to act on native instinct even amidst the refractive system of media mirrors is, in itself, a heroic enterprise:

> The man who can stand the megagaze is a walking imago, a certain type of transcendent semihuman who, in Emerson's phrase, "carries the holiday in his eye." The Emersonian holiday that television actors' eyes carry is the promise of a vacation from human self-consciousness. Not worrying about how you come across. A total unallergy to gazes. It is contemporarily heroic. It is frightening and strong. It is also, of course, an act, for you have to be just abnormally self-conscious and self-controlled to appear unwatched before cameras and lenses and men with clipboards. (25)

Drawing explicitly on the work of Harvard philosopher of aesthetics Stanley Cavell, whose 1981 book *Pursuits of Happiness* similarly traced signs of Emersonian self-reliance on the faces of film actors in Hollywood screwball comedies, Wallace here works his way through the paradox whereby, within the digital world, inner independence and media masquerade can be seen as not necessarily antithetical: "This self-conscious appearance of unself-consciousness," says Wallace, "is the real door to TV's whole mirror-hall of illusions" (25–6).

Like Emerson, then, and indeed like Cavell, Wallace sought throughout his work forms of reconciliation between the transcendent and the simulacrum. To put this another way, his texts seek to locate inherent meaning and purpose even amidst the razzmatazz of contemporary popular culture, which is generally accepted in his work as a donnée for the world within which any ethical impulse has to operate. Stephen Railton has suggested that the generic model for classic "American Renaissance" narratives — Emerson's "Nature," Henry David Thoreau's *Walden*, Walt Whitman's *Leaves of Grass*, and others — is "unmistakably the Protestant sermon" (107), since they all embody a performative dimension that situates the author in, as it were, the pulpit. Railton points to how the specific legacy of revivalist preaching manifests itself in more secular forms in mid-nineteenth-century American culture, so that, for example, Melville's fictional representation of Father Mapple's sermon in *Moby-Dick* comes to epitomize that novel's strange blend of worldly description and metaphysical rumination.

Despite the obliquities of his style, Wallace shares with these famous writers the propensity for an implicitly proselytizing idiom, where questions of moral imperative carry as much weight as their fictional correlatives, and he also has in common with Emerson and Thoreau an ambivalence toward the ontological reality of other people. Thoreau's *Walden* is of course a notoriously self-centered text, where the existence of others is admitted only on sufferance, while Van Wyck Brooks accused Emerson of having no idea of the relationship between abstract and concrete, and of writing about figures such as Plutarch and Spinoza as if they had no human bodies and were merely manifestations of what Emerson called the "Over-Soul." Since the publication of Emerson's "The American Scholar," complained Brooks, "the whole of American literature has had the semblance of one vast, all-embracing baccalaureate sermon" (117). Wallace's narratives suffer from a similar kind of conundrum, whereby the combination of ethical interrogation and technical language tends to create a theoretical momentum that effectively deflects the social world into abstract terms. The defamiliarizing strain in Wallace, as in Emerson and Thoreau, similarly has the effect of deliberately alienating readers from social situations they can immediately identify with. This might be one reason that responses to Wallace's work, as to that of Emerson, have tended to divide along gender lines, with some women readers finding it difficult to empathize in particular with the more schematic and apparently dehumanizing aspects of Wallace's early style. Reading *Infinite Jest* within a theoretical framework of gender, for example, Catherine Toal relates the novel to a crisis of masculinity, turning upon the displacement of social formation by darker forces of recreational addiction: "the grip of narcotic or media stimulation; the collapse of fatherly authority; and the rise of a dislocated, disoriented adult selfhood" (306).

But despite such psychological disorientations, Wallace's writing was morally and philosophically committed, no less than was that of Thoreau, to a phenomenology of place. It was this sense of being grounded in specific local environments that became, for Wallace, a central source of ethical value and affective attachment. In his essay "Derivative Sport in Tornado Alley," the author recalls growing up in central Illinois, which he used to contrast in his mind with the "tall hills and serpentine one-ways of upstate NY" (8), where he had been an infant. For Wallace, there were structural analogies between the "vectors, lines and lines athwart lines" of Midwestern topographies (3) and his own youthful skill as a tennis player, an expertise which similarly "requires geometric thinking" (9) as well as an instinctive capacity to measure "angles" (9) within the "straight lines" (8) of a rectangular tennis court. Indeed, Wallace in this piece attributes his later academic interest in the language of mathematics to "a Midwesterner's sickness for home" (3), the nostalgia for linear "grids" (3) that operated for him on a subliminal level. Despite the fact that Wallace's father has claimed that much of "Derivative Sport" is simply "feigned autobiography" and that "David never played tennis in a tornado" (Harris 185–6), the essay can nevertheless be understood as a poignant tribute not only to his own local landscape, real or imagined, but also to the idea of local landscapes in general. The author here sardonically attributes his success as a "near-great" tennis player when (and only when) "in and around my township" (14) to his practiced skill in factoring into his play the notorious central Illinois wind, a climatic variable that other competitors found impossible to handle.

Another tribute to Midwestern community is "Getting Away from Already Pretty Much Being Away from It All," Wallace's journalistic account of the 1993 Illinois State Fair, where throughout the essay there is an implied contrast between the values of the East Coast and the Midwest. Wallace presents himself here as returning to rural Illinois from New York after a long absence, and, despite the admission of his own "East-Coast cynicism" (89), he comes to recognize the state fair as "a conscious affirmation of real community, of state solidarity and fellow-feeling and pride" (91). One aspect of this communitarianism involves Wallace's perception of how rural Midwesterners find themselves normally so "surrounded by unpopulated land, marooned in a space whose emptiness starts to become both physical and spiritual" (91), that these social rituals take on for them an air of "sacredness" (108). But another dimension to this occasion, so far as the author himself is concerned, lies again in the way this state fair provides a counterbalance to the specific fear of isolation and solipsism, the "weird, deluded but unshakable conviction" that he recalls from his "Midwest childhood" of how "everything around me existed all and only *For Me*" (89).

From this perspective, much of Wallace's writing might be seen to operate allegorically as an attempt to make connections with a world outside of himself, a deliberate exploration in both psychological and theoretical terms of how an isolated self enters into dialogue and conversation with a wider community. This principled escape from solipsism manifests itself in the affiliations drawn self-consciously between the individual and his broader social context, something that effectively links Wallace's philosophical redescription of selfhood with the sentiment of "union" and fellow-feeling that has a long and venerable history in the American political tradition. There are interesting parallels, for example, between Wallace's description of the 1993 Illinois State Fair and Abraham Lincoln's Address to the Wisconsin State Agricultural Society at Milwaukee, Wisconsin, in 1859. Lincoln, like Wallace, declares that the "institution" of agricultural fairs is "useful" because

they bring us together, and thereby make us better acquainted, and better friends than we otherwise would be. From the first appearance of man upon the earth, down to very recent times, the words *"stranger"* and *"enemy"* were *quite* or *almost*, synonymous. Long after civilized nations had defined robbery and murder as high crimes, and had affixed severe punishments to them, when practiced among and upon their own people respectively, it was deemed no offence, but even meritorious, to rob, and murder, and enslave *strangers*, whether as nations or as individuals. Even yet, this has not totally disappeared. The man of the highest moral cultivation, in spite of all which abstract principle can do, likes him whom he *does* know, much better than him whom he does *not* know. To correct the evils, great and small, which spring from want of sympathy, and from positive enmity, among *strangers*, as nations, or as individuals, is one of the highest functions of civilization. To this end our Agricultural Fairs contribute in no small degree. They make more pleasant, and more strong, and more durable, the bond of social and political union among us. (150–1)

Lincoln goes on to extol state fairs for fostering the uses of new technology to expedite agricultural labor, and he consequently concludes that such democratic events serve to facilitate "individual, social, and political prosperity and happiness" (162). Wallace pays a discreet if double-edged homage to Lincoln in his own essay on the Illinois fair, where he describes how the "Fairgrounds take up 300+ acres on the east side of Springfield, a depressed capital of 109,000 where you can't spit without hitting some sort of Lincoln-site plaque" (91); and the efficacy of this Midwestern ritual — which, for Wallace, carries an ominous as well as a celebratory side — lies in its power to encompass all within its charge. Looking at the livestock "chewing cuds" while destined to be "judged and applauded as future food," Wallace comments: "In a way, we're all here to be swallowed up" (131). Just as the cattle will win prizes and then promptly be slaughtered, so their human owners share the fate of ultimately being incorporated as components within the Ferris wheel of this community ritual.

Wallace cites Lincoln again in a short piece he wrote in November 2007 for the *Atlantic*, where he asks whether it might be worth choosing "to regard the 2,973 innocents killed in the atrocities of 9/11 not as victims but as democratic martyrs, 'sacrifices on the altar of freedom'?" ("Just Asking" 25). Wallace points out in a footnote that "this phrase is Lincoln's, more or less" (25), and it is in fact taken from the president's letter to Mrs. Lydia Bixby on 21 November 1864, where he commiserates with her loss of five sons in the Civil War. Lincoln's letter ends: "I pray that our Heavenly Father may assuage the anguish of your bereavement, and leave you only the cherished memory of the loved and lost, and the solemn pride that must be yours, to have laid so costly a sacrifice upon the altar of Freedom" (318). Wallace's argument here is that just as the regularly high number of "domestic highway deaths" in the United States is deemed an acceptable price to pay for "the mobility and autonomy" that the car offers (25), so those killed on 9/11 might be understood as a "sacrifice" to the "incalculably precious . . . American idea" of freedom, an idea that the executive orders, "military functions," and "warrantless surveillance" introduced by George W. Bush have served to undermine (30). This contribution to the *Atlantic*'s symposium, "The American Idea," suggests not only Wallace's commitment to time-honored American traditions but also his darker awareness of how such ideals were compromised by the repressive political reactions of the Bush administration after the Al Qaeda strike. In "The View from Mrs. Thompson's," his essay recording the experience of watching the events of 9/11 unfold on television in Illinois, he critiques the elderly neighbors watching these broadcasts with him not for being "stupid, or ignorant" but rather for being "innocent" (139): too willing, that is to say, to accept at face value the explanatory narratives proffered to them by national television networks on behalf of the U.S. body politic.

If there is one thing Wallace's writing is not, it is innocent. Hedged around by ironic retractions and self-subverting footnotes, he projects a vision of the world whose somberness derives in large part from its very lack of stability. It is the labyrinthine nature of the seemingly "infinite" perspectives embedded within the textual and social environment that represents such a challenge to both writer and reader. Infinity is of course a central trope in the Wallace lexicon, betokening not only a mathematical concept with varied implications through the ages, as outlined in *Everything and More: A Compact History of* ∞, but also the dizzying *mise-en-abîme* of computer technology in *Infinite Jest*, where boundaries distinguishing empirical from virtual reality are destabilized. It is this kind of erasure of any comfortable correspondence theory of truth that also darkens the mood in Wallace's short story "Philosophy and the Mirror of Nature," whose title directly echoes Richard Rorty's celebrated book of philosophy, published in 1980. Rorty's work sought explicitly to abolish metaphysical ideas of epistemology and what the philosopher called "shopworn mirror-metaphors" (333) invested in an absurdly regressive "Platonic notion of Truth" (377). Wallace himself majored in philosophy (as well as English) at Amherst College, and he shared with Rorty a radical skepticism about what the latter called "a deep, hidden, metaphysically significant nature" (373), along with a consequent openness to regard knowledge as a form not of truth but of edifying "conversation" (373). But whereas for Rorty such an abolition of metaphysics opened the horizon to welcome forms of intellectual pragmatism, in Wallace's story of the same name such an erasure of stable signifiers comes to carry a more sinister valence. The central character is a woman whose face has been ruined by "botched" cosmetic surgery intended to remove the crow's-feet around her eyes, causing her face to take on an "insanely frightened" look at all times (182), something that alarms everyone she happens casually to come into contact with. Having set out artificially to improve her worldly image, the unfortunate woman now finds herself hoisted on her own petard, and she subsequently seeks redress in the form of a lawsuit against the incompetent surgeon who did the cosmetic damage. The irony here is that her legal case, based around a hyperbolic account of "repair's callous butchery" and her own "chronic mask of crazed suffering and terror" (188), is no less beholden to a world of rhetorical manipulation and melodramatic affect than the compulsion that drove her to get her face fixed in the first place. Deprived of any correspondence theory of truth, Wallace's characters find themselves cast adrift in a fallen world of false appearances and "special effects" (186), with the comic references in this story to films such as *Bride of Frankenstein* (182) emphasizing how the author conceives of America's corporate marketplace as a theatre of gothic masquerade.

All this, of course, contrasts tellingly with the folksy innocence that Wallace observed among the bewildered citizens of Illinois in the immediate aftermath of 9/11, and it suggests how his stance toward this social world is one of dramatic irony, whereby he as author is empowered to perceive forms of disturbance to which his protagonists remain blind. In this sense, the air of impending doom that hangs over a story such as "The Suffering Channel"—carefully set "early in the afternoon of 1 July 2001" in the editorial office of *Style* magazine "on the sixteenth floor of 1 World Trade Center, New York" (241), where the youthful protagonists are naturally unaware of "the tragedy by which *Style* would enter history two months hence" (245)—might be understood as synecdochic of Wallace's ominous universe as a whole.

Whereas Rorty's pragmatism led him ultimately to celebrate the domestic possibilities of American culture, an activist potential expressed most explicitly in his late work *Achieving Our Country* (1998), Wallace's extrapolation of a political community from social networks tends to operate in a more ambivalent fashion. All of his writing, both fiction and nonfiction, gives the impression of being immersed within its own labyrinthine world, and part of the dilemma Wallace's characters customarily face is their inability to get any lucid perspective or purchase on the information fields that encompass them. Wallace himself admitted in a 1998 interview that he did not at that time hold a U.S. passport ("A Fun Thing"), and his writing is committed, both intellectually and emotionally, to locations and positions within the American system. In this same conversation, Wallace nominated William James, Ernest Hemingway, John Steinbeck, and Tobias Wolff as American authors with whom he felt a special affinity, while in an earlier interview with Larry McCaffery he also cited Vladimir Nabokov, Donald Barthelme, and Don DeLillo as major influences, along with canonical English writers such as John Donne, Gerard Manley Hopkins, and Philip Larkin (McCaffery 139). Wallace was markedly more enthusiastic about British poets than British novelists, with the metaphysical propensities and innovative language of Donne, Hopkins, and Larkin speaking to his interests more clearly than the ossified emphasis on social class and hierarchy in traditional English novels.

There is also a reference in Wallace's first novel, *The Broom of the System* (1987), to Frank Norris's "stunning novel *McTeague*" (430), another novel of systematic enclosure published in 1899, where the bureaucracy of medical licensing finally catches up with the frontier spirit of the eponymous San Francisco dentist. In this sense, many of Wallace's fictional narratives both embody and struggle against the encircling brooms of the system, deploying experimental language in an effort putatively to transcend the multiple information networks that his world of electronic artifice meticulously inscribes. Sometimes, as in the minimalist short story "Incarnations of Burned Children," this language takes on self-consciously apocalyptic dimensions, as if the author were linguistically wrestling, in a state of compulsion or even desperation, with states of worldly matter. In "E Unibus Pluram," Wallace describes his generation as residing within a televisual "world whose defining boundaries have been deformed by electric signal" (51), and this can be seen as analogous to living within a Midwest defined inexorably by "lines" and "vectors," such as he evokes in "Derivative Sport in Tornado Alley" (3). Many of Wallace's nonfiction pieces are also marked by jokey, self-referential asides that highlight how he as a paid journalist is necessarily implicated within the world he describes. Indeed, a self-subverting sense of ironic entrapment, where it appears almost impossible to go beyond the contours of preexisting limits, is characteristic of his writing more generally. For Wallace, one of the defining aspects of being an American author at the turn of the twenty-first century was a need to respond to how human experience had been modified in complex ways by the ubiquitous worlds of mass media: not only the "electric signal" of television but also the labyrinthine tentacles of the so-called infotainment industry.

In this sense, the bitter humor of *Infinite Jest* lies in the way it illuminates the inherent contradictions of a national system founded explicitly on an American's cherished freedom to pursue his own desires, in an environment where such gestures have relapsed into patterns of obsessive repetition, what the novel calls "autopilot ritual" (965). Tennis is presented in *Infinite Jest* as one of the many forms of addiction in Wallace's work, while in his later journalistic piece "How Tracy Austin Broke My Heart" he describes how the brilliant young tennis player's physical gestures, which carry "a transcendent beauty that makes manifest God in man" (142–3), are contradicted by the empty clichés that emerge in sports autobiographies and interviews, as if "blindness and dumbness are the price of the gift" (155). Again, Wallace evokes a world of psychological fragmentation and ontological contradiction, where a spiritual yearning to transcend worldly systems goes along with a sardonic awareness of the banal material conditions within which they are necessarily incarnated. In the "Adult World" diptych from *Brief Interviews with Hideous Men*, such contradiction becomes overtly schizophrenic, with the "Stochastic Currency Analyst" (141) purportedly checking foreign exchange markets during the night as a cover story for his secret compulsive masturbation and visits to sample the merchandise at the local porn emporium. This leads the protagonists' marriage into alien territory, where commercial sex and electronic "financescapes," to use Arjun Appadurai's term (34), impinge equally upon their domestic arrangements, which in turn highlights the more general point made by Timothy Brennan, about how in the new world generated by information technology, where the cartographies of proximate and distant are not mutually antithetical but symbiotically intertwined, the point "is not to flee from the global, but to socialize it" (307), to explore ways in which American identity might be transnationally remapped. In *Infinite Jest*, a war game called "Eschaton" is played on four contiguous tennis courts every year on "Interdependence Day" (325), with the students teaming up into geopolitical entities and lobbing tennis balls symbolizing nuclear warheads at each other, and all of Wallace's fiction turns upon ways in which such spectral forms of globalization have permeated the American domestic mindset in strange and often darkly comic ways.

It is the brilliance of Wallace's work to express such disorienting situations not just moralistically but also experientially, to show ways in which, at the turn of the twenty-first century, electronic abstraction has entered into the force field of human consciousness. In the short story "Oblivion," an unnamed "Assistant Systems Supervisor" (194) responds to sleeping problems by attending the "Edmund R. and Meredith R. Darling Sleep Clinic" (216), where his nocturnal brain waves are recorded in the clinic's sleep chamber: "The waves' white 'line' was discomfiting, being palsied, bumpy and arrhythmic rather than regular or consistent, as well as being trended with dramatic troughs and spikes or 'nodes' suggestive in appearance of an arrhythmic heart or financially troubled or erratic 'Cash flow' graph" (228). Although this is mordantly funny, its structure of defamiliarization is not merely satiric; instead, in a more sinister fashion, it exposes aspects of human behavior that are normally concealed from citizens' purview. By dramatizing in this way the character's night consciousness, and by displacing his cerebral reflexes into the form of an abstract graph or chart that is linked here again to a financial metaphor, the author illuminates the latent mechanical and economic systems that keep all human bodies in the United States functioning. Yet this corporeal condition does not become in Wallace simply a passive or fatalistic reflex: in the story "My Appearance," an aging television actress appears on NBC's *David Letterman Show* and astounds her chat-show host, accustomed as he is to the slick ironies of postmodern performance, by her determination to speak the truth about the ups and downs of her media career. The language she uses here is resolutely ethical, indeed Emersonian, in its principled emphasis on self-reliance: "Months later, after I'd come through something by being in its center, survived in the stillness created by great disturbance from which I, as cause, perfectly circled, was exempt, I'd be struck all over again by what a real and simply *right* thing it was for a person in such a place to say" (200–1).

Balancing such ethical imperatives against an intuitive sense of corporate immersion, Wallace was always conscious of speaking from a place inside his native culture. Such positioning could be experienced, as it were, horizontally: Wallace was eloquent on how as an author he was part of a television generation, influenced by writers such as DeLillo and Thomas Pynchon, whose works "revolve metaphorically off the concept of interference . . . and . . . seas of signal" ("E Unibus" 73). He also acknowledged his kinship with contemporary American novelists and filmmakers such as Jonathan Franzen, Gus Van Sant, and David Lynch, paying tribute in particular to Lynch's 1986 film *Blue Velvet*, which he credited with having first given him the sense of how experimental art could find its own level of inner integrity: "if it's authentic and true," remarked Wallace in relation to *Blue Velvet*, "you will feel it in your nerve endings" (Rose). All this suggests a willingness to acknowledge generational bonding not simply as a form of contingent or casual influence but, more significantly, as the artistic manifestation of a necessary world, where the "authentic" becomes that which is inescapable. For Wallace, though, such acknowledgment of a necessary world also extended back in time, through the historical legacies of American literature and culture, the worlds of Emerson and Lincoln, William James and Richard Rorty, and it could be argued that this vertical relationship to American tradition was as important to him intellectually as the more obvious bonding with his own peer group. The American cultural tradition, in other words, became another of those rectangular spaces within whose confining vectors the author found himself perpetually returning serve. In this sense, Wallace's observations at the Illinois State Fair of how they were all there, humans and animals, to be "swallowed up" ("Getting Away" 131) speaks to his awareness, from a geographical position at the heart of the country, of being immersed within the cartographic grid of the United States, even while simultaneously finding himself estranged from it. The ethical impulses that help to drive Wallace's narratives are themselves indebted to American intellectual traditions of Transcendentalism and Pragmatism that ironically reinscribe the author as enunciating from a position within the belly of the beast, and the critical paradox here, as so often with Wallace, turns upon how his aspirations to states of lucidity and probity are themselves always already framed by a shared national culture.

The unusual power of Wallace's writing, then, derived from his capacity to make it personal and impersonal, emotionally affective and ruthlessly abstract, both at once. Such an odd mixture of distance and engagement in both his fictional and nonfictional narratives speaks to the global repositioning of American literature and culture within a wider sphere, where the local protagonists can no longer properly map the vectors and coordinates by which they are shaped. If the more austere geometries of mathematics and philosophy formed the point of intellectual departure for Wallace's fictions, one enduring legacy from his later work, in particular, is the sense of its author as a hesitant public intellectual, an oddly self-effacing presence on the college lecture circuit and in the nation's media outlets, a reticence impelled in part by his recognition of how American values themselves were being held in check by modulations in the traditional shape of the country. To be sure, Wallace's reluctance to appear at Oxford exemplified how he preferred to keep his distance from the more ossified realms of higher education and from the cumbersome publicity apparatus associated with contemporary culture in all its synthetic forms, but it was his ultimately self-immolating willingness to wrestle with these behemoths of corporate life, to seek to identify some spirit of authenticity even amidst such disheartening narratives of alienation and simulation, that constituted the profound genius of his art.

Works Cited

Appadurai, Arjun. *Modernity at Large: Cultural Dimensions of Globalization.* Minneapolis: University of Minnesota Press, 1996. Print.

Brennan, Timothy. *At Home in the World: Cosmopolitanism Now.* Cambridge, MA: Harvard University Press, 1997. Print.

Brooks, Van Wyck. "America's Coming-of-Age." 1915. In *Van Wyck Brooks: The Early Years. A Selection from his Works, 1908–21.* Ed. Claire Sprague. New York: Harper Torchbooks, 1968. 79–158. Print.

Emerson, Ralph Waldo. "The American Scholar." 1837. In *Collected Works I* 49–70. Print.

———. *The Collected Works of Ralph Waldo Emerson, I: Nature, Addresses, and Lectures.* Ed. Robert E. Spiller and Alfred R. Ferguson. Cambridge, MA: Harvard University Press, 1971. Print.

———. "Nature." 1836. In *Collected Works I* 1–45. Print.

———. "The Over-Soul." 1841. In *The Collected Works of Ralph Waldo Emerson, II: Essays: First Series.* Ed. Alfred R. Ferguson and Jean Ferguson Carr. Cambridge, MA: Harvard University Press, 1980. 157–76. Print.

———. "The Poet." 1844. In *The Collected Works of Ralph Waldo Emerson, III: Essays, Second Series.* Ed. Alfred R. Ferguson and Jean Ferguson Carr. Cambridge, MA: Harvard University Press, 1984. 1–24. Print.

Foerster, Norman. "Factors in American Literary History." In *The Reinterpretation of American Literature.* Ed. Norman Foerster. New York: Harcourt, Brace and Company, 1928. 23–38. Print.

Graff, Gerald. *Professing Literature: An Institutional History.* Chicago: University of Chicago Press, 1987. Print.

Harris, Charles B. "David Foster Wallace's Hometown: A Correction." *Critique* 51.3 (2010): 185–6. Print.

Lincoln, Abraham. "Address to the Wisconsin State Agricultural Society, Milwaukee, Wisconsin, September 30, 1859." In *Portable Lincoln* 150–62. Print.

———. *The Portable Abraham Lincoln*. Ed. Andrew Delbanco. New York: Viking Penguin, 1992. Print.

———. "To Mrs. Lydia Bixby." 21 November 1864. In *Portable Lincoln* 318. Print.

McCaffery, Larry. "An Interview with David Foster Wallace." *Review of Contemporary Fiction* 13.2 (Summer 1993): 127–50. Print.

Melville, Herman. "Hawthorne and His Mosses." 1850. In *The Piazza Tales and Other Prose Pieces, 1839–1860*. Ed. Harrison Hayford et al. Evanston: Northwestern University Press, 1987. 239–53. Print.

———. *Moby-Dick; or, The Whale*. 1851. Ed. Harrison Hayford et al. Evanston: Northwestern University Press, 1968. Print.

Railton, Stephen. *Authorship and Audience: Literary Performance in the American Renaissance*. Princeton: Princeton University Press, 1991. Print.

Rorty, Richard. *Achieving Our Country: Leftist Thought in Twentieth-Century America*. Cambridge, MA: Harvard University Press, 1998. Print.

———. *Philosophy and the Mirror of Nature*. Oxford: Blackwell, 1980. Print.

Rose, Charlie. "Charlie Rose Interviews David Foster Wallace." *The Charlie Rose Show*. PBS. 27 March 1997. Web.

Thoreau, Henry David. *Walden*. 1854. Ed. J. Lyndon Shanley. Princeton, NJ: Princeton University Press, 1973. Print.

Toal, Catherine. "Corrections: Contemporary American Melancholy." *Journal of European Studies* 33.3/4 (December 2003): 305–22. Print.

Wallace, David Foster. "Adult World (I)." In *Brief Interviews* 137–55. Print.

———. "Adult World (II)." In *Brief Interviews* 156–61. Print.

———. *Brief Interviews with Hideous Men*. 1999. London: Abacus–Little, Brown, 2000. Print.

———. *The Broom of the System*. 1987. London: Abacus–Time Warner, 1997. Print.

———. *Consider the Lobster and Other Essays*. London: Abacus–Time Warner, 2005. Print.

———. "Derivative Sport in Tornado Alley." In *A Supposedly Fun* 3–20. Print.

———. E-mail to author. 5 May 2007.

———. E-mail to author. 15 May 2007.

———. E-mail to author. 18 May 2007.

———. "E Unibus Pluram: Television and U.S. Fiction." 1994. In *A Supposedly Fun* 21–82. Print.

———. *Everything and More: A Compact History of* ∞. New York: Norton, 2003. Print.

———. "A Fun Thing They'll Never Do Again: Gus Van Sant Meets David Foster Wallace." *Dazed and Confused* May 1998. Web.

———. "Getting Away from Already Pretty Much Being Away from It All." In *A Supposedly Fun* 83–137. Print.

———. "How Tracy Austin Broke My Heart." In *Consider the Lobster* 141–55. Print.

———. "Incarnations of Burned Children." In *Oblivion* 114–6. Print.

———. *Infinite Jest: A Novel.* Boston: Little, Brown, 1996. Print.

———. "Just Asking." *Atlantic* November 2007: 25–30. Print.

———. "My Appearance." In *Girl with Curious Hair.* 1989. London: Abacus–Little, Brown, 1997. 173–201. Print.

———. "Oblivion." In *Oblivion* 190–237. Print.

———. *Oblivion: Stories.* London: Abacus–Time Warner, 2004. Print.

———. "Philosophy and the Mirror of Nature." In *Oblivion* 182–9. Print.

———. "The Suffering Channel." In *Oblivion* 238–329. Print.

———. *A Supposedly Fun Thing I'll Never Do Again: Essays and Arguments.* 1997. London: Abacus–Little, Brown, 1998. Print.

———. *This Is Water: Some Thoughts, Delivered on a Significant Occasion, about Living a Compassionate Life.* New York: Little, Brown and Company, 2009. Print.

———. "The View from Mrs. Thompson's." In *Consider the Lobster* 128–40. Print.

Whitman, Walt. *Leaves of Grass.* 1855. Ed. Sculley Bradley and Harold W. Blodgett. New York: Norton, 1973. Print.

Wilson, Edmund, ed. *The Shock of Recognition: The Development of Literature in the United States Recorded by the Men Who Made It.* Garden City, NY: Doubleday, 1943. Print.

DON DeLILLO

INFORMAL REMARKS FROM THE
DAVID FOSTER WALLACE MEMORIAL
SERVICE IN NEW YORK ON
OCTOBER 23, 2008

INFINITY. This is the subject of David Wallace's book on the mathematics, the philosophy, and the history of a vast, beautiful, abstract concept. There are references in the book to Zeno's dichotomy and Goldbach's conjecture, to Hausdorff's maximal principle. There is also the offsetting breeze of Dave's plainsong — *OK then* and *sort of* and *no kidding* and *stuff like this.*

His work, everywhere, tends to reconcile what is difficult and consequential with a level of address that's youthful, unstudied and often funny, marked at times by the small odd sentence that wanders in off the street.

"Her photograph tastes bitter to me."

"Almost Talmudically self-conscious."

"The tiny little keyhole of himself."

A vitality persists, a stunned vigor in the face of the complex humanity we find in his fiction, the loss and anxiety, darkening mind, self-doubt. There are sentences that shoot rays of energy in seven directions. There are stories that trail a character's spiraling sense of isolation.

Everything and More. This is the title of his book on infinity. It might also be a description of the novel *Infinite Jest*, his dead serious frolic of addicted humanity. We can imagine his fiction and essays as the scroll fragments of a distant future. We already know this work as current news — writer to reader, intimately, obsessively. He did not channel his talents to narrower patterns. He wanted to be equal to the vast, babbling, spin-out sweep of contemporary culture.

We see him now as a brave writer who struggled against the force that wanted him to shed himself. Years from now, we'll still feel the chill that attended news of his death. One of his recent stories ends in the finality of this half sentence: *Not another word.*

But there is always another word. There is always another reader to regenerate these words. The words won't stop coming. Youth and loss. This is Dave's voice, American.

JOSH ROILAND

GETTING AWAY FROM IT ALL:
THE LITERARY JOURNALISM OF
DAVID FOSTER WALLACE AND
NIETZSCHE'S CONCEPT
OF OBLIVION

ON A DRY Saturday morning in late May 2005, David Foster Wallace delivered the commencement address to the graduating class at Kenyon College in central Ohio. He sought to tell them why their liberal arts degree had "actual human value instead of just a material payoff" (*This Is Water* 11). For Wallace that value lay not in the old cliché of learning how to think, but rather in learning how to exercise control over what to think about: "It means being conscious and aware enough to choose what you pay attention to and to choose how you construct meaning from experience. Because if you cannot or will not exercise this kind of choice in adult life, you will be totally hosed" (55). The speech, both colloquial and compassionate, was the clearest articulation of a philosophy that guided Wallace's writing life — and is a useful point of departure for understanding an understudied aspect of his writing: his journalism.[1]

Although Wallace is best known for *Infinite Jest*, critics also greeted his collections of nonfiction with equal enthusiasm, often noting their irreverence. Reviewers described *A Supposedly Fun Thing I'll Never Do Again* as a collection of "vivid, hilarious essays" and "irrefutable proof of his comic genius" (Miller, "The Road to Babbittville"; Begley). Equally, Wallace garnered praise for "holding up the high comic tradition — passed down from Sterne to Swift to Pynchon" with the publication of his second collection of nonfiction, *Consider the Lobster* (Eugenides). But none of his reviews or obituaries describe his magazine and newspaper stories as literary journalism. Although this omission may point more to a mainstream marginalization of the term rather than a willful oversight on behalf of critics, it is nonetheless important to understand that Wallace wrote in that tradition. Literary journalism is a form of nonfiction writing that adheres to all of the reportorial and truth-telling covenants of traditional journalism, while employing rhetorical and storytelling techniques more commonly associated with fiction. In short, it is *journalism as literature.* The form and its field of study provide a whole catalog of approaches for understanding Wallace's stories in relation to his reviews, speeches, and essays. Specifically, Norman Sims has said, "Literary journalists recognize the need for a consciousness on the page through which the objects in view are filtered" (*True Stories* 7). Wallace was awash in this consciousness; it compelled him to be curious and caused him to chronicle nearly everything he encountered.

Although Wallace himself never commented explicitly about literary journalism, there is evidence that he knew the form and that he regarded it highly. In his introduction, as guest editor of *The Best American Essays 2007,* he cited Mark Danner's story, "Iraq: The War of the Imagination," as one of several pieces of literary journalism in the collection. He lumped many of these stories with other essays into a subgenre he called the "'service essay,' with 'service' here referring to both professionalism and virtue . . . but what renders them most valuable to me is a special kind of integrity in their handling of fact. An absence of dogmatic cant" ("Deciderization" xxiii). For Wallace, such journalistic dependability was in woefully short supply. In a 2003 *Believer* interview with Dave Eggers, he lamented that "there's no more complex, messy, community-wide argument (or 'dialogue'); political discourse is now a formulaic matter of preaching to one's own choir and demonizing the opposition. . . . How can any of this possibly help me, the average citizen, deliberate" about any number of complicated political issues? Of course, not all literary journalism attempts or achieves this service, but Wallace believed that stories which did, helped readers live the type of conscious life that he advocated in his Kenyon speech. He called the stories he selected for the collection "models — not templates, but models — of ways I wish I could think and live in what seems to me this world" ("Deciderization" xxiv).

Wallace's beliefs about this style of writing are congruent with what some of the leading scholars in the field have said about the power and purpose of literary journalism. In a foundational statement, Sims wrote, "Whether or not literary journalism equips me for living differently than other forms of literature, I read it as if it might" (*The Literary Journalists* 6). Later, in his historiography of the form, John Hartsock claimed that literary journalism's "purpose is to narrow the distance between subjectivity and the object, not divorce them" (132). And most recently, Kathy Roberts Forde promoted the idea that literary journalism realizes a Deweyian relationship between art and politics: "To my way of thinking, the American profession of journalism would better serve democratic ends by giving up its quixotic claim of representing 'objective truth' in news reports and working instead toward the discovery and presentation of pragmatic truth (or truths)" (205). Wallace both affirmed and practiced these ideas in his own journalism. His reporting does not simply chronicle who, what, when, and where; rather, it examines the larger cultural assumptions and significances embedded within a topic. He believed in the power that Sims identifies. He abided by Hartsock's purpose. And he sought the type of contingent truth, and its attendant political consequences, that Forde advocated. The paradox, unfortunately, is that while Wallace was professionally and politically compelled to ask and interpret, he was also personally troubled by much of what he encountered. What made him a great journalist also caused him great anxiety.

Moreover, I submit that the best way to understand that anxiety — which is to say, the best way to understand his journalism — is to view it through the lens of Friedrich Nietzsche's idea of *oblivion*, defined in his second essay of *The Genealogy of Morals* as "an active screening device, responsible for the fact that what we experience and digest psychologically does not, in the stage of digestion, emerge into consciousness any more than what we ingest physically" (189). Nietzsche is useful here because Wallace's journalism displays his extreme consciousness, both in the details of the observable world and in the impressions they make on his psyche. Often, he was plagued by what he could not let go. And his stories are beset by digressions and introspections, many of which are collected in footnotes. He suffered from an absence of oblivion, whose active role, according to Nietzsche, is "that of a concierge: to shut temporarily the doors and windows of consciousness; to protect us from the noise and agitation . . . to introduce a little quiet into our consciousness" (189). But as a journalist, Wallace's job was to collect and organize the noise and agitation of the phenomenal world.

For example, reporting from the 2003 Maine Lobster Festival for *Gourmet* magazine, Wallace faces a question that he says is unavoidable: "Is it alright to boil a sentient creature alive just for our gustatory pleasure?" ("Consider" 243). He admits that addressing this question opens up a Pandora's box of related concerns that are not only complex but uncomfortable, especially for anyone, himself included, who "enjoys a variety of foods and yet does not want to see herself as cruel and unfeeling" (246). Wallace confesses that his main way of dealing with conflicts, such as this one, is to dissociate, to "avoid thinking about the whole unpleasant thing" (246). Nonetheless, his professional obligation trumps his attempts at oblivion and since the "assigned subject of this article is what it's like to attend the 2003 MLF . . . it turns out there is no honest way to avoid certain moral questions" (247). If dissociation brings peace, then journalism brings pain, as Wallace admitted years later, saying, "Writing-wise, fiction is scarier, but nonfiction is harder—because nonfiction's based in reality, and today's felt reality is overwhelmingly, circuit-blowingly huge and complex" ("Deciderization" xiv). But as a journalist he must explore that reality, and his stories bear the marks of that process's psychic pain.

That story, "Consider the Lobster," is one of the eleven pieces of literary journalism among dozens of other works of nonfiction that Wallace authored in his lifetime.[2] Although the topics ranged widely from the Adult Video News Awards, which he covered for *Premiere*, to riding the Straight Talk Express for *Rolling Stone* during John McCain's failed bid for the 2000 Republican presidential nomination, the trope that structures these stories is escape, which, for Wallace, was a desire born of sadness. Pornography is sad: "Much of the cold, dead, mechanical quality of adult films is attributable, really, to the performers' faces" ("Big Red Son" 17). Politics are sad: "Modern politicians make us sad, hurt us deep down in ways that are hard even to name, much less talk about" ("Up, Simba" 187). Sports are sad: "Midwest junior tennis was also my initiation into true adult sadness" ("Derivative Sport" 12). And vacations are sad: "There is something about a mass-market Luxury Cruise that's unbearably sad" ("A Supposedly Fun" 261). All of these subjects involve supplanting everyday reality with fantasy, which Wallace believed was a too common American phenomenon.

Vacations are the most literal embodiment of that escape trope, and Wallace wrote three stories that explored getaways. Along with the aforementioned "Consider the Lobster," which he wrote for *Gourmet* in 2003, Wallace also penned pieces on the 1994 Illinois State Fair ("Getting Away from Already Being Pretty Much Away from It All") and a 1996 Caribbean cruise ("A Supposedly Fun Thing I'll Never Do Again") for *Harper's*.[3] David Lipsky called the two *Harper's* stories "some of the most famous pieces of journalism of the past decade and a half" ("The Lost Years"). Vacations for Wallace are not relaxing. He describes them as "radically constricting and humbling in the hardest way" ("Consider" 240). The point of a vacation is to escape the everyday, to be oblivious to the attendant concerns and responsibilities of daily life, which is something Wallace is both unwilling and unable to do. Consequently, he believes mass tourists are "alien, ignorant, greedy for something you cannot ever have, disappointed in a way you can never admit" (240). The key to understanding this contempt comes in that second adjective: ignorant. To be ignorant is to lack consciousness, which is why vacationers cannot admit their disappointment: they cannot recognize it. But for Wallace a lack of consciousness has larger ramifications. To get away from it all is to abdicate a moral responsibility, to dire effect. In 2007, with the country embattled in two wars, still reeling from the aftermath of Hurricane Katrina, and on the verge of a historic economic collapse, Wallace wrote: "We are in a state of three-alarm emergency —'we' basically meaning America as a polity and culture." He believed such an emergency would not have happened "if we had been paying attention and handling information in a competent grown-up way" ("Decideriza-tion" xxi).

Wallace's appeal for awareness is an instructive moment to note how he conceives morality in a very different way than Nietzsche. For Nietzsche, responsiveness was actually a sign of the weak-willed man. In the first essay of *The Genealogy of Morals* he wrote that "it is a sign of strong, rich temperaments that they cannot for long take seriously their enemies, their misfortunes, their misdeeds; for such characters have in them an excess of plastic curative power, and also a power of oblivion" (173). Nietzsche believed that those who could not let go of the past were plagued by *ressentiment*: the transference of the pain from one's own weak will onto an external object. Moreover, Nietzsche believed that *ressentiment* was actually the psychological motor powering the modern conception of morality. He arrived at this valuation by tracing the etymology of the terms "good" and "bad" in various languages and finding "the same conceptual transformation. The basic concept is always *noble* in the hierarchical, class sense, and from this has developed, by historical necessity, the concept *good* embracing nobility of mind, spiritual distinction. This development is strictly parallel to that other which eventually converted the notions *common, plebian, base* into the notion *bad*" (162). In time, this power dynamic created a sense of bitterness in commoners and compelled them to look upon the nobility not as *good* but, in fact, as *evil*, and in turn to view *themselves* as *good*: "The slave revolt in morals begins by rancor turning creative and giving birth to values — the rancor of beings who, deprived of the direct outlet of action, compensate by an imaginary vengeance" (170). Whole ethical systems of belief and action developed out of this transvaluation, leading Nietzsche to conclude not only that there is no a priori reason for associating "good" with altruistic deeds but also that conceptions of virtue and morality actually develop out of rancor and *ressentiment*.

For Nietzsche, the only way to overcome these sentiments was the will to power; the strong man acts while the weak reacts. And oblivion is what clears the way for action and allows for "the nobler functions and functionaries of our organism which do governing and planning" (189).

Without oblivion we are slaves to our memory, which mostly recalls a past that is grave, serious, and hurting (192). Wallace acknowledged the existence of weaker psychological elements like *ressentiment* within himself. In his essay "Joseph Frank's Dostoevsky" he lists several of the Russian author's characters who exude vitality, including the "unbelievably repellent Smerdyakov [from *The Brothers Karamozov*], that living engine of slimy resentment in whom I personally see parts of myself I can barely stand to look at" (265). Reading Wallace's nonfiction through these lenses of lasting resentment and an inability to forget, one can understand, perhaps, the earnestness with which he writes about consciousness. After all, what is awareness but the present tense of memory?

An imperative to be present is a clear thread that runs through all of Wallace's nonfiction, from his reviews, speeches, and essays, to his literary journalism. For instance, the people in all three of his vacation stories indulge in escapism. They have allowed oblivion to close the door on their consciousness, and in exchange they are happy — but Wallace believes it is a false consciousness. Rural Midwesterners get away from their isolated existences by flocking to public events like state fairs to share in community and celebrate land ("Getting Away" 108). Passengers aboard the *Zenith* luxury cruise ship — which Wallace immediately rechristens the *Nadir*, an ironic joke that loses its humor in the aftermath of his suicide — get away from their landlocked worries via onboard pampering and "Managed Fun," which infantilizes them to a preconscious state ("A Supposedly Fun" 320). And carnivores at the Maine Lobster Festival indulge gourmet fantasies by consuming discounted lobster en masse and thus lose their class consciousness ("Consider" 239). Each embodiment of escape, however, unsettles Wallace. Unconsciousness leads to groupthink, gluttony, and self-delusion. He notes that the fairgoers exhibit a herdlike quality as they unconsciously react to the fair's various stimuli. Cruise passengers mistake pampering for actual human compassion, and, worse, are never satisfied with the amount of indulgences they receive. And lobster eaters attain a false sense of taste (and class) because they deny the essential questions at the heart of the gourmet experience.

Despite these perditions, the vacationers' countenance is unchanged because the very structure of these vacations discourages awareness. Of the "Managed Fun" aboard the *Nadir*, Wallace notes bitterly: "They'll micromanage every iota of every pleasure-option so that not even the dreadful corrosive action of your own adult consciousness and agency and dread can fuck up your fun. Your troublesome capacities for choice, error, regret, dissatisfaction, and despair will be removed from the equation" ("A Supposedly Fun" 267). Thus, the vacationers are unaware and unbothered by these contradictions. Wallace, however, is aware of them and feels doubly burdened. Not only is he troubled by their lack of consciousness, but the excess of his own weighs on him. During his cruise, Wallace becomes agitated by the insincerity of the staff's "Professional Smile," the affected disposition that he calls "the pandemic of the service industry" (289). He spends three hundred twenty-two words in a footnote chronicling not only the despair-inducing effects of its insincerity but also how the absence of sincerity now causes him psychic harm. He wends through various hypothetical situations to reach the conclusion that "the Professional Smile has now even skewed my resentment at the dreaded Professional Scowl" (289). Clearly shaken by his mind's capacity to dwell, Wallace ends the footnote despairingly: "What a fucking mess" (290). This mess embodies what Nietzsche makes clear: a surfeit of consciousness is unhealthy.[4] He wrote, "The concierge maintains order and etiquette in the household of the psyche; which immediately suggests that there can be no happiness, no serenity, no hope, no pride, no *present*, without oblivion" (189).

One can find further evidence of the paralyzing effects of consciousness in Wallace's sports journalism. Wallace wrote one memoirish essay ("Derivative Sport in Tornado Alley"), one book review ("How Tracy Austin Broke My Heart"), and three pieces of literary journalism ("Tennis Player Michael Joyce's Professional Artistry as a Paradigm of Certain Stuff about Choice, Freedom, Discipline, Joy, Grotesquerie, and Human Completeness," "Democracy and Commerce at the U.S. Open," and "Federer as Religious Experience") about tennis, which he told Laura Miller was "the one sport I know enough about for it to be beautiful to me" (*Salon* interview). In all of these pieces, Wallace belabors the point of the sport's difficulty, but he identifies a trait that he believes allows top-tier players to perform at such a high level: like the happy vacationers, successful tennis pros possess an ability to suspend consciousness. He is fascinated by the fact that top athletes bypass their heads and simply act. For example, in a footnote in "Tennis Player Michael Joyce," Wallace admits that he is "kind of awed by Joyce's evident ability to shut down lines of thinking that aren't to his advantage" (222). Wallace himself was a regionally ranked junior tennis player growing up outside of Champaign-Urbana, Illinois, but he said the experience "was also my initiation into true adult sadness" ("Derivative Sport" 12). This sadness occurred because he lacked Joyce's ability to close out all distractions; consequently, he never excelled beyond a certain level. In his review of Austin's book, he included a sample meditation on how hard it is not to be consumed by one's thoughts while under both the pressure of an important moment and the gaze of a watchful audience: "Don't think about it . . . yeah but except if I'm consciously not thinking about it then doesn't part of me have to think about it in order for me to remember what I'm not supposed to think about . . . shut up, quit thinking about it and serve the goddamn ball" (154). Wallace knew what it took to be a great tennis player, but he could not replicate it in himself.[5] He possessed the physical but not the psychic ability to excel; his lack of oblivion always got in the way. Conversely, while oblivion helps athletes perform, Wallace also believes it prevents them from offering any meaningful insight into their own achievements. He concludes that "blindness and dumbness" are not the price for great athletic gifts but are actually "its essence," and to write well is to be aware and have access to one's consciousness and to present honestly life with all its flaws and imperfections; Austin does not have this, and Wallace skewers her in a review of her autobiography (155).

Wallace's own excess of consciousness presents itself stylistically in the form of footnotes, which may be the most outwardly identifiable aspect of both his nonfiction and fiction.[6] When considered as literary journalism, Wallace's appropriation of this academic practice broadens the definitional characteristics of the genre, which also include "immersion reporting, complicated story structures, character development, symbolism, voice, a focus on ordinary people . . . and accuracy" (Sims, *True Stories* 6–7).[7] The notes become an embodiment of those other characteristics; within them Wallace is able to achieve and accentuate each individual feature. At the same time, the notes allow Wallace to mirror his vision of American culture in his writing style:

> There's a way, it seems to me, that reality is fractured right now, at least the reality I live; the difficulty about writing about that reality is that text is very linear, it's very unified. I, anyway, am constantly on the lookout for ways to fracture the text that aren't totally disorienting. I mean, you can take the lines and jumble them up and that's nicely fractured, but nobody's going to read it, right? So, there's got to be some interplay between how difficult you make it for the reader and how seductive it is for the reader to do it. (Charlie Rose interview)[8]

Some critics, however, argued that the numerous footnotes were arrogant and evidence that Wallace needed a better editor.[9] The point that these critics miss, however, is that Wallace could have easily integrated many of the footnotes into the body of his main text. By designating them as notes, he not only complicates the narrative structure but also indicates that they are pieces of information that are important but not integral. In other words, they are remnants of his consciousness that he cannot part with. Wallace told Charlie Rose that the "footnotes get very, very addictive and it's almost like having a second voice in your head." They illustrate not only his physical need but also his psychic inability to chronicle and interpret all of the stimuli he encounters during his reporting. He once told David Lipsky that he "received 500,000 discrete bits of information today, of which maybe 25 are important. My job is to make some sense of it" (Lipsky). This job becomes increasingly important when a magazine assignment institutionalizes it.

Nietzsche characterizes this sense-making as a desire for perfection. He writes that people without oblivion "can't be done with anything," but not in a way that is "purely passive succumbing to past impressions"; rather, they exhibit "active not wishing to be done with it" (190). He believed oblivion was an instinctive — although not impervious — part of the psyche, calling man a "naturally forgetful animal for whom oblivion represents a power, a form of strong health" (189). Anachronistically speaking, Nietzsche would have regarded Wallace as a "dyspeptic" whose "screen is damaged and inoperative" (189). Unable to digest what his consciousness encounters, Wallace stores the excess information in his footnotes.

Nietzsche was a trained philologist who scrutinized etymologies in order to unmask firmly held truths and metanarratives (and in that sense, he was a forerunner of deconstruction and postmodern philosophy). Wallace shared that obsession with genealogies and was, in fact, considered by many as his generation's foremost practitioner of postmodern aesthetics.[10] But despite having a philosophy degree and not being shy about incorporating past thinkers into his work,[11] he only mentioned Nietzsche once in all of his nonfiction. It comes in a parenthetical aside, embedded in the fourteenth footnote, in his review of literary scholar Joseph Frank's five-volume study of Fyodor Dostoevsky. But the note is instructive. Wallace writes, "In our own culture of 'enlightened atheism' we are very much Nietzsche's children, his ideological heirs" ("Joseph Frank's Dostoevsky" 264). When Wallace says we are all "Nietzsche's children," he is referring to an atomized culture where individuals eschew metanarratives and will their ethical belief systems. But Wallace makes it clear in his Kenyon speech that such "enlightened atheism" is, in fact, a false prophet: "In the day-to-day trenches of adult life, there is actually no such thing as atheism. There is no such thing as not worshipping. Everybody worships. The only choice we get is what to worship." For Wallace, it is important to revere "some spiritual-type thing" and not material, ideological, or status gods because "anything else you worship will eat you alive. . . . It's the truth" (*This Is Water* 98–101, 105). This earnest appeal for "keeping the truth up front in daily consciousness" is actually an antidote to the irony that Wallace felt was pervasive and corrosive in American literature and culture, causing him to wonder "why we seem to require of our art an ironic distance from deep convictions or desperate questions" ("Joseph Frank's Dostoevsky" 271). Early in his writing career Wallace noted that irony is "not a rhetorical mode that wears well" because it "serves an almost exclusively negative function. It's critical and destructive; a ground clearing. . . . But irony's singularly unuseful when it comes to constructing anything to replace the hypocrisies it debunks" ("E Unibus Pluram" 67). Likewise, irony is not a useful tool in his literary journalism. If the entire point is to write "stuff about what it feels like to live, instead of being a relief from what it feels like to live," then irony is, in fact, an impediment to that goal because it widens that gulf between subjectivity and its object (Lipsky, "The Lost Years").

It is perhaps ironic that Wallace argues so vehemently against irony, because many critics felt that it was the defining feature of his literary aesthetic.[12] And while his short stories and novels do exhibit a fractured style and an arch, self-knowing tone, such an overarching label is an easy caricature. Critics who label Wallace an ironist privilege his writing style and ignore his ideology. Moreover, Wallace's nonfiction is decidedly not postmodern, ironic, or avant-garde. Although it does share the same maximalist writing style as his fiction, and utilizes rhetorical techniques like parody and pastiche, the narratives are also linear, realistic, and, most important, earnest. For example, near the end of his story about John McCain's 2000 presidential run, Wallace stops the article "for a quick *Rolling Stone* PSA" in which he directly addresses young voters:

> If you are bored and disgusted by politics and don't bother to vote, you are in effect voting for the entrenched Establishments of the two major parties, who please rest assured are not dumb, and who are keenly aware that it is in their interests to keep you disgusted and bored and cynical and to give you every possible psychological reason to stay at home doing one-hitters and watching MTV on primary day. By all means stay at home if you want, but don't bullshit yourself that you're not voting. In reality, there is *no such thing as not voting*: you either vote by voting, or you vote by staying home and tacitly doubling the value of some Diehard's vote. ("Up, Simba" 207)

This public service announcement is decidedly unironic and exemplifies the ideological gravity that undergirds Wallace's journalism.

In a 2006 interview in Italy, Wallace described his writing style as "using postmodern techniques, postmodern aesthetic but using that to discuss or represent very old traditional human verities that have to do with spirituality and emotion and community and ideas that the avant-garde would consider very old-fashioned so that there's a kind of melding, it's using postmodern formal techniques for very traditional ends, if there is group... that's the group I want to belong to" (*Le Conversazioni* interview). This distinction helps explain why one critic called Wallace an "old-fashioned moralist in postmodern disguise all along" (Mishra). Still, I would argue that the disguise was as much a projection by critics as it was a cloak to cover Wallace's true intentions. Both modern and postmodern writers have examined fractured cultural landscapes. The difference is that "the modernist laments fragmentation, while the postmodernist celebrates it" (Barry 84). And like the modernist, Wallace makes it clear throughout his literary journalism that he is not at all happy to be witnessing the events that he does. Of his onboard experience during the Caribbean cruise, Wallace wrote: "I have felt as bleak as I've felt since puberty," later adding, "there's something deeply mind-fucking about the Type-A-personality service and pampering on the *Nadir*" ("A Supposedly Fun" 258, 298). And yet, those comments and that story do not come across as smug or condescending. During a radio interview about his Caribbean cruise with Steve Paulson on *To the Best of Our Knowledge*, Wallace explained how "it's very easy just to be mean. Let's make some very easy, mordant comments about Sybaritic pleasure and commercial American culture." Instead, Wallace displayed a strong fidelity to the reader by casting himself as complicit in culture. He spells his writing philosophy out clearly in letters he wrote to Anne Fadiman's (herself a literary journalist) creative nonfiction writing class at Yale. In two of the letters, published posthumously in *Harper's*, Wallace once again emphasizes his obligation to his readers:

> Maybe the root challenge here is to form and honor a fairly rigorous contract with the reader, one that involves honesty and unblinkingness (if the latter's a word). So that the reader gets the overall impression that here's a narrator who's primarily engaged in trying to Tell the Truth ... and if that truth involves the putziness of other people or events, so be it, but if it involves the narra-

tor's own schmuckiness, limitations, prejudices, foibles, screw-ups at the event, etc., then these get told too — because the truth-as-seen is the whole project here (as opposed to just mockery, or just self-ridicule, or just self-superiority, etc.). ("It All Gets Quite Tricky" 32)[13]

Wallace's commitment to an empathetic awareness of the humanness of himself and his subjects epitomizes Thomas B. Connery's belief that "literary journalism attempts to show readers life and human behavior, even if what actually emerges is life's incomprehensibility and the inexplicability of human behavior" (8).

Wallace never considered himself a journalist. And he often made sport of this fact throughout his *reportage*, usually by projecting a self-conscious and naïve view of the profession. For example, as he begins his reporting from the Illinois State Fair, he reflects, "I imagine credentials to be a small white card in the band of a Fedora. I've never been considered Press before. My main interest in credentials is getting into rides and stuff for free" ("Getting Away" 83). This blend of nostalgia and indifference humorously frames Wallace as an amateur (which, of course, he was[14]), but it also establishes him as an outsider — a journalistic Other — distinct from other reporters and freed from the constraints of conventional journalism. He reinforces this naïve view by paying similar attention to his attire at the beginning of his coverage of John McCain's 2000 presidential run:

> I was absurdly proud of my *Rolling Stone* press badge and of the fact that most of the pencils and campaign staff referred to me as "the guy from *Rolling Stone*." I will confess that I even borrowed a friend's battered old black leather jacket to wear on the Trail so I'd better project the kind of edgy, vaguely dangerous vibe I imagined an *RS* reporter ought to give off. (You have to understand that I hadn't read *Rolling Stone* in quite some time.) ("Up, Simba" 158)

The symbolism in these two passages is evident: Both the clothes and the conventions of old journalists are outdated. And by positioning himself as an obtuse outsider, Wallace creates space for a new journalism.[15]

Wallace uses his interloper status to both his reportorial and rhetorical advantage. While profiling the filmmaker David Lynch for *Premiere*, he confesses: "One of the minor reasons Aysymmetrical Productions let me onto the set is that I don't even pretend to be a journalist and have no idea how to interview somebody" ("David Lynch Keeps His Head" 147). And he includes his inability to interview during a passage from the state fair story: "I ask a kid to describe the taste of his Funnel Cake and he runs away" ("Getting Away" 128). However, there is more going on in these self-conscious admissions than an ironic send-up of the profession.[16] Wallace offers a metacommentary on his job as a way to indicate to the reader that the traditional topics and tendencies of journalism fail to capture much beyond surface-level description. While examining yearly prize-winning vegetable displays, he encounters a 17.6-pound zucchini. All he can say is, "One big zucchini, alright" ("Getting Away" 128). By highlighting his reportorial ineptitude, Wallace draws attention to the professional challenges faced by conventional journalists: access, the need to use "official sources" to "objectify" what he already knows (Carey 181), and the banality of trivial facts (how else to respond to such a sizable squash?). The difference is that Wallace has the editorial freedom to work around the conventions of sourcing and objectivity and third-person point of view. He makes the reader aware of the problem and then offers a solution.

Wallace's literary journalism embodies a principle that John Dewey wrote about long ago: "Artists have always been the real purveyors of news, for it is not the outward happening in itself which is new, but the kindling by it of emotion, perception and appreciation" (184). Wallace himself sketched out a similar summary of the benefits of alternative forms of journalism in his introduction to *The Best American Essays 2007*. He also addressed the limitations of conventional journalism in presenting a story's deeper meaning[17] in his Caribbean cruise story a decade earlier. He begins the third section of "A Supposedly Fun Thing I'll Never Do Again" with an anecdote about a 16-year-old man who had recently jumped to his death from an upper deck of a similar cruise ship. Wallace concludes, "The news version was that it had been an unhappy adolescent love thing, a shipboard romance gone bad, etc. I think part of it was something else, something there's no way a real news story could cover" (261). Here the intimation is that traditional methods of reporting and writing are inadequate to offer more than prima facie conclusions, and that what is needed is a style of journalistic writing that "broadly and subjectively explores how and why, reaching beyond the institutional parameters of those categories to produce prose characterized by" what Alan Trachtenberg called "a rendering of felt detail" (Connery 3).

The literary journalists whom Wallace most closely resembles are Hunter S. Thompson and Joan Didion. Wallace shares Thompson's dark worldview and manic prose style. Thompson's 1973 piece, "The Kentucky Derby Is Decadent and Depraved," chronicles "the inexplicability of human behavior" (Connery 8) in much the same way as Wallace's later stories about the state fair and his Caribbean cruise. Similarly, Wallace shares Didion's sharp eye for revealing details as well as her personal dread. In much the same way that Didion's "The White Album" chronicles the peculiarly personal anomie of the late 1960s and early 1970s, Wallace's journalism of the last two decades examines the "lostness" of Generation X.[18] In his taxonomic essay, "The New Journalism and the Image-World," David Eason categorizes Thompson and Didion as modernists, in contrast to realist writers like Tom Wolfe and Gay Talese. According to Eason, "realism assures its readers that traditional ways of making sense still apply in society," whereas modernist texts "describe the inability of traditional cultural distinctions to order experience" (194). Extending Eason's classification beyond the 1960s, and continuing my earlier argument that he is not postmodern, I would also place Wallace in that modernist camp. Similar to Connery's description, Wallace had little faith that his observations or interpretations would reveal a larger symbolic truth. He once said that writing fiction (and presumably nonfiction) is "about what it is to be a fucking human being" (McCaffery 131). And that existence, as Wallace's own life showed, is often confusing and complicated.

As Norman Sims has written: literary journalism stands as "a humanistic approach to culture as compared to the scientific, abstract, or indirect approach taken by much standard journalism" (*True Stories* 12).

Such an understanding helps explain why pieces such as "Consider the Lobster" are more than just individual digressions packed around a central journalistic purpose: "Consider the Lobster" is as much about defining what it means to be a gourmet as it is about animal rights. Although he goes to great lengths to discuss the neurological, bioethical, and philosophical factors that come into play when deciding the ethics of cooking lobsters, he ultimately leaves the matter unresolved — except to resign and say that the decision is still, ultimately, up to an individual's principles. (And that lackluster conclusion doesn't come until the second paragraph of footnote 20, two pages from the article's end.) For Wallace, the bigger question is whether or not we should think about these matters at all; whether we should be conscious. He ends the essay with a series of earnest rhetorical questions directed at *Gourmet* readers. "After all," he asks, "isn't being extra aware and attentive and thoughtful about one's food and its overall context part of what distinguishes a real gourmet?" (254). Here Wallace elevates taste to the level of consciousness — and it's not hard to make the leap from that question to the larger ontological question: Isn't questioning everything the essence of what it means to be alive? But just as soon as he raises the proposition he resigns and ends the piece by saying, "There are limits to what even interested persons can ask of each other" (254). Translation: Although these questions may be important, he recognizes that it's too much to ask readers, much less vacationers, to also shed their oblivion.[19]

Wallace's death sent critics and fans alike scrambling back to his texts in search of clues and explanations. But this is a mistake. I abide by *New York Times* critic A. O. Scott's admonition that "the temptation to regard Mr. Wallace's suicide last weekend as anything other than a private tragedy must be resisted." But, Scott admits, "the strength of the temptation should nonetheless be acknowledged. Mr. Wallace was hardly one to conceal himself within his work; on the contrary, his personality is stamped on every page — so much so that the life and the work can seem not just connected but continuous" (Scott). This is nowhere truer than in his literary journalism, as he told Lipsky: "The *Harper's* pieces were me peeling back my skull. You know, welcome to my mind for 20 pages, see through my eyes." It is easy to see this anxiety and sadness in Wallace's stories now that he is dead. But the despair, of course, like his decades-long battle with clinical depression, was there all along. And Wallace, in fact, did little to hide it. In this regard, Wallace's two biographers Lipsky and Max misread his nonfiction in their profiles. Lipsky said "the difference between the fiction and the nonfiction reads as the difference between Wallace's social self and his private self. The essays were endlessly charming. . . . Wallace's fiction, especially *Infinite Jest*, would turn chilly, dark, abstract. You could imagine the author of the fiction sinking into a depression. The nonfiction writer was an impervious sun" ("The Lost Years"). And early in his profile, Max claimed that "depression often figured in his work" (Max 48). He then cited copious details from one alarmingly sad short story called "The Depressed Person." As a counterpoint, Max added: "He never published a word about his own mental illness" (48). While technically correct, it is inaccurate to say that his depression was not apparent in Wallace's nonfiction. For example, early in "A Supposedly Fun Thing I'll Never Do Again" he devotes an entire section to explaining how being on the ship leaves him suicidal:

> The word's overused and banalified now, despair, but it's a serious word, and I'm using it seriously. For me it denotes a simple admixture — a weird yearning for death combined with a crushing sense of my own smallness and futility that presents as a fear of death. It's maybe close to what people call dread or angst. But it's not these things, quite. It's more like wanting to die in order to escape the unbearable feeling of becoming aware that I'm small and weak and selfish and going without any doubt at all to die. It's wanting to jump overboard. (261)

Critics often overlooked the darker elements of Wallace's journalism because he supplanted his anguish in both the readers' and reviewers' minds through his unexpected descriptions (at the Illinois State Fair he notes that horses' faces are "long and somehow suggestive of coffins"), his humor (on the first night of his Caribbean cruise he confesses to an "atavistic shark fetish" and asks the wait staff for "a spare bucket of *au jus* drippings from supper so I could try chumming for sharks off the back rail of the top deck"), and his intelligence (in Maine he says that solving the lobster question requires "metaphysics, epistemology, value theory, ethics") ("Getting Away" 92; "A Supposedly Fun" 261; "Consider" 246). These are the descriptions that readers and critics remember, but it is equally important not to forget that, as Wallace told Charlie Rose, "unfortunately a lot of [the stories] I think are about me."

Wallace often attributed the source of his anxiety to his particular geography. He blames his unease at the fair to the fact that he is "not spiritually Midwestern anymore" ("Getting Away" 132). Aboard the *Nadir*, he sublimates his nervousness onto the ship's confined space and his semi-agoraphobia, and at the Maine Lobster Festival, he blames his unhappiness on his inability to understand why "so many people's idea of a fun vacation is to don flip-flops and sunglasses and crawl through maddening traffic to loud, hot, crowded tourist venues" ("Consider" 240). Perhaps a more accurate location for his disquietude rests in what he calls his "default setting, hardwired into our boards at birth" (*This Is Water* 38). In fact, Wallace alludes to his nervous psychological state in several stories. Early in "Getting Away from Already Being Pretty Much Away from It All" he half-jokingly admits that his neurological makeup is "extremely sensitive: carsick, airsick, height sick," before adding hauntingly, "my sister likes to say I'm 'life sick'" (99). What Wallace meant as a joking aside reveals, when probed, a "great and terrible truth." His sister, Amy Havens Wallace, told *Rolling Stone* that in high school her brother had "pinned an article about Kafka to [his bedroom] wall, with the headline THE DISEASE WAS LIFE ITSELF" (Lipsky). As an adult, Wallace taught and admired Kafka's literature. In 1998, he delivered a speech entitled "Laughing with Kafka" to the PEN American Center. In that speech Wallace claimed that the central joke in Kafka's fiction is "that the horrific struggle to establish a human self results in a self whose humanity is inseparable from that horrific struggle. That our endless and impossible journey toward home is in fact our home" ("Some Remarks" 64–5). The joke, of course, is terrifying, and it does not take a substantial leap to recognize that the same paradox presided over Wallace's life and is reflected in his writing.

Although his journalism illustrates how despair results from consciousness, his Kenyon College commencement address argues that consciousness can also be a way to alter or get free "of my natural, hardwired, default setting" (*This is Water* 44). Wallace begins his speech by retelling a familiar parable: Two young fish encounter an older fish swimming the opposite direction. He greets them, saying, "Morning, boys. How's the water?" The younger fish swim on for a bit and then one asks the other, "What the hell is water?" Wallace explains that the point of this story is to illustrate that "the most obvious, ubiquitous, important realities are often the ones that are hardest to see and talk about." Wallace uses the rest of the speech to argue that the value of consciousness is to "keep from going through your comfortable, prosperous, respectable, adult life dead, unconscious, a slave to your head and to your natural default setting of being uniquely, completely, imperially alone day in and day out." He ends the speech by urging the students to cultivate simple awareness of the seemingly obvious; to repeat the mantra of the enlightened older fish: "This is water. This is water" (3–4, 8, 60, 132–133).

But Wallace's advice takes on a darker resonance when it's read against his introduction to *The Best American Essays 2007*. Again imploring readers to be more conscious of their surroundings, Wallace invokes another water metaphor, this time to emphasize the difficulty in processing all the information necessary to be a mindful, moral adult: "Or let's not even mention the amount of research, background, crosschecking, corroboration, and rhetorical parsing required to understand [it all]. . . . There's simply no way. You'd simply drown. We all would" ("Deciderization" xxii). This contradiction epitomizes the insufferable paradox of Wallace's philosophical worldview: It is imperative to be conscious, but to be conscious is to be impaired.

In the end, two words resonate for Wallace more than any other: infinite and oblivion. These words not only factor into book and story titles but also signify an ongoing tension in his work. They are the warring themes that bookend his prose. The endless, limitless, and immeasurable competing with the need to limit, close off, and forget. Infinite consciousness leads to an infinitesimal amount of oblivion. Wallace reconciled these two forces, if only for a moment, at the end of his state fair story. In the original *Harper's* publication, he ends the piece with a revelation that the real draw for fairgoers is not the rides and shows, but the crowd itself. In the collected essays edition, however, Wallace moved that insight to the middle of the story and instead allowed his final experience at the fair to resonate with the reader. The fact that Wallace changed the ending underscores the resonance of this final scene where he witnesses a thrill seeker being harnessed and hoisted into the air on a ride called the SKYCOASTER. A crane raises the man hundreds of feet off the ground, suspending him above the onlookers, before a clip is released and the man is dispatched to swing like a pendulum across the fairgrounds. The tension is too much for Wallace. Just before the man drops, Wallace dissociates. He closes his eyes. He confesses, "Just then I lose my nerve, in my very last moment at the Fair . . . and I decline to be part of this, even as witness — and I find, again, in extremis, access to childhood's other worst nightmare, the only sure way to obliterate all; and the sun and the sky and plummeting go out like a light" ("Getting Away" 137). And that's how the story ends. A foreshadow of a more lasting getaway, a more permanent oblivion.

Notes

1. In the three intervening years between that address and his death, the speech existed in relative anonymity. An unofficial transcript survived online and was later printed in *Best American Nonrequired Reading 2006*. In the aftermath of Wallace's death, however, the speech, with its overt references to suicide, became a touchstone for critics who sought answers to why one of the world's most renowned writers would take his own life. The renewed interest in the speech led Little, Brown and Company to publish the work in a devotional-sized book under the title *This Is Water: Some Thoughts, Delivered on a Significant Occasion, about Living a Compassionate Life* (2009). A year later, an audio recording of the speech became available for purchase on iTunes; and while some still cleaved to the darker elements of the address, others gravitated with near religiosity toward the homiletic aspects of the talk. It became a spiritual tract on the New Sincerity by Saint Dave. There was, however, a backlash to this sanctification. Wallace's friend Jonathan Franzen, who in the fall of 2008 had told the audience at one of the four public memorials given for Wallace that he was "as passionate and precise a punctuator of prose as has ever walked this earth," later wrote in a 2011 piece for the *New*

Yorker that readers only had a superficial understanding of Wallace, the person: "People who had never read his fiction, or had never even heard of him, read his Kenyon College commencement address in the *Wall Street Journal* and mourned the loss of a great and gentle soul" (*Celebrating the Life* 16; "Farther Away" 90).

2. In chronological order, those pieces are: "Getting Away from Already Being Pretty Much Away from It All," "Democracy and Commerce at the U.S. Open," "David Lynch Keeps His Head," "Tennis Player Michael Joyce's Professional Artistry as a Paradigm of Certain Stuff about Choice, Freedom, Discipline, Joy, Grotesquerie, and Human Completeness," "A Supposedly Fun Thing I'll Never Do Again," "Big Red Son," "Up, Simba: Seven Days on the Trail of an Anticandidate," "The View from Mrs. Thompson's," "Consider the Lobster," "Host," and "Federer as Religious Experience." All of these pieces, except "Democracy and Commerce at the U.S. Open" and "Federer as Religious Experience," are collected in either *A Supposedly Fun Thing I'll Never Do Again* or *Consider the Lobster and Other Essays.* Wallace revised and renamed nearly all of his nonfiction from its original publication form to its collected book form. He made it clear on the copyright page of both books that he preferred the book versions of his pieces. In *Consider the Lobster* he wrote, "The following pieces were originally published in edited, heavily edited, or (in at least one instance) bowdlerized form in the following books and periodicals." Therefore, all of my citations will refer to the book versions of his essays and journalism because they represent Wallace's vision for them.

3. Their respective *Harper's* titles are "Ticket to the Fair" and "Shipping Out: On the (Nearly Lethal) Comforts of a Luxury Cruise."

4. Wallace once told Lipsky: "There's good self-consciousness, and then there's toxic, paralyzing, raped-by-psychic-Bedouins self-consciousness" ("The Lost Years").

5. This theme is also evident in Wallace's short story, "Good Old Neon," from the aptly named collection *Oblivion.* Early in the story, the narrator responds to his analyst's question about whether he plays chess by saying, "I used to in middle school but quit because I couldn't be as good as I eventually wanted to be, how frustrating it was to get just good enough to know what getting really good at it would be like but not being able to get that good, etc" (146).

6. In fact, Wallace footnotes his footnotes and then occasionally appends those notes with asterisks and daggers and whole mini-essay interpolations.

7. Wallace, himself the son of two professors, believed that actual academic prose was the epitome of bad writing. In a footnote in his review of Bryan Garner's *A Dictionary of Modern American Usage*, he both excoriated and lam-

pooned the genre: "The truth is that most of U.S. academic prose is appalling — pompous, abstruse, claustral, inflated, euphuistic, pleonastic, solecistic, sesquipedalian, Heliogabaline, occluded, obscure, jargon-ridden, empty: resplendently dead" ("Authority and American Usage" 81).

8. Wallace had a tendency to repeat himself in his interviews, often drawing his responses from his written work. Several years after his appearance on *Charlie Rose*, he told Steve Paulson, of the public radio program *To the Best of Our Knowledge*: "I often feel very fragmented and as if I have a symphony of different voices and voiceovers and factoids going on all the time and digressions on digressions on digressions. I know that people who don't much care for my stuff see a lot of the stuff as just sort of vomiting it out. That's at least my intent. What's hard is to seem very digressive and bent in on yourself and diffracted and also have there be patterns and significances about it and it takes a lot of drafts, but it probably comes out just looking like a manic, mad monologue."

9. "A Supposedly Fun Thing I'll Never Do Again" contains 137 footnotes in 97 pages of text, while the 388 endnotes in his novel *Infinite Jest* span 96 pages, leading Michiko Kakutani, in her *New York Times* review, to quote Henry James in calling the novel a "loose baggy monster" ("A Country Dying of Laughter").

10. For a stunning example of Wallace's interest in and command of U.S. lexicography, see his 61-page review of Garner's *A Dictionary of Modern American Usage*, first published in *Harper's* as "Tense Present: Democracy, English, and the Wars Over Usage" (April 2001) and then collected in *Consider the Lobster* as "Authority and American Usage."

11. The title of Wallace's senior philosophy thesis at Amherst is "Richard Taylor's 'Fatalism' and the Semantics of Physical Modality."

12. In her somewhat controversial review of *Infinite Jest*, Kakutani called Wallace a "pushing-the-envelope postmodernist." In her "Appreciation" of him after his death, she referenced his "mastery of postmodern pyrotechnics" ("A Country Dying of Laughter"; "Exhuberant Riffs on a Land Run Amok").

13. In an interview with David Lipsky in the late 1990s, Wallace admitted that in his journalism "there's a certain persona created, that's a little stupider and schmuckier than I am." Yet his allegiance to the reader is real. In "A Supposedly Fun Thing I'll Never Do Again" he spends a substantial amount of time criticizing the acclaimed author Frank Conroy for a promotional essay he wrote on behalf of the cruise ship. The *Nadir*'s brochure does not present the essay as an advertisement but rather as an "authentic response" to his experience aboard. Part of what bothers Wallace is his admiration of Conroy, especially of his memoir *Stop Time*, which Wallace confesses "is one of the books

that first made poor old yours truly want to try to be a writer." Wallace finds
Conroy's essaymercial "graceful and lapidary and attractive and assuasive. I
submit that it is also completely sinister and despair-producing and bad" because "an essay's fundamental obligations are supposed to be to the reader. The
reader, on however unconscious a level, understands this, and thus tends to
approach an essay with a relatively high level of openness and credulity." The
essay is one more instance of the ship's dubious advertisements which "don't
flatter your adult agency, or even ignore it — they supplant it." The Conroy
essay is a prime example of this loss of control. The attempt is to "micromanage not only one's perception of a *7NC Luxury Cruise*, but even one's own
interpretation and articulation of those perceptions. . . . As my week on the
Nadir wore on, I began to see this essaymercial as a perfect ironic reflection of
the mass-market-Cruise experience itself" (288–91).

14. Wallace includes a running joke throughout "Getting Away from Already Being Pretty Much Away from It All" about his lack of proper journalistic resources. As he talks with the fair's unofficial historian he reflects: "It
occurs to me I probably ought to have brought a notebook." The next day he
provides an update: "I'd bought a notebook, but I left the car windows down
last night and it got ruined by rain." Finally, near the end of the piece he concludes the joke, noting that he was finally prepared to take notes: "All they had
was a little kid's tablet with that weird soft gray paper and some kind of purple
brontosaurus-type character named Barney on the cover" (85, 91, 112).

15. And much like the New Journalism of the 1960s and 1970s, there is
nothing really "new" in what Wallace is doing. Like previous literary journalists before him, Wallace "conveys impressions, ideas, and emotions and draws
upon themes and motifs identified by the writer and revealed in the details
of an event or in the manners, morals, and actions of people" (Connery 6).
Literary journalism in America stretches back to at least the mid-1800s, with
roots in the newspaper sketch. The form has flourished during several distinct periods in U.S history: the 1890s, 1930s–1940s, 1960s–1970s, and today.
Each of these historical moments fomented an alternative method of reporting
and writing because of an epistemological crisis within conventional journalism with regard to the profession's ability to adequately report on the rapidly
changing phenomenal world (Hartsock 15). The two most informative books
on the history of the form are John Hartsock's critical historiography *A History of American Literary Journalism: The Emergence of a Modern Narrative
Form* (2000) and Norman Sims's narrative history *True Stories: A Century of
Literary Journalism* (2008).

16. There are, however, moments when Wallace is sardonic, especially when
describing his methodology as "solid bent-over investigative journalism,"

"dogged journalistic querying," "serious journalistic phone inquiries," and a "William T. Vollmannish bit of journalistic derring-do," which usually lead to such revelations as noting the grass inside the governor's tent at the Illinois State Fair is, in fact, artificial turf ("Getting Away" 89; "A Supposedly Fun" 266, 288, 315).

17. The terminology here is problematic. Other synonyms for "deeper meaning" (such as: true, honest, complete, whole, and contingent) are equally problematic in the nettlesome relativism of the postmodern age. The whole point is that they convey a sense or feeling beyond what one normally associates with straight facts. Perhaps the best way to say it is that it tells a story as opposed to offering a report.

18. In an interview with Laura Miller of *Salon.com*, Wallace described living in America at the turn of the millennium as "particularly sad . . . something that doesn't have very much to do with physical circumstances, or the economy, or any of the stuff that gets talked about in the news. It's more like stomach-level sadness. I see it in myself and my friends in different ways. It manifests itself as a kind of lostness."

19. Wallace's conclusions at the Maine Lobster Festival are variations on a theme he chronicled earlier in his career. He came to the same conclusion during his Caribbean cruise: "Here's the thing: A vacation is a respite from unpleasantness, and since consciousness of death and decay are unpleasant, it may seem weird that Americans' ultimate fantasy vacation involves being plunked down in an enormous primordial engine of death and decay" ("A Supposedly Fun" 263). He believes it is also the reason why David Lynch's film *Fire Walk with Me* got terrible reviews: "It required of us an empathetic confrontation with the exact same muddy *both*ness in ourselves and our intimates that makes the real world of moral selves so tense and uncomfortable, a *both*ness we go to the movies to get a couple hours fucking relief from" ("David Lynch Keeps His Head" 211).

Works Cited

Barry, Peter. *Beginning Theory: An Introduction to Literary and Cultural Theory*. Manchester, UK: Manchester University Press, 1995. Print.

Begley, Adam. Dust jacket. In *A Supposedly Fun* by David Foster Wallace. Print.

Carey, James. "The Dark Continent of American Journalism." In *The James Carey Reader*. Ed. Eve Stryker Munson and Catherine A. Warren. Minneapolis: University of Minnesota Press, 1997. 144–88. Print.

Connery, Thomas B. *A Sourcebook of American Literary Journalism: Representative Writers in an Emerging Genre*. Westport, CT: Greenwood Press,

1992. Print.

Dewey, John. *The Public and Its Problems*. New York: Henry Holt, 1927; reprint, Athens, OH: Swallow Press, 1954. Print.

Eason, David. "The New Journalism and the Image-World." In *Literary Journalism in the Twentieth Century*. Ed. Norman Sims. Oxford: Oxford University Press, 1990; reprint, Evanston: Northwestern University Press, 2008. Print.

Eugenides, Jeffrey. Dust jacket. In *Consider the Lobster* by David Foster Wallace. Print.

Forde, Kathy Roberts. *Literary Journalism on Trial: Masson v. New Yorker and the First Amendment*. Amherst: University of Massachusetts Press, 2008. Print.

Franzen, Jonathan. In *Five Dials: Celebrating the Life and Work of David Foster Wallace*. London: Hamish Hamilton, 2008. 16–7. Print.

———. "Farther Away." *New Yorker* 18 April 2011. 80–95. Print.

Hartsock, John C. *A History of American Literary Journalism: The Emergence of a Modern Narrative Form*. Amherst: University of Massachusetts Press, 2000. Print.

Kakutani, Michiko. "A Country Dying of Laughter." *New York Times* 13 February 1996. Web.

———. "Exuberant Riffs on a Land Run Amok." *New York Times* 14 September 2008. Web.

Lipsky, David. "The Lost Years & Last Days of David Foster Wallace." *Rolling Stone* 30 October 2008. Web.

Max, D. T. "The Unfinished." *New Yorker* 9 March 2009: 48–61. Print.

McCaffery, Larry. "An Interview with David Foster Wallace." *Review of Contemporary Fiction* 13.2 (Summer 1993): 127–50. Print.

Miller, Laura. "The Horror, The Horror." *Salon.com* 30 June 2004. Web.

———. "The Road to Babbittville." *New York Times* 16 March 1997. Web.

Mishra, Pankaj. "The Postmodern Moralist." *New York Times* 12 March 2006. Web.

Nietzsche, Friedrich. *The Genealogy of Morals*. 1956. Trans. Francis Golffing. New York: Anchor Books, 1990. Print.

Scott, A. O. "The Best Mind of His Generation." *New York Times* 20 September 2008. Web.

Sims, Norman. *True Stories: A Century of Literary Journalism*. Evanston: Northwestern University Press, 2007. Print.

Sims, Norman, ed. *The Literary Journalists*. New York: Ballantine Books, 1984. Print.

Wallace, David Foster. "Authority and American Usage." In *Consider the Lobster* 66–127. Print.

———. "Big Red Son." In *Consider the Lobster* 3–50. Print.

———. "Consider the Lobster." In *Consider the Lobster* 235–54. Print.

———. *Consider the Lobster and Other Essays*. New York: Little, Brown and Company, 2005. Print.

———. "David Lynch Keeps His Head." In *A Supposedly Fun* 146–212. Print.

———. "Deciderization 2007 — A Special Report." In *The Best American Essays 2007*. Series Ed. Robert Atwan. New York: Houghton Mifflin Company, 2007. xii–xxiv. Print.

———. "Derivative Sport in Tornado Alley." In *A Supposedly Fun* 3–20. Print.

———. "E Unibus Pluram: Television and U.S. Fiction." In *A Supposedly Fun* 21–82. Print.

———. "Getting Away from Already Being Pretty Much Away from It All." In *A Supposedly Fun* 83–137. Print.

———. "Good Old Neon." In *Oblivion* 141–81. Print.

———. "How Tracy Austin Broke My Heart." In *Consider the Lobster* 141–55. Print.

———. Interview by Charlie Rose. *Charlie Rose* 27 March 1997. Web.

———. Interview by *Le Conversazioni* 2 July 2006. Web.

———. Interview by Dave Eggers. *Believer* November 2003. Web.

———. Interview by Laura Miller. *Salon.com* 8 March 1996. Web.

———. Interview by Steve Paulson. *To the Best of Our Knowledge* 19 July 1998. Web.

———. "It All Gets Quite Tricky." *Harper's* November 2008. 31–2. Print.

———. "Joseph Frank's Dostoevsky." In *Consider the Lobster* 255–74. Print.

———. "Oblivion." In *Oblivion* 190–237. Print.

———. *Oblivion*. New York: Little, Brown and Company, 2004. Print.

———. "Some Remarks on Kafka's Funniness from Which Probably Not Enough Has Been Removed." In *Consider the Lobster* 60–5. Print.

———. "A Supposedly Fun Thing I'll Never Do Again." In *A Supposedly Fun* 256–353. Print.

———. *A Supposedly Fun Thing I'll Never Do Again: Essays and Arguments*. New York: Little, Brown and Company, 1997. Print.

———. "Tennis Player Michael Joyce's Professional Artistry as a Paradigm of Certain Stuff about Choice, Freedom, Discipline, Joy, Grotesquerie, and Human Completeness." In *A Supposedly Fun* 213–55. Print.

———. *This Is Water: Some Thoughts, Delivered on a Significant Occasion, about Living a Compassionate Life*. New York: Little, Brown and Company, 2009. Print.
———. "Up, Simba: Seven Days on the Trail of an Anticandidate." In *Consider the Lobster* 156–234. Print.

GEORGE SAUNDERS

INFORMAL REMARKS FROM THE
DAVID FOSTER WALLACE MEMORIAL
SERVICE IN NEW YORK ON
OCTOBER 23, 2008

A FEW YEARS BACK I was flying out to California, reading *Brief Interviews with Hideous Men*. I found the book was doing weird things to my mind and body. Suddenly, up there over the Midwest, I felt agitated and flinchy, on the brink of tears. When I tried to describe what was going on, I came up with this: if the reader was a guy standing outdoors, Dave's prose had the effect of stripping the guy's clothes away and leaving him naked, with super-sensitized skin, newly susceptible to the weather, whatever that weather might be. If it was a sunny day, he was going to feel the sun more. If it was a blizzard, it was going to really sting. Something about the prose itself was inducing a special variety of openness that I might call *terrified-tenderness*: a sudden new awareness of what a fix we're in on this earth, stuck in these bodies, with these minds.

This alteration seemed more spiritual than aesthetic. I wasn't just "reading a great story"— what was happening was more primal and important: my mind was being altered in the direction of compassion by a shock methodology that was, in its subject matter, actually very dark. I was undergoing a kind of ritual stripping away of the habitual. The reading was waking me up, making me feel more vulnerable, more alive.

The person who had induced this complicated feeling was one of the sweetest, most generous, *dearest* people I've ever known.

I first met Dave at the home of a mutual friend in Syracuse. I'd just read *Girl with Curious Hair* and was terrified that this breakfast might veer off into, say, a discussion of Foucault or something, and I'd be humiliated in front of my wife and kids. But no: I seem to remember Dave was wearing a Mighty Mouse T-shirt. Like Chekhov in those famous anecdotes, who put his nervous provincial visitors at ease by asking them about pie-baking and the local school system, Dave diffused the tension by turning the conversation to us. Our kids' interests, what life was like in Syracuse, our experience of family life. He was about as open and curious and accepting a person as I'd ever met, and I left feeling I'd made a great new friend.

And I had. We were together only occasionally, corresponded occasionally, but every meeting felt super-charged, almost — if this isn't too corny — sacramental.

I don't know much about Dave's spiritual life but I see him as a great American Buddhist writer, in the lineage of Whitman and Ginsberg. He was a wake-up artist. That was his work, as I see it, both on the page and off it: he went around waking people up. He was, if this is even a word, a *celebrationist*, who gave us new respect for the world through his reverence for it, a reverence that manifested as attention, an attention that produced that electrifying, all-chips-in, aware-in-all-directions prose of his.

Over the last few weeks, as I've thought about what I might say up here, I've heard my internalized Dave, and what he's been saying is: don't look for consolation yet. That would be dishonest. And I think that voice is right. In time — but not yet — the sadness that there will be no new stories from him will be replaced by a deepening awareness of what a treasure we have in the existing work. In time — but not yet — the disaster of his loss will fade, and be replaced by the realization of what a miracle it was that he ever existed in the first place.

For now, there's just grief. Grief is, in a sense, the bill that comes due for love. The sadness in this room amounts to a kind of proof: proof of the power of Dave's work; proof of the softening effect his tenderness of spirit had on us; proof, in a larger sense, of the power of the Word itself: look at how this man got inside the world's mind and changed it for the better. Our sadness is proof of the power of a single original human consciousness. Dave — let's just say it — was first among us. The most talented, most daring, most energetic and original, the funniest, the least inclined to rest on his laurels or believe all the praise. His was a spacious, loving heart, and when someone this precious leaves us, especially so early, love converts on the spot to a deep, almost nauseating sadness, and there's no way around it.

But in closing, a pledge, or maybe a prayer: every one of us in this room has, at some point, had our consciousness altered by Dave. Dave has left seeds in our minds. It is up to us to nurture these seeds and bring them out, in positive form, into the living world, through our work, in our actions, by our engagement with others and our engagement with our own minds. So the pledge and the prayer is this: we'll continue to love him, we'll never forget him, and we'll honor him by keeping alive the principal lesson of his work: mostly we're asleep, but we can wake up. And waking up is not only possible, it is our birthright, and our nature, and, as Dave showed us, we can help one another do it.

PART TWO

AESTHETICS

SAMUEL COHEN

TO WISH TO TRY TO SING
TO THE NEXT GENERATION:
INFINITE JEST'S HISTORY

WHEN DAVID FOSTER WALLACE committed suicide in 2008, his death became part of his legacy. The fact of his suicide illuminates his work for some readers but threatens to overshadow it for others. The difference between these two reactions is in part about the tension between the belief in the explanatory power of biography and the conviction that the application of the facts of a writer's life to the writing can only be reductive and can even be a betrayal of the imaginative work writers do. It is also about the fear, which I share, that Wallace's work will forever be read through the way that he died.[1]

In spite of my wariness about using Wallace's life to read his work, I don't think it's possible to fully understand *Infinite Jest* without reckoning in what Wallace was feeling and thinking about writing and about himself as a writer at the time he wrote it. The novel is not only informed by these feelings and thoughts: it is as much about them as it is about any of the many other things with which it is often rightly said to be concerned.

AS AN UNDERGRADUATE at Amherst College, David Foster Wallace became disenchanted with his major, philosophy, a development that figured in his decision to take the leave of absence during which he began writing fiction (and which he described as "a midlife crisis at twenty") (McCaffery interview 139). He eventually returned to school and in 1985 completed an honors thesis in philosophy while also writing one in creative writing. Although he thought about continuing with both pursuits at the time of his graduation, following the model of philosophy professor and novelist William Gass, he ultimately decided to get an MFA (Ryerson 16). By 1987, the year he finished his MFA, Wallace's award-winning first novel *The Broom of the System* (which began as his undergraduate creative writing thesis) had been published. By 1989, a story collection, *Girl with Curious Hair*, appeared, and Wallace was at work on a second novel with the working title "A Failed Entertainment" (which would become *Infinite Jest*). That fall, Wallace matriculated in the graduate program in philosophy at Harvard University.

In spite of his long interest in philosophy, this move could be seen as curious; at least from the point of view of the course of a promising fiction writing career, it might seem a step backward or at the very least in a different direction than might be expected. It turned out that Wallace's career at Harvard lasted only a year; after two semesters of coursework, he left, and resumed work on "A Failed Entertainment" while teaching English at Emerson College and then at Illinois State University. The step back turned out to be merely a detour. As a detour on the road to the writing of such an important novel, however, it is interesting for what it might tell us about that writing. Wallace's reasons for taking it, then, are important.

During the time between finishing his MFA in 1987 and returning to school in 1989, his recurring problems with depression had resurfaced. Wallace struggled with depression for decades, and his death in 2008 was the result of that struggle. He first went on the antidepressant Nardil in 1989 (after a suicide attempt a year earlier, which was followed by electroconvulsive therapy); it was his going off of it in 2007 that led to his suicide (Max, Green). It is reasonable to think, then, that Wallace's decision to put aside his novel and go to graduate school in philosophy was motivated by these problems. In addition to being someone who suffered through depression and dealt with the effects and side effects of antidepression medication, though, Wallace was of course a writer. And he was by no account a writer who took his work lightly; rather, he sweated through draft after draft, wrestling not only with manuscripts but with what kind of writer he wanted to be and what he wanted his writing to do (Pietsch 63–4). Of course, it is impossible to know how much of what went into Wallace's decision to go back to school in philosophy was about depression and how much was about writing. That Wallace was abandoning and restarting "A Failed Entertainment" at the time is known. That the difficulty he experienced in writing it was one factor in his decision to change course, interrupting his life and writing career, seems a reasonable supposition. As D. T. Max puts it, "Wallace had decided that writing was not worth the risk to his mental health"; in Wallace's own words, the reason he went to graduate school in philosophy "is I remembered that I had flourished in an academic environment," implying that he did not feel that he was flourishing at the time in his writing (Max).

Reading *Infinite Jest* as the product of a creative process marked by great difficulties requires inquiring into the nature of those difficulties. My inquiry here depends on the idea that the nature of these difficulties can best be understood by considering *Infinite Jest* in the interrelated contexts of Wallace's own life as a writer, of literary history, and of late twentieth-century America. The position of the novel's composition in these histories is crucial to understanding not only how it comes out of its time but also how it comes out of its author's reflections on that time. The particular way in which *Infinite Jest* looks at each of these pasts from its present, and how it wonders about each of these futures, helps explain not only the difficulties Wallace encountered in writing it but also why it seems to have meant so much to so many of its readers and why it will be read long into the future.

A QUICK DESCRIPTION of the shape of *Infinite Jest*: the novel is set in the early twenty-first century and tells not one but three stories which do and do not converge. The first is the story of Hal Incandenza, student at Enfield Tennis Academy, athletic and intellectual prodigy, increasingly addicted marijuana user, and son of late physicist, experimental filmmaker, and grisly suicide (by microwave) James Incandenza. The second is the story of Don Gately, former criminal and current resident at Ennet House, a halfway house down the hill in Enfield from the academy where he goes to hide but stays to recover from his own drug addiction. The third story is about the struggle between agents of the U.S. government[2] and Québecois separatists for possession of a movie (whose title might be "Infinite Jest" but is often referred to as the Entertainment or the *samizdat*) that was the last made by Hal's father and that is rumored to be fatal to the viewer (who is rendered catatonic watching it), thus making it an attractive weapon to those who would like to see the U.S. addiction to entertainment literalized and lethalized. This third story links the first two through, among other connections, the film's maker and its star, Joelle van Dyne, who is an ex-lover of Hal's brother Orin and currently a resident of Ennet House with Don Gately. Among many, many subplots, there are stories involving Orin, Hal's other brother Mario, his mother and her lover, the various students at the academy, and an elaborate tennis war game played at the academy. Threads connecting the three separate stories also exist or are suggested everywhere in these and in the three main narrative threads, including through the synchronicity between them, as Stephen Burn has pointed out (29).

What these smaller suggested and actual connections do not do is fully bring these three stories together. And they fail to do this in spite of the promise offered by the book's structure. *Infinite Jest* opens with a scene whose relation to the rest of the novel is either present frame to nearly book-length flashback or flash-forward to main narrative. Either way, as the novel continues, the story progresses chronologically and in terms of the unfolding plot and sense-making process in such a way that it encourages the expectation that these three different stories will fully converge and the various mysteries will be explained. They are not. The questions that go unanswered are myriad and concern elements from each of the stories, but foremost among these is the one introduced in this crucial first scene.

As the book opens, the narrating Hal is meeting with administrators at the University of Arizona, including admissions officers, who are, in their effort to give Hal a tennis scholarship, working to reconcile the incredible sophistication of his essays with his low test scores and also, once the meeting begins, with his apparent inability to speak. Instead of answering their questions about his academic record, he emits a series of grunts and squeals accompanied by grimaces and flailing, thus presenting the appearance of, as one attendee puts it, a "writhing animal with a knife in its eye" (14). Readers themselves are forced to try to reconcile Hal's hyperarticulate, observant, and deliberate narrating voice with the exterior he seems to be presenting, which, as his erratic behavior escalates, results in his being pinned to the floor of the men's room until an ambulance arrives.

While the university officials hazard guesses as to the causes of Hal's condition, the novel provides nothing in the way of explanation at the time. The question isn't just not answered at the time, though; the question of what happened to Hal after the time of the end of the novel and the time of its opening, about a year later, is never answered. What the novel seems to promise at the end of this opening, when Hal imagines an orderly in the emergency room asking, "So yo then man what's *your* story?" (17) — Hal's story, with all that the word "story" implies in this context about how he came to be in the state he's in — the novel withholds. There are a number of possible answers to the question of what happened to Hal over which academic critics, reviewers, and online aficionados have struggled, including the possibility that Hal has taken DMZ, the drug acquired by a fellow student, the possibility that Hal has viewed his father's lethal cartridge, or the possibility that the effects of marijuana withdrawal are responsible for his condition (Burn 37).

The novel also chooses, ignoring Chekhov's rule about the loaded rifle, not to fire another seemingly crucial reference from the opening scene — Hal digging up what remains of his father's head (which may have inside it a copy of his film) with Don Gately while fellow academy student John N. R. (No Relation) Wayne stands watch. This second loose end, if it had been conclusively integrated into the narrative, could have tied up the three primary story lines, but it is left hanging, and so the promised convergence of the main narrative threads, which itself might have explained Hal's condition at the novel's opening, never materializes. Instead, we are left on the last page with Hal wandering the halls of the Academy, smiling unsettlingly; with Don Gately still clean but in the hospital, having been shot and having what might be a hallucination of death induced by the pain that is the result of his refusal of pain meds; and with the Wheelchair Assassins (part of the movement of Québecois separatists) headed toward Enfield, possibly having gotten their hands on a copy of the Entertainment.

The result is that, at the end of *Infinite Jest*, the thing that readers in general and readers of this very long novel in particular wait for — the final revelation of meaning, the simultaneous end of the chain of events that constitute the plot and the moment when we can look back and see that whole chain in light of its end — isn't there. What's there instead is a nonending, an inconclusion — a number of possible but unprovable hypotheses, interpretations of what occurs in this gap in the chain between where the novel ends and where the story or stories that constitute it end. A further question we are left with, the answer or answers to which become part of the activity of figuring out what to make of *Infinite Jest*, is why this should be, what it means that the book leaves us hanging in this way.

Wallace's choice to end *Infinite Jest* in this way can be seen in a number of ways — to cite only a few examples: as an invitation to circle back to the beginning that illustrates a number of circles of addiction and/or retribution (Burn); as a challenge to "discover the text's recursive pattern," which is designed to "puncture the illusion of autonomous selfhood" (Hayles 695); or as the culmination of the novel's "disturbing text" performance, aimed at causing readers to virtually experience addiction, generally, and the Entertainment specifically (Cioffi). While there is something to all of these interpretations, I think we also can look to this aspect of *Infinite Jest*'s structure for the answers to the question of the relation between the early difficulties Wallace had writing the book and the form the book ultimately took. In particular, the shape of *Infinite Jest*'s narrative is about what it is like to live "in the middest" of history; this is what connects Wallace's experience of his personal crisis as a writer, his moment in literary history, and his moment in American history. To sketch out these connections, I will now consider three corresponding intertwining historical narratives *Infinite*

Jest implicitly constructs: a *Künstlerroman*, or the portrait of an artist as a young man; a history of contemporary fiction; and a history of contemporary America.

INFINITE JEST is no *Catcher in the Rye*, though it is amusing to imagine Holden in Hal's place, or vice versa. Still, given that much of Wallace's novel is set in a boarding school, that it follows a cast of adolescents around for many, many pages, and that it is centrally concerned with a main character's struggle to grow up, it is certainly a *Catcher*-esque *Bildungsroman* (and surely has Salinger's novel in its DNA). The Hal plot, in Boswell's words, "constitutes a more or less traditional bildungsroman . . . a reading that is particularly apt in view of the many similarities between Hal and Wallace," chief among which is Hal's tennis career (122). While a *Bildungsroman* does not definitionally require that the story of development's roots lie in its author's own biography, the fact that *Infinite Jest*'s seems to, allows us to make an interpretive leap and read the novel not simply as a *Bildungsroman* but as a kind of *Künstlerroman*. Reading Wallace's novel as a portrait of the artist as a young man requires reading the story of the main character's tennis as a figure for writing. While at first this connection might seem a stretch, Wallace was a regionally ranked junior tennis player, and so it makes sense to imagine that his novel about the development of a young tennis player could also be about his own development as a writer.

In *Infinite Jest*, we see Hal Incandenza as a strong but not top junior tennis player who develops somewhat suddenly into the number two player at Enfield. While always talented and hard working, Hal has hit something of a plateau in the level of his success, until he makes a competitive leap. The novel, then, is in part the story of his pursuing an education, possibly a sentimental one, which allows him to develop further in what he hopes will be his adult career, making his place in the world. In this sense it is identifiably a *Bildungsroman*. The question of just what it is that allows this leap to happen, though, leads to the further question of how we are to think of this development, of whether it is positive or enabled by something that is ultimately injurious to Hal as a person. In Stephen Burn's reading, the fact that Hal's competitive leap happens when he's become addicted to marijuana, "the coincidence of Hal's competitive explosion and the year of his addiction," indicates that "both have drawn on the same erasure of self" (50). He bases this reading on the parallel he sees between the athletic philosophy Hal inherits from his father and grandfather, at the core of which is the turning of self into machine, soul into body, and the erasure of self he sees as at the core of addiction. For Burn, this parallel suggests not a negative valuation of Hal's improvement on the court but rather a rethinking of what genre Hal's story belongs to: "Although at times *Infinite Jest* may suggest the outlines of a conventional *bildungsroman*, tracing the development of a sensitive prodigy through an institutional upbringing, the movement of the novel is actually away from fully-realized selfhood" (50). If what seems like positive development is not, this argument goes, then Hal's story cannot be understood as belonging to the genre.

Certainly there are ways in which Hal's story does not seem to run in a positive direction. While the tennis improves, he descends into addiction and ends up hospitalized with an unexplained condition that has rendered him incapable of intelligible speech. One element of Burn's support for his argument against seeing *Infinite Jest* as a *Bildungsroman*, however, can help us see the course of Hal's story differently. For evidence of the novel's ending with the erasure of Hal's self, Burn invokes Joyce, writing, "it is notable that while Joyce's *A Portrait of the Artist*, which is perhaps the ultimate template of a sophisticated twentieth-century development narrative, begins in the third-person and ends in the first, *Infinite Jest* reverses this pattern. Beginning with a confident 'I' the narrative proper ends with 'he'" (51). He further adds that if you consider the end of the novel not the end of the text proper but the end of the footnotes on page 1079, you can say that the novel ends even more impersonally, not with a third-person reference to the protagonist but with a corporation (complete, I would add, with a registered trademark symbol,®). While Burn characterizes one movement in the novel accurately, it is worth considering whether Hal's story actually ends this way. If we separate *fabula* from *sjuzhet*, the last moments in the portion of

Hal's life *Infinite Jest* follows are not in fact those with which the book ends but those with which it opens.

And where it opens, in time, is not a moment of self-erasure. Four of the novel's first five paragraphs begin with the first-person singular pronoun. Hal is, as he says, "in here"— he is a soul trapped inside a body, literally strapped down, struggling to express himself, to bring what is inside out into the open so that he can be understood. Whatever has brought him to this moment, Hal is, at his story's end — and the novel's end returns readers to this opening/ending — struggling to move forward, to find a new way to speak. Read in this way, the arc of Hal's story can still be said to follow an arc of development, even if the nature of the change that has led to its final moments is unclear and the development is largely prospective. And it is an arc whose ultimate stakes are about expression, about finding a way to speak. It is in this connection — this moment when Hal has moved in his own story not from first person to third, as Burn would have it, but from third to first — that his story seems most like a kind of *Künstlerroman* to me, and closest to Wallace's biography.

As was Joyce when he wrote *Portrait*, Wallace was in his early thirties when he finished *Infinite Jest*. He had behind him his own *Dubliners*, *Girl with Curious Hair*, as well as his widely praised first novel, *The Broom of the System*. The struggle to write this second novel — the difficulties with which seem to have been at least part of what motivated Wallace to abandon the manuscript and make an abortive return to school and the study of philosophy — can be seen in Hal's struggles. The feeling of having plateaued that Wallace experienced in his own tennis career and the anxiety of taking the next step as a writer of fiction that he faced in writing "A Failed Entertainment" can be seen as informing the story of Hal's careers as tennis player and adolescent (*Supposedly* 15). The place where we see Hal at the end of his story, struggling to find a new way to speak again, could be seen as analogous to the place where Wallace found himself in 1989 as a writer. If a writer's late twenties and early thirties are often like a tennis phenom's late teens — that is, the time when youthful promise either does or does not blossom into full-blown success — then Wallace, like Hal, stood poised either on the threshold of stardom or at the edge of a precipice. The anxiety of being in this place surely contributed to making writing feel, as Max puts it, like a risk to Wallace's mental health. What makes this story a kind of *Künstlerroman* is the way in which Hal's story offers an analogy for its author's development. What makes this analogy important for our understanding of *Infinite Jest* is the way in which that development is expressed not only in the content of the novel but also in its form.

THE NATURE of this development is itself shaped by the second of the histories I want to examine in connection to *Infinite Jest* — literary history. As Stephen Daedalus, after his mythical namesake, escaped the labyrinthine confines of his inherited cultural traditions in order to free himself as a writer, so Wallace (as has been noted by many critics and admitted extensively by Wallace) struggled to be free from his own inherited literary influences. While it has become a critical commonplace that this struggle happened early in his career — that *Broom* is the postmodernist apprentice novel and that the fiction and nonfiction (especially *Girl*, particularly the long story "Westward the Course of Empire Takes Its Way," and the essay "E Unibus Pluram") are the places where he explicitly works out a way to break free of influence and so to write *Infinite Jest* — I think it is worth considering the idea that the struggle didn't end, making an anxiety-free *Infinite Jest* possible, but instead continued in the writing of the novel. The difficulty of breaking free of the powerful influence of the writers of the previous generation who so shaped his earlier work, then, could be seen to be at the root of the struggle Wallace experienced in trying to write *Infinite Jest*, and the shape the novel finally took could be seen to express the nature of that struggle.

Of *Infinite Jest* and the question of influence, Marshall Boswell writes:

> Whereas the earlier books are frankly anxious about the various debts they owe to the preceding generation of postmodern writers, *IJ*, perhaps more so than anything else Wallace has so far published, stands on its own as a work of tireless invention and last-

ing importance, standing shoulder to shoulder with such works
as Pynchon's *Gravity's Rainbow*, Gaddis's *The Recognitions*, and
Barth's *Giles Goat-Boy* without for a moment seeming derivative
or ancillary. (118)

Wallace's earlier fiction is very much about this anxiety of the preceding generation's influence, so evidently that I don't need to rehearse the
argument here. However, I will take a quick look at these early works
in order to highlight what's important in their struggle with influence
for my understanding of *Infinite Jest* as not standing on its own, not
the product of Wallace's having resolved the problem, but rather as a
continuation, even a dramatization of it.

Though seen as a "declaration of independence" (in Boswell's words,
5) from the minimalist aesthetic of Raymond Carver and Ann Beattie
and its later iteration in the work of the "Brat Pack" of Jay McIner-
ney, Bret Easton Ellis, and Tama Janowitz then dominating the literary
scene, *The Broom of the System* might also be described as a hearken-
ing back to the older aesthetic of Thomas Pynchon, William Gaddis,
and Don DeLillo. Early reviews noted these influences, as Michiko Kakutani did in the *New York Times*, drawing out thematic and stylistic
similarities to Pynchon's 1964 *The Crying of Lot 49*. Although *Broom*
has its own ideas about Wittgenstein and entropy, much of the influence
of Pynchon almost appears to be homage, from the Pynchonian names
to the Pynchonian open ending—for the uncried *Lot 49*, substitute
Broom's unended last sentence, "I'm a man of my" (467). It is more than
understandable that a novel started as an undergraduate thesis and published when its author was twenty-five would display its influences in
high relief, and though the novel does more than that, including establishing an early version of Wallace's characteristic style, it is undoubtedly heavily under the influence of earlier writers, and of Wallace's
own not untypical young writer's desire to be clever. Wallace himself
described it, in a 1989 letter to Jonathan Franzen, as feeling as if it had
been written by "a very smart fourteen-year-old" (Max).

Wallace has similarly less than positive words for *Girl with Curious
Hair*'s concluding novella, "Westward the Course of Empire Takes Its

Way," which he called "a permanent migraine" (McCaffery interview 142). While the entire collection can be seen to continue Wallace's engagement with his literary inheritance — individual stories can be read as critiques of Philip Roth ("Say Never") and Brat Pack–style minimalism ("Everything Is Green") — "Westward" is the story in which he most fully and explicitly takes on the metafiction of the previous generation, in the form of John Barth's "Lost in the Funhouse." In a copyright page disclaimer, he describes it as "written in the margins" of Barth's story, but it might be more accurate to describe it as a kind of palimpsest, written over the text of "Funhouse," from its details to its purpose. It features a hero, Mark Nechtr, whose last name parallels that of the Barth story's main character, Ambrose, whose name is also echoed in that of the teacher of the creative writing workshop Nechtr is taking, Professor Ambrose (as is Barth's Hopkins by the location of that workshop at the East Chesapeake Tradeschool).[3] And this rewriting isn't limited to allusion: Professor Ambrose himself proclaims his genealogy, saying that he "*is* a character in and the object of the seminal 'Lost in the Funhouse'" (*Girl* 261). The novella also explicitly implicates Wallace in this drama with the fact of Nechtr's future writing of an autobiographical fiction whose main character will be named Dave.

Beyond these and many other details, the story's larger purpose is to overwrite "Funhouse" by showing what it sees as the emptiness at its core (and by extension the postwar metafiction it's meant to stand for) and to lay out a vision of a new kind of fiction that uses metafiction's technical innovations for different ends. It attempts to do this by itself adopting those innovations, constructing its own funhouse, as Barth did, but pushing those techniques until they exhaust themselves, displaying what Wallace believes to be their solipsistic self-regard. This was a dangerous move aesthetically, however, and in the end the story seems to get lost in its own funhouse. As Wallace himself put it in an interview, "I got trapped just trying to expose the illusions of metafiction the same way metafiction had tried to expose the illusions of the pseudo-unmediated realist fiction that had come before it. It was a horror show" (McCaffery interview 142). The effort to extricate himself from influence, from his literary fathers, continued to produce fiction that, while successful in some spots and joyously inventive in others, was ultimately stillborn.

1989's *Girl* failed to receive the positive notices Wallace had hoped for; as D. T. Max has reported, Wallace was crushed by *Girl's* reception, and that, along with the difficulties in writing the new novel and the abortive return to school and philosophy, may have contributed to a breakdown at Harvard and time in a halfway house. From there, in a letter to Franzen, he wrote:

> Right now, I am a pathetic and very confused young man, a failed writer at 28 who is so jealous, so sickly searingly envious of you and [William] Vollmann and Mark Leyner and even David fuckwad Leavitt and any young man who is right now producing pages with which he can live, and even approving them off some base clause of conviction about the enterprise's meaning and end. (Max)

At the root of Wallace's difficulties in writing, at least in this description of them, was the problem of not knowing what fiction was supposed to be and do, the lack of a "base clause of conviction" about what he wrote for. In this same letter, he described suicide as "a reasonable if not at this point a desirable option with respect to the whole wretched problem." It seems clear from this account of his troubles that Wallace had not resolved to his own satisfaction the problem of how to write after Gaddis, Pynchon, and DeLillo, and that this fact was a source of great pain.

After he returned to the Midwest and resumed writing, Wallace continued to think and write about "the whole wretched problem" of how to produce pages of fiction in a style appropriate to his times. He most thoroughly laid out these ideas about how contemporary fiction should confront its postmodernist inheritance in "E Unibus Pluram: Television and U.S. Fiction," an essay originally appearing in the *Review of Contemporary Fiction* in 1993 and reprinted in the nonfiction collection *A Supposedly Fun Thing I'll Never Do Again* in 1997. While this essay has been taken as the culmination of Wallace's working through his struggle with influence, with how to write in his moment in literary history, and so as the necessary final step in his enabling himself to produce *Infinite Jest*, it is more than possible to see it, like *Broom* and *Girl*, as containing earnest, sophisticated, and sometimes very funny attempts to take this step but as ultimately failing to move from critique to alternative.

As *Girl*'s "Westward the Course of Empire Takes Its Way" attempts to rewrite Barth's "Lost in the Funhouse" for its own moment in literary history, "E Unibus Pluram" serves as Wallace's version of Barth's 1967 essay, "The Literature of Exhaustion," a kind of manifesto for postmodernism as the formal strategy best suited to a time when the traditional forms of literary expression seemed used up. Arguing that postmodernism has become mainstream in American culture (in part through its central role in contemporary television) and so has lost its literary power to make meaning, instead becoming an empty, purely cynical pose, Wallace calls for a turn toward sincerity and sentiment. He calls for a new generation of "anti-rebels . . . who dare somehow to back away from ironic watching, who have the childish gall to actually endorse and instantiate single-entendre principles" (*Supposedly* 81). But again, as the characters in "Westward" and the story itself argue, the key to getting past endless ironic self-consciousness is to be conscious of it — to critique the critique, to be meta-aware of meta-awareness — and again, as A. O. Scott, Mary Holland, and others have noted, "E Unibus Pluram" seems stuck in the same loop of self-directed irony. The desire for "single-entendre principles" that Wallace thinks the new antirebels should work from, their "base clause of conviction," is overwhelmed by his attraction to doubleness, to play.

These moments in Wallace's earlier career, often read as steps on his road to artistic maturity, a destination at which he arrived with *Infinite Jest*, can instead be read as successive enactments of his struggle to find his place in literary history. In "Westward," Mark is described as "a boy hotly cocky enough to think he might inherit Ambrose's bald crown and ballpoint scepter, to wish to try to sing to the *next* generation" (348). At the time he undertook the writing of what became *Infinite Jest*, Wallace may have still been that cocky boy, producing confident diagnoses of contemporary fiction's ailments, but by 1989 and the early 1990s he was also someone who described himself as a failed writer, someone so panicked by influence, to borrow a formulation of A. O. Scott's, that he tried to turn away from fiction entirely. *Infinite Jest*, then, can be read not as the product of Wallace's finally finding the way to sing to a new generation but instead as both another part of a long, difficult engagement with the problem of how to do such a thing and also a reflection on that engagement itself. As such, it can be understood not only as a *Künstlerroman* but as a kind of literary history.

If Hal's story is a kind of *Künstlerroman*, one that ends with the young writer-figure on the verge of maturity, incoherent but full of things to say, and if the generic expectation of a story of artistic development combines with the discontinuous and open-ended form of the narrative in such a way that we don't quite know how the hero got to be in the condition he's in or what's going to happen to him, then it makes sense to ask what kind of literary history the shape of Hal's story suggests. The generic expectation of literary history — a story of innovation, of radical breaks driven by the Bloomian urge to slay the literary father or by historical changes that render current forms unusable — combines with the discontinuous and open-ended form of the narrative in such a way that we don't know how contemporary fiction got to be in the condition it's in or what it is going to look like in the future.[4]

Patricia Waugh's useful definition of metafiction holds that "*Metafictional* writers all explore *a theory of fiction* through the practice of writing fiction" (2); similarly, *Infinite Jest* could be said to suggest not only a literary history but also a theory of literary history. In the very shape of Hal's story, the novel could be said to offer a critique of the way the history of innovation is understood by writers and critics not only but especially of the modern novel. This regularly criticized model, with artistic change exploding around moments of historical change at the beginning and middle of the previous century, assumes a theory of literary succession based on radical breaks, repudiations, and serial creations of new forms in the context of refusal of old forms. Boswell's placing of Wallace in literary history relies on the model:

> [Wallace] confidently situates himself as the direct heir to a tra-
> dition of aesthetic development that began with the modernist
> overturning of nineteenth-century bourgeois realism and contin-
> ued with the postwar critique of modernist aesthetics. Yet Wal-
> lace proceeds from the assumption that *both* modernism and
> postmodernism are essentially "done." Rather, his work resolutely
> moves forward while hoisting the baggage of modernism and
> postmodernism heavily, but respectfully, on its back. (1)

This account, confusing in itself and in its context (immediately following Boswell's description of Wallace as "a nervous member of some still-
unnamed ... third wave of modernism," he is called confident), is nonetheless recognizable in its following the model of innovation described
above. It is recognizable from our training in school, reading Norton
anthologies and other accounts of the history of American literature's
three stages of development, and from Wallace's own accounts of the
writing of his predecessors and his prescriptions for succeeding them.
This model is the cause of a great deal of incoherence in criticism and a
great deal of anxiety among writers such as Wallace, and along with the
murky psychodramatic account Bloom offers us, leads in *Infinite Jest* to
both a reproduction of its expectations and an implicit, perhaps inadver-
tent critique in the novel's form. The novel doesn't provide a continuous
linear story ending with a new stage of literary development; instead,
it offers a story whose shape expresses the difficulty of understanding
how what we have in the present came out of the work of the past and
the impossibility of knowing what comes next. And this shape, following Waugh, suggests a critique not only of the historical account of our
present literary moment's relation to the recent past but also of the way
we construct literary histories generally.

A year after the publication of the tenth anniversary edition of *Infinite Jest* and a year before Wallace's suicide, *Harper's* published an
essay by Jonathan Lethem, "The Ecstasy of Influence: A Plagiarism,"
that proposed an alternative way of thinking about literary history and
artistic succession. From its title's (borrowed) play on Bloom's "anxiety
of influence" to its very form — an essay composed mostly of text lifted

from other writers (a fact not revealed until the appearance of a key to sources, ten pages in) — Lethem's essay offers correctives to long- (and still-) held notions about intellectual property and the nature of artistic innovation. In a long, expertly pieced-together collage/disquisition on the differences between the idea of art as de novo creation and the idea of art as common property, freely exchanged, Lethem implicitly argues against the bedrock assumption on which traditional literary histories rest and asks if there isn't another way to think about the whole thing:

> Undiscovered public knowledge emboldens us to question the extreme claims to originality made in press releases and publishers' notices: Is an intellectual or creative offering truly novel, or have we just forgotten a worthy precursor? . . . Does our appetite for creative vitality require the violence and exasperation of another avant-garde, with its wearisome killing-the-father imperatives, or might we be better off ratifying the *ecstasy of influence* — and deepening our willingness to understand the commonality and timelessness of the methods and motifs available to artists? (67)

The anxiety Wallace manifests about his place in literary history is tied up not only in his own personal *Künstlerroman* but also in the larger story of contemporary American fiction. This is a lot for one writer to solve, and the strain of trying might have been avoidable. The joyousness of Wallace's pastiches, his perfect ear not only for the way other people talk but also for the way other writers write, his inclination to take in all of the culture in which he swims, to borrow his own metaphor (and, to follow it through, to which he rarely seems blind), are all proof that there is another way to think about influence. The image of Hal unable to speak is a terribly anxious one, familiar to us from those dreams in which we are unable to scream, but it can also be seen as hopeful: while Hal hasn't yet found a way to express what he has to express, he is in there, hyperobservant, struggling to share what he sees. Not-quoting Lewis Hyde's *The Gift*, Lethem writes: "Most artists are brought to their vocation when their own nascent gifts are awakened by the work of a master. That is to say, most artists are converted to art by art itself. Finding one's voice isn't just an emptying and purifying oneself of the words of others but an adopting and embracing of filiations, communities, and discourses" (61). Thinking that his work must represent a radical break, Wallace asks the impossible of himself, as many literary histories ask the impossible of their writers. *Infinite Jest* gives form to the potentially paralyzing anxiety of living in the middle of history — to the doubt that Hal will deal with his family history and reach his maturity, that the artist will ever escape his influences and grow out of his clever youth, that the contemporary American novel will ever reckon with its postmodern inheritance and find whatever form it will take next. One of many ironies here is that it may have already found that form.

THE ANXIETY of living in the middle of a history that seems endless and at the same time closed, claustrophobic, could be said to be endemic to Wallace's generation. A. O. Scott puts his finger on this: "Like many other Americans who grew up in the wake of 1960s, [Wallace] seems haunted by a feeling of belatedess." Though Scott is here talking more about literary than social history — he is writing specifically about Wallace's feeling that as a writer he came after the moment when rebellion was more than just a "style"— his framing of that observation in the larger social history of postwar America helps us see how *Infinite Jest* is also about being in the middle of another kind of history, a condition in some respects quite similar. *Infinite Jest* came after the 1960s and after the end of the Cold War, or, as some would have it, the End of History. As the influence of Barth, Coover, and others weighed on his shoulders, so the weight of history is felt by writers of his cohort. While many writers of this earlier generation turned in the 1990s to history, taking the opportunity in that retrospective decade to revisit the past and see how it looked in this "after" time (often arguing against the notion that history had done anything like "ending"), younger writers equally concerned with the past seemed even in their historical fiction to be especially concerned with the future, which seemed to stretch endlessly and uncertainly before them (see Cohen).[5]

This state of feeling not at the end of history but in its middle, between a more meaningful, authentic-seeming past and a future that lacked the dark but defining shadow of the Cold War, doesn't only help explain the shape of *Infinite Jest* — it also helps account for *Infinite Jest*'s reception by readers of the time who shared that feeling of being in the middle of things. The story it tells of a young man struggling to grow up, to find a way to deal with a past that seems to overwhelm him and move forward into an uncertain future, is its story. The devoted readership Wallace's novel earned was certainly due to a number of factors — but chief among them, to return to the *Catcher in the Rye* DNA it carries, was the distinctiveness of Wallace's voice, the way it sang to a new generation. The voice with which it sang may not have been the entirely new voice Wallace thought was necessary, the pursuit of which caused him great frustration and, evidently, pain; it was a voice built out of old voices, recombined and repurposed. But the anxiety that shapes Hal's story also informs Wallace's voice, and that anxiety is key to the chord it has struck with readers — along with the curiosity and close attention, the humor, and the joy of playing with words. While we can never know what was in Wallace's mind during the period when he stepped away from the writing of *Infinite Jest*, it is hard not to wish, for his psychic well-being, that he had been able to better appreciate the ecstasy of repurposing influence to make something new. Without the anxiety of trying to forge a new place in history, however, *Infinite Jest* might not have sung so well and so loudly, and might not have been positioned to speak to future generations as the voice of its own anxious age.

Notes

1. This is perhaps especially a fear for *The Pale King*, Wallace's unfinished novel, which was published in April 2011. It is a fear expressed by Wallace's widow, Karen Green, for that book and for all of his work; of interviews she gave after Wallace's death, she has said, "I know journalism is journalism and maybe people want to read that I discovered the body over and over again, but that doesn't define David or his work. It all turns him into a celebrity writer dude, which I think would have made him wince, the good part of him" (Adams interview). As Laura Miller puts it, "Only after his death could David Foster Wallace be properly misunderstood."

2. In the novel the U.S. government is working in the ostensible interests of all three nations of O.N.A.N., the Organization of North American Nations formed after the end of the Cold War and around the same time as the estab-

lishment of the Great Concavity, the giant dump comprised of parts of New York, New Hampshire, and Vermont that former-singer-turned-President Johnny Gentle created as part of his campaign against dirt, the new common enemy the nation needed after the Cold War's end, to which the U.S. sends its toxic waste and which he forced Canada to accept as its own territory.

3. I am indebted to Marshall Boswell for the nectar/ambrosia observation (105) and for his detailed and nuanced reading of the story generally.

4. Though Bloom claims that his theory of the anxiety of influence is meant to concern only the relation of one text to another, precursor text, it is commonly taken to be about the relationship between later writers and their precursors; it is in this broader sense (one that I find more helpful than Bloom's insisted-upon textual stance, which seems to defy his own imagery in the book, full of strong poets wrestling with their strong precursors) that I am using it.

5. See the historical and historically minded novels of Bachelder, Eugenides, Foer, Krauss, Lethem, Millet, and Whitehead.

Works Cited

Bachelder, Chris. *U.S.!* New York: Bloomsbury, 2006. Print.

Bloom, Harold. *The Anxiety of Influence: A Theory of Poetry*. New York: Oxford University Press, 1973. Print.

Boswell, Marshall. *Understanding David Foster Wallace*. Columbia: University of South Carolina Press, 2003. Print.

Burn, Stephen. *David Foster Wallace's* Infinite Jest: *A Reader's Guide*. New York: Continuum, 2003. Print.

Cioffi, Frank Louis. "'An Anguish Become Thing': Narrative as Performance in David Foster Wallace's *Infinite Jest*." *Narrative* 8.2 (2000): 161–81. Print.

Cohen, Samuel. *After the End of History: American Fiction in the 1990s*. Iowa City: University of Iowa Press, 2009. Print.

Eugenides, Jeffrey. *Middlesex*. New York: Farrar, Straus and Giroux, 2002. Print.

Foer, Jonathan Safran. *Everything Is Illuminated*. Boston: Houghton Mifflin, 2002. Print.

———. *Extremely Loud and Incredibly Close*. Boston: Houghton Mifflin, 2005. Print.

Green, Karen. Interview by Tim Adams. *Guardian* 10 April 2011. Web.

Hayles, N. Katherine. "The Illusion of Autonomy and the Fact of Recursivity: Virtual Ecologies, Entertainment, and *Infinite Jest*." *New Literary History* 30.3 (1999): 675–97. Print.

Holland, Mary K. "'The Art's Heart's Purpose': Braving the Narcissistic Loop of David Foster Wallace's *Infinite Jest*." *Critique* 47.3 (Spring 2006): 218–42. Print.

Joyce, James. *Dubliners*. 1914. Ed. Robert Scholes and A. Walton Litz. New York: Penguin, 1969. Print.

———. *A Portrait of the Artist as a Young Man*. 1916. Ed. and introduction, Seamus Deane. New York: Penguin, 1992. Print.

Kakutani, Michiko. "Life in Cleveland, 1990." Review of *The Broom of the System,* David Foster Wallace. *New York Times* 27 December 1986, sec. 1: 14. Print.

Krauss, Nicole. *The History of Love*. New York: Norton, 2005. Print.

Lethem, Jonathan. "The Ecstasy of Influence: A Plagiarism." *Harper's* February 2007, 59–71. Print.

———. *The Fortress of Solitude*. New York: Doubleday, 2003. Print.

Max, D. T. "The Unfinished: David Foster Wallace's Struggle to Surpass *Infinite Jest*." *New Yorker* 9 March 2009. Web.

Miller, Laura. "'The Pale King': David Foster Wallace's Last Battle." Review of *The Pale King*. *Salon* 10 April 2011. Web.

Millet, Lydia. *Oh Pure and Radiant Heart*. New York: Soft Skull, 2005.

Pietsch, Michael. Interview by Rick Moody. *Sonora Review* 55/56 (2009): 59–66. Print.

Ryerson, James. Introduction. In *Fate, Time, and Language: An Essay on Free Will*. By David Foster Wallace. New York: Columbia University Press, 2011. 1–33. Print.

Salinger, J. D. *The Catcher in the Rye*. New York: Little, Brown, 1951. Print.

Scott, A. O. "The Panic of Influence." *New York Review of Books* 47, 10 February 2000. Web.

Wallace, David Foster. *The Broom of the System*. New York: Penguin, 1987. Print.

———. *Girl with Curious Hair*. New York: Norton, 1989. Print.

———. *Infinite Jest*. Boston: Little, Brown, 1996. Print.

———. Interview by Larry McCaffery. *Review of Contemporary Fiction* 13.2 (Summer 1993): 127–50. Print.

———. *A Supposedly Fun Thing I'll Never Do Again*. New York: Little, Brown and Company, 1997. Print.

Waugh, Patricia. *Metafiction: The Theory and Practice of Self-Conscious Fiction*. London: Routledge, 1984. Print.

Whitehead, Colson. *The Intuitionist*. New York: Bantam, 1999. Print.

———. *John Henry Days*. New York: Doubleday, 2001. Print.

RICK MOODY

TRIBUTE WRITTEN FOR WALLACE
FAMILY MEMORIAL BOOK, 2008

I HAD A younger brother's awe about David, because he was so graceful
and hilarious and solicitous in person — as well as intellectually imposing. I treasure the times I got to spend with him.

Among others, there was the time we were in Toronto together, reading for the Harbourfront Festival. His receiving line was about four
times as long as mine, and he was a little sheepish about it. In the course
of waiting for him to finish signing books, I listened to him dress down
some guy who couldn't understand why the ending of *Infinite Jest* didn't
have more closure. He was really good-natured about it, but that didn't
mean he was going to give any ground — "Maybe you're just not reading
it right." Later, we went up in the space needle they have in Toronto, and
David lampooned my inability to walk across some transparent flooring
at the very top. Fear of heights!

The photo shoot we did together, along with Junot Díaz and Ed-
widge Danticat and A. M. Homes for an issue of the *New Yorker* devoted to writers under forty. It was a very *long* photo shoot, the worst
kind. We were all crammed on some rotating playground device, so
that the photographer could get a smeary background, and I remember
David yelling out, "Is anyone here familiar with the word *frottage*?"

The two of us did a live interview in San Francisco for the publication of my novel *The Diviners*. It was the first time I got to meet his
wife. We had a great dinner together, and then I went and botched the

event. I was so intimidated by David onstage that I got tongue-tied, even though I'd given him a list of tolerable questions to ask me in advance . . .

I actually met him for the first time when he did a reading with Bill Vollmann at Dixon Place in New York City, sometime just after *Girl with Curious Hair* came out. 1989, maybe. Almost twenty years ago. Vollmann fired a starter pistol during the reading, and Dave read for about forty-five or fifty minutes, unable, it seemed, to find a punctuation mark at which he might stop, without managing (nonetheless) ever to be less than galvanizing. My whole idea of how to engage with contemporary fiction came into being that night. There was a reason to try to do what I was hoping I'd be able to do.

Not too many years after that, I had dinner with David and Jonathan Franzen in the Village when they competed with one another to spot quote from Don DeLillo's *Americana*. From memory.

I'd had problems that were not unlike Dave's problems, and there was also one night when we went to one of those meetings that people go to when they have certain kinds of problems, and that's a night I often think about now. It made it easier for me to keep doing what I was doing — working hard, hanging in there — knowing he was out in the world doing the same. We talked about our recovered lives glancingly, from time to time, over the years — making sure the other was okay. Trying to maintain a certain reasonable privacy. I guess it's impossible in these dark days not to wish I had been able to help more.

Still, when the ache is overpowering, there's the work. None of this personal stuff, however worthy of recollection, however moving, is as important as the writing, the legacy. I think writers are always failed social animals. I certainly am. I never feel comfortable in public, and there aren't too many people I feel comfortable with, certainly not many writers. That I cared so passionately about David's work, that it left such a mark on me, is the truest measure of how much I loved the guy, because that's where I found the fullest, and most complex evocation of who he was. He wasn't able, with me, to allow in all of those paradoxes, and complexities, and I suspect this was true with many of his other professional acquaintances as well. His work had all these things, though, and more, and I, for one, am not done reading and wrestling with what he accomplished there. I treasure the work as I treasured the man. He had a significant impact on my life and work, an almost incalculable impact. I miss him a lot.

LEE KONSTANTINOU

NO BULL:

DAVID FOSTER WALLACE AND

POSTIRONIC BELIEF

Belief, Irony, Metafiction

The American 1990s saw the reinvigoration of two popular eschato-
logical visions, the first explicitly Christian — associated with the new
right — the second socioeconomic but no less millenarian in temper. In
the fall of 1989, in the *National Interest*, Francis Fukuyama published
his famous inquiry into the question of whether we had reached "The
End of History?"[1] His essay is famous for its optimistic conclusion: the
process of ideological tumult that had characterized the first nine decades of the twentieth century (and, really, all recorded human history)
had arrived at its inevitable end with liberal, consumer-oriented capitalist democracies; all rivals had proven themselves to be not only morally
bankrupt but pragmatically unworkable. Though all countries everywhere had yet to arrive at the ideological Promised Land, there could
be little doubt that they would in due course hear the Good News.
Whatever else we might think about Fukuyama's claim that history is
coherent and directional, his arguments were something like historical
common sense at the end of the Cold War. It is against this sort of te-
leological talk — the total triumph of the market, the utter collapse of
all alternative visions — that the career of David Foster Wallace must
be situated. In the midst of this "end of history" discourse, which celebrated the West's triumph, life in the U.S. and Britain came to seem
listless and without flavor, especially for those not enamored of the consumerist Utopia Fukuyama described. Many convinced themselves that

in the wake of the Cold War nothing much was going to change, that loneliness and a kind of bland sadness was all one could expect of the new world order. In a 1994 issue of the *Modern Review*, a London-based magazine, Toby Young put it this way: "It's difficult to imagine what a post-ironic sensibility would be like. It's a bit like finding yourself at the end of history. You're bored because you're not participating in any historic events but you can't very well up sticks and go and fight in a war in a less evolved society. To do so would be *untrue to your own historical experience*; it would require you to *unlearn the lessons history has already taught you*. And what would be the point?" (Young and Vanderbilt 7, emphasis mine).

The "end of history" was, after all, even in Fukuyama's telling "a very sad time," an era where "daring, courage, imagination, and idealism, will be replaced by economic calculation, the endless solving of technical problems, environmental concerns, and the satisfaction of sophisticated consumer demands" ("The End of History?" 18). Our desire for idealistic struggle and courageous achievement might never be fulfilled, but the market would churn out in great quantities the antidepressants that would help us forget our sad reality. This common interpretation of the cultural situation of post–Cold War America is, I think, also the source of the weary tone we find among writers like Richard Rorty, who in *Contingency, Irony, and Solidarity* (1989) works hard to deflate whatever grand ambitions we might have had about discovering a relationship between our private and public lives, leaving us in a theoretical position where our public commitment to liberalism is undergirded by the (for some) disheartening realization that we're only pretending for strategic reasons to hold our essentialist or foundationalist opinions. Though he would reject any claim for the *necessity* of liberalism's final victory, Rorty very much endorses the desirability of the "bourgeois freedom" afforded by history's end (Rorty 84). The twin contexts of late 1980s and early 1990s market triumphalism and theoretical anti-foundationalism — which Fredric Jameson famously linked together — shed considerable light on the stakes of Wallace's literary project, which have already been thoroughly cataloged in the previous chapters of this collection. Above all, Wallace wanted to discover or invent a viable postironic ethos for U.S. literature and culture at the End of History, that is, for an America in the thrall of full-blown postmodernism. In this chapter, I will demonstrate how Wallace sought to use techniques historically associated with metafiction to generate forms of affect that theory held to be impossible and to relink private and public life, in something like Rorty's sense of those terms, via an ethos of postironic belief.

For Wallace, creating postironic belief was the goal of literary communication. This is why Wallace polemically railed against "death of the author" arguments and constructed his fictions, and especially his epochal *Infinite Jest* (1996), around the unfulfilled desire to communicate. Indeed, when James O. Incandenza appears as a wraith to the convalescing Don Gately, late in the novel, he explains that he created the irresistibly addictive avant-garde film, "Infinite Jest," in order "to contrive a medium via which he [James] and the muted son [Hal] could simply *converse*," a form of entertainment that "would reverse thrust on a young self's fall into the womb of solipsism, anhedonia, death in life" (*IJ* 838, 839, emphasis in original). Wallace claims to know in his "gut that writing is an act of communication between one human being and another," and justifies his conviction with reference to an idiosyncratic reading of Wittgenstein as a sort of incipient post-postmodernist, someone who understands the deadly necessity of transcending narcissistic relativism ("Greatly Exaggerated" 144).[2] Wallace writes out of a conviction that we live in a society and culture of indefinable but ubiquitous sadness — crippled by a complex of solipsism, anhedonia, cynicism, snark, and toxic irony, a culture whose aimless meandering can be traced back, in one way or another, to the consumerist End of History. Such was life in the secular millennial kingdom. Perhaps impossibly, Wallace wanted to use literary form to construct ethical countertypes to the incredulous ironist.

I call this ethical countertype "the believer." When he calls for the rise of an "anti-rebel" — a kind of post-countercultural or newly earnest countercultural figure, a figure that stands in an oppositional relationship to mass counterculture, against a now dominant postmodernist irony — Wallace does not give a positive content to this figure, and he certainly doesn't embrace some simple return to a pre-ironic sensibility, associated for him with the suburban television reality of *Leave It to Beaver* or the new right.[3] What Wallace wants is not so much a religious correction to secular skepticism allegedly run amok as *new forms of belief*— the adoption of a kind of religious vocabulary (God, prayer, etc.) emptied out of specific content, a vocabulary engineered to confront the possibly insuperable condition of postmodernity. Recovering drug addict Don Gately, for example, has no personal conception of God— members of AA and NA "get to make up [their] own understanding of God or a Higher Power or Whom-/Whatever"— but he "takes one of AA's very rare specific suggestions and hits the knees in the a.m. and asks for Help and then hits the knees again at bedtime and says Thank You, whether he believes he's talking to Anything/-body or not, and he somehow gets through that day clean" (*IJ* 443). As Wallace puts it earlier in his novel, answering the question "how can you pray to a 'God' you believe only morons believe in, still?": "The old guys say it doesn't yet matter what you believe or don't believe, Just Do It they say, and like a shock-trained organism without any kind of independent human will you do exactly like you're told, you keep coming and coming, nightly" (350). Though some critics have interpreted *Infinite Jest* as harshly critical of the ideology of AA,[4] I would suggest that the formal situation of Gately relative to God resembles the relationship Wallace wants to posit between the reader and belief.

Understood this way, Wallace's postironic stance differs from that of writers who produce what James Wood has called "hysterical realism," a category Wood associates with traditional postmodernists such as Don DeLillo and Thomas Pynchon and more recent writers such as Salman Rushdie and Zadie Smith. What is most interesting about Wood's dismissive reading of these authors— including Wallace, whom Wood describes as a hysterical realist, and whose short story collection *Oblivion* he excoriated in the *New Republic*— is that his attack very much resembles the postironic critique of 1960s and 1970s metafiction Wallace himself proffers. In a review of Toni Morrison's *Paradise* (1997), Wood argues that fiction constitutes an invitation to belief, or rather— in a secular age— an invitation to act as if one believed in fiction: "Fiction demands belief from us, and this request is demanding in part because

we can choose not to believe" ("The Color Purple" 236, my emphasis).
Wood here distinguishes between the ontological faith that religion
requires and belief in fiction, which can only "gently request" that readers act "as if" they believed. Belief in fiction, by this account, is only
a metaphorical sort of belief.[5] This argument suffers from an obvious
flaw: the concept of belief stands by its very constitution against choice.
You cannot "choose" to act "as if" you believed in a work of fiction; nor
can you choose to stop believing in what you read. A believer is someone
who in some sense cannot help but hold his or her ontological convictions.[6] Wood might counter by suggesting that we use some synonym
for "belief" or another more accurate description of what he is trying to
get at, such as "pretense."[7] The problem with such a counterargument
would be that Wood is actually right that fiction demands belief of us,
but he shies away from the implications of his own argument and therefore misreads the project of Wallace and other recent writers grouped
with so-called hysterical realists.

We do judge novels on the basis of what they can convince us to believe. This is the only reason why writing can sensibly be described as
"plausible" or "implausible": because, in its mode of worldbuilding, a
story touches some part of us that makes these sorts of judgments and
distinctions. Moreover, not only do we always judge what we read using
ontological criteria, but what we read often makes ontological demands
of us, can try to transform our beliefs, can demand that we become believers. Thus, if the job of the novel is to make a persuasive appeal to
the reader to believe in the events depicted, then "hysterical realism"
fails for Wood because its too rapid accretion of interesting detail breaks
the trance of believability. "[Zadie] Smith does not lack for powers of
invention," Wood writes, with reference to a characteristic passage in
White Teeth. "The problem is that there is too much of it . . . on its own,
almost any of these details . . . might be persuasive. Together, they van-
dalize each other. . . . As realism, it is incredible; as satire, it is cartoonish;
as cartoon, it is too realistic" ("Hysterical Realism" 172). What Wood
decries is the sort of novel that, in its particulars, cannot be faulted for
lacking realism but whose overall pattern takes on an implausible shape.
This global implausibility disrupts the local pleasure one might take

in a work of fiction that more judiciously doled out its implausibilities. Novels of hysterical realism thus simultaneously feel allegorical and do not allegorize; they present characters that almost but do not quite rise to the level of the identifiably human. Because the hysteria of hysterical realism short-circuits its realism, we cannot take seriously the alleged claim of the hysterical realist to seriousness or merit.[8]

But isn't disrupting realism exactly the point of this kind of fiction? Wasn't realism very precisely the primary target of advanced art, and especially that curious subgenre known as metafiction? How can one critique a genre for successfully achieving its aims, unless one feels those aims aren't worthy of pursuit in the first place? Relatedly, in what sense can Wallace and the other postironists, who seek to cultivate an ethos of belief among their readers, be accused of undermining realism and belief? To understand the origin of Wood's misunderstanding of Wallace, we need to notice that what the historical metafictionists saw as liberation — the demolition of a false and oppressive prisonhouse of belief — Wallace experienced as a source of suffering. And yet, despite the pain disbelief engendered, Wallace felt he was forced to write as he did. For Wallace, postmodernism (and specifically metafiction) *was* the cultural logic of late capitalism, and like his contemporaries at the *Modern Review* he couldn't just ignore this oppressive reality, as Wood would ask him to do. I would suggest that Wallace and other aspiring postironists are reacting to a picture of metafiction and postmodernist zaniness developed primarily in university literature departments. That is, the critically produced concept of metafiction is a cognitive mediator standing between Wallace and his interpretation of postmodernist fiction from the 1960s and 1970s. Patricia Waugh's *Metafiction*, published in 1984, can serve as a synecdoche of the consensus view of the mission of metafiction. Waugh's study wants to suggest "the extent to which the dominant issues of contemporary critical and sociological thought are shared by writers of fiction" (60), but leaves the nature of this suggestion ambiguous. Are postmodernists and metafiction writers studying contemporary sociological literature and seeking to allegorize or otherwise draw attention to these findings? Is the turn to metafiction a coincidental development? Or does some underlying shift in the world — economic or epistemic — cause both changes?

Whatever the answers to these questions, metafiction "self-consciously and systematically draws attention to its status as an artifact in order to pose questions about the relationship between fiction and reality," in Waugh's account (2). Though there are many quite different techniques associated with metafiction, all draw attention to practices of reading and writing, very often by exposing how worlds of fiction are embedded within higher-order worlds. When we read characters reading, we are supposed to become aware of how our own reading process is homologous to the inscribed practice of reading. In the most extreme interpretations of this homology, often inspired by deconstructive discourse, we discover ourselves to be unreal in a sense, to be purely functional or discursive actants (rather than agents). Waugh distinguishes between "two poles of metafiction," one which "finally accepts a substantial real world whose significance is not entirely composed of relationships within language; and one which suggests that there can never be an escape from the prisonhouse of language" (53). Despite these differences, all metafiction is a sort of critique or revelation, an unveiling of falsity or of the impossibility of ever finding the truth or of the very incoherence of the concept of truth. In other words, either metafiction is an allegory for the breakdown of master narratives and coherent frames in the social world (the weak interpretation) or metafiction, because it changes our relation with language, actually breaks down our confidence in norms, values, and conventions, such that we're thrown into a bottomless well of relativistic doubt (the strong interpretation). This latter, strong interpretation has often been compared to a version of critical self-consciousness associated with Romantic irony, and especially Friedrich Schlegel's fragmentary commentary on irony as a mode of "permanent parabasis."

Metafiction is a form of irony because, like irony, it forces the reader/subject to ceaselessly question all grounds for understanding, up to and including the epistemic grounds one uses to justify being an ironist in the first place, a mode of questioning that Hegel, and Kierkegaard after him, called irony's "infinite absolute negativity," its self-negating nature.

The result is that metafiction doesn't undermine this or that belief, but *belief as such*. It operates on something like an inverted technical principle from that of religious belief. Metafictionists assume that if a range of vocabulary could be mapped cleanly to a domain of content (in the world), then a form of epistemic or ontological realism would be justified. Taking this syllogism for granted, metafictionists attempt to show that such a mapping is impossible, and by foregrounding the bottomless self-referentiality of language or the unbounded connotative range of words, writers of metafiction supposedly undermine the reader's previously firm stance of belief. Metafiction removes the foundations for belief in realism. By contrast, postironists attempt to use metafictional form as a way of reconnecting form and content, as a way of strengthening belief. What is paradoxical about this attempt is the *emptiness* of the proposed "postironic belief." Postironists don't advocate a stance of belief toward some aspect of the world but rather the ethos of belief in and of itself.

Wallace's metafiction has a complicated relationship to the concept of belief, which has led some critics astray in their interpretation of his aims. In a survey of Wallace's career, A. O. Scott argues that Wallace is "less anti-ironic than (forgive me) meta-ironic." "Meta-irony," for Scott, is "a gambit . . . to turn irony back on itself, to make . . . fiction relentlessly conscious of its own self-consciousness, and thus to produce work that will be at once unassailably sophisticated and doggedly down to earth." Scott expressed clearly what many critics assume in their writing about Wallace, that he is engaging in yet another turn of metafiction's ironic dialectic, beginning to question the basis or ground of metafiction itself, another step down the pathway of Hegel's "infinite absolute negativity." Marshall Boswell claims that Wallace "opens the cage of irony by *ironizing* it, the same way he uses self-reflexivity to disclose the subtle deceptions at work in literary self-reflexivity" (207, emphasis in original). Iannis Goerlandt, meanwhile, "scans the text [*Infinite Jest*] for 'meta-ironic' markers" and concludes that Wallace fails to transcend irony by means of irony (320). But Boswell's and Goerlandt's analyses — and the term "meta-ironic"— incorrectly suggest that Wallace's fiction performs yet another iteration in an endless process of ironic commentary, turning irony back destructively onto itself. I have suggested that "postirony" is the better term for Wallace's project, and I will stipulate that postirony is not an effort to make fiction paradoxically self-conscious of its own self-consciousness but rather something more modest: an effort to decouple the academic and cultural association between metafictional form and ironic knowingness and cynicism. Thus in "Westward the Course of Empire Takes Its Way" (in *Girl with Curious Hair*), *Infinite Jest*, and "E Unibus Pluram: Television and U.S. Fiction," Wallace takes great pains to deny that "cynicism and naiveté are mutually incompatible" (*Girl* 304) and in "Westward" overtly links the belief in the importance and power of irony to the university, the creative writing workshop, and critical theories of postmodernity.[9] If a cynic can be naïve, then someone nonnaïve can be a noncynic. Wallace attempts to persuade his reader to adopt a stance of nonnaïve noncynicism by means of metafiction.

Beyond the Fourth Wall

"E Unibus Pluram" describes the relationship between television and metafiction in terms of their respective stances toward irony, credulity, and belief. By Wallace's account, television is a technology that by its nature stands in a position of domination or authority over those who view it in "high doses" (34); it is a device that cannot help but displace all authority beyond itself, putting itself at the center of the world of media addicts (like himself). Though he demonstrates a clear awareness of the socioeconomic contexts within which television programming is created, Wallace nonetheless identifies his target not only with a form of economic organization — the capitalist context of television production — but also with the intrinsic properties of visual media. When critiquing the technologist George Gilder's Utopian vision of the coming of the networked "telecomputer," for instance, Wallace insists that transforming "passive reception of facsimiles of experience to active manipulation of facsimiles of experience" will do nothing to solve the fundamental problem with television (74). The problem for Wallace, in this essay and in *Infinite Jest*, is a problem of addiction: "Whether I'm 'passive' or 'active' as a viewer, I still must cynically pretend [not to be dependent on TV], because I'm still dependent, because my real dependency here is not on a single show or a few networks. . . . My real dependence is on the fantasies and the images that enable them, and thus on any technology that can make images both available and fantastic" (75).

By Wallace's account, TV presents images of actors pretending to unself-consciously go through their lives, which leads viewers (and fiction writers) to confuse their experience viewing scripted performances with voyeurism, the authentically secret "espial" of everyday people living their lives. "A problem with so many of us fiction writers under 40 using television as a substitute for true espial, however, is that TV 'voyeurism' involves a whole *gorgeous orgy of illusions* for the pseudo-spy, when we watch" (24), a gorgeous illusion orgy that is built on denial, the systematic suspension of disbelief.[10] Television viewers ignore a range of mediations and hard truths: that watching television is not a true form of voyeurism; that viewers and fiction writers pathologically treat the sorts of people we see on television as models of what we ought to want to be; that the previous illusions are emerging from "our own *furniture*," from our television sets; and so on (24). These are the sorts of "disbelief we suspend" when we watch people on television, people who are "absolute *geniuses* at seeming unwatched . . . a certain type of transcendent semihuman who, in Emerson's phrase, 'carries the holiday in his eye'" (24–5). In the terms I am using, what Wallace says we are addicted to is credulity, a helpless belief in fantastic or fabricated images.

But if the television addict is addicted to facsimiles and fantasies and fantastic images, why wouldn't metafiction or ironic inoculation against belief-making technologies serve a positive function? Wallace's answer to this question is complex, and it informs the way that he constructs his fictions, especially *Infinite Jest*. Those who produce content for television demand that we suspend disbelief and desperately fear that we might critically disbelieve in the authority of television, and so television producers incorporate viewer disbelief into television programming itself, inoculating this programming to disbelieving ironic critique. Wallace writes that "junior advertising executives, aspiring filmmakers, and grad-school poets are in my experience especially prone to this condition, where they simultaneously hate, fear, and need television, and try to disinfect themselves of whatever so much viewing might do to them by watching TV with weary contempt instead of the rapt credulity most of us grew up with" (29). And yet, television has the ability to mirror the "weary contempt" of the cynical viewer, while also preemptively neutralizing the critical gaze of the experimental writer, in such a way that critique via irony becomes impossible or ineffective, leaving latter-day postmodernist fiction (what Wallace calls "Image-Fiction") "dead on the page" (81). These are the problems that drive Wallace's call for a new generation of experimental and oppositional writers:

> The next real literary "rebels" in this country might well emerge as some weird bunch of anti-rebels, born oglers who dare somehow to back away from ironic watching, who have the childish gall actually to endorse and instantiate single-entendre principles. Who treat of plain old untrendy human troubles and emotions in U.S. life with reverence and conviction. Who eschew self-consciousness and hip fatigue. These anti-rebels would be outdated, of course, before they even started. Dead on the page. Too sincere. Clearly repressed. Backward, quaint, naïve, anachronistic. Maybe that'll be the point. Maybe that's why they'll be the next real rebels. Real rebels, as far as I can see, risk disapproval. . . . The new rebels might be artists willing to risk the yawn, the rolled eyes, the cool smile, the nudged ribs, the parody of gifted ironists, the "Oh how *banal*." (81, emphasis in original)

The next real literary "rebel" is, in short, someone who risks accusations of credulity. That is, the antirebel Wallace is seeking is a type of *believer*. Whereas Wood rejects hysterical realism or literary postmodernism because of its remoteness from something called "reality," the postironic response — both to critics of postmodernism and to postmodernism itself — is to attempt to demonstrate that the form of metafiction can produce the opposite effect: belief.

This is the context in which we should understand what Wallace is up to in his short story "Octet," part of the collection *Brief Inter-*

views with Hideous Men (1999). In "Octet," Wallace inverts the procedures of metafiction, asking not that we become aware of the artifice
of his fictional exercise, the artifice of the artificer, but rather that we
believe in the total, genuine honesty, the "100% candor" (148) of the
author — not the narrator, but *the author*, Wallace. The story begins as a
series of numbered, seemingly unrelated "pop quizzes" asking the reader
questions about "late-stage terminal drug addicts," quarrelling friends,
divorcing couples, etc. Wallace designates many of the characters in this
story with letters, like X and Y, instead of proper names. Pop Quiz 6
fails to culminate with a clear question, concluding with a metacom-
ment that "the whole *mise en scène* here seems too shot through with
ambiguity to make a very good Pop Quiz" (134). Wallace's narrator tries
to rewrite this scenario as Pop Quiz 6(A), which ends with the injunction: "X now finds himself, behind his commiserative expression and
solicitous gestures, secretly angry at his wife over an ignorance he has
made every effort to cultivate in her, and sustain. Evaluate" (145). The
quizzes, though numbered, skip around — the first quiz we encounter
is "Pop Quiz 4"—and ultimately the quizzes do not seem related to
one another. Pop Quiz 9 (of the "octet") takes a radically different turn,
beginning, "You are, unfortunately, a fiction writer" who is "attempting a cycle of very short belletristic pieces" as a means through which to
"compose a certain sort of 'interrogation' of the person reading them,
somehow — i.e. palpations, feelers into the interstices of her [the reader's] sense of something, etc. . . . though what that 'something' is remains
maddeningly hard to pin down" (145).

   After attempting to revise the stories, and realizing that they are
something like an "aesthetic disaster," you (the aforementioned "fiction
writer") attempt to acknowledge the disastrous nature of the Pop Quizzes openly but find that "these intranarrative acknowledgements have . . .
the disadvantage of flirting with metafictional self-reference . . . which
in the late 1990s, when even Wes Craven is cashing in on metafictional
self-reference, might come off as lame and tired and facile, and also runs
the risk of compromising the queer *urgency* about whatever it is you feel
you want the pieces to interrogate in whoever's reading them" (146–7,
emphasis in original). A footnote to the text of Pop Quiz 9 explains that

part of what you want these little Pop Quizzes to do is to break the textual fourth wall and kind of address (or "interrogate") the reader directly, which desire is somehow related to the old "meta"-device desire to puncture some sort of fourth wall of realist pretense, although it seems like the latter is less a puncturing of any sort of real wall and more a puncturing of the veil of impersonality or effacement around the writer himself. (147)

The "latter" form of fourth-wall puncturing — a.k.a. traditional metafiction — is scathingly critiqued by the narrator/Wallace as little more than a "rhetorical sham-honesty," because the desire to puncture said fourth wall originates fundamentally from a desire to be liked, to make one's reader feel flattered "that he [the sham metafiction writer] apparently thinks you're enough of a grownup to handle being reminded that what you're in the middle of is artificial (like you didn't know that already, like you needed to be reminded of it over and over again as if you were a myopic child who couldn't see what was right in front of you)" (147).

Initially, the pop quizzes begin for the writer as an attempt at a Hegelian sublation of metafiction into metafiction critical of its own impulses, an attempt to interrogate "the reader's initial inclination to dismiss the pieces as 'shallow formal exercises' simply on the basis of their shared formal features, forcing the reader to see that such a dismissal would be based on precisely the same sorts of shallow formalistic concerns she was (at least at first) inclined to accuse the octet of," but the effort of the interpellated "fiction writer" (a.k.a. "you") fails, and "you know that this is a very bad corner to have painted yourself into" (152). The solution Wallace (or his narrator) hits upon to resolve this paradox is less to sublate irony by means of higher order irony than to directly address the reader, to "ask her straight out whether she's feeling anything like what you feel," a "trick" that requires you "to be 100% honest. Meaning not just sincere but almost naked — more like unarmed. Defenseless" (154). The great danger in this approach is that "it might . . . come off like [you are] the sort of person who not only goes to a party all obsessed about whether he'll be liked or not but actually goes around the party and goes up to strangers and asks them whether they like him or not" (158). Despite these fears, Wallace ends the last quiz of "Octet" in just the way all the other pop quizzes end, with a request: "So decide" (160). What we are supposed to decide remains ambiguous, though the key decision we seem to have to make is whether or not to directly address the reader. Remember: Wallace positions the second-person subject of the last quiz as a fiction writer.

Wallace's last quiz invites us to understand that the interpolated fiction writer who is considering addressing the audience is identical to Wallace himself, that we are reading about Wallace's experience writing the story we're reading. However, his use of the second person, and his presentation of the final section as yet another pop quiz, interferes with directly conflating the character ("you") with Wallace. The block between "you" and Wallace necessitates that readers decide whether to make the identification. Nonetheless, the last quiz is so long, detailed, and specific when compared to the previous quizzes that it is hard not to understand it as a direct commentary on Wallace's experience writing "Octet."

The narrative technique Wallace is using bears much in common with what Raoul Eshelman has called the "double framing" of post-postmodern art (he invents the term "performatism" to describe this art). "Performatist works are set up in such a way that the reader or viewer at first has no choice but to opt for a single, compulsory solution to the problems within the work at hand," Eshelman writes (2). Allowing us to have our "postmetaphysical cake and eat it too," the performativist work of art sets up two frames of reference: "The outer frame imposes some sort of unequivocal resolution to the problems raised in the work on the reader or viewer," forcing us to take seriously the outer frame's "coercive" interpretation of the inner frame. "Either some sort of irony will undercut the outer frame from within and break up the artificially framed unity, or we will find a crucial scene (or inner frame) confirming the outer frame's coercive logic" (3). Building on Eric Gans's generative anthropology, and tracing the technique of "double framing" in the film *American Beauty* and in the novel *The Life of Pi*, among other works, Eshelman argues that the outer frame embeds the content of diegesis within an "originary scene" that reduces "human behavior to what seems to be a very basic or elementary circle of unity with nature and/or with other people" (4). In the case of "Octet," the inner frame of the pop quizzes is offered as the natural form "you" might employ if you, the hypothetical fiction writer described in Pop Quiz 9, wanted to be "100% honest" with your reader. Whereas the "fourth wall" of traditional metafiction opens onto the situation of the reader (revealing that what the reader reads ought to be disbelieved), Wallace's "fourth wall" opens onto the situation of the writer (whom we are asked to believe in).

Another version of this metafictional validation of the real — one that tries even more forcefully to tear down the fourth wall in a way that converts fiction into a sort of nonfiction — can be found in Wallace's short story "Good Old Neon," part of his 2004 collection *Oblivion*. "Good Old Neon" begins as an apparently fictional story about a character who claims to have committed suicide. The story is narrated in the first person and is presented as the recollection of the suicide victim told from after the time of his death; this character promises early in "Good Old Neon" to "explain what happens immediately after a person dies," and he informs us that he committed suicide because of his conviction that he is an irreparable fraud, a victim of what he calls the "fraudulence paradox" (143, 147). Those who suffer from the "fraudulence paradox" discover how "the more time and effort you put into trying to appear impressive or attractive to other people, the less impressive or attractive you felt inside — you were a fraud. And the more of a fraud you felt like, the harder you tried to convey an impression or likable image of yourself so that other people wouldn't find out what a hollow fraudulent person you really were" (147). When the narrator finally commits suicide, we learn that "dying isn't bad, but it takes forever" (180). Wallace constructs a formal analog to the character's experience of death by depicting a runaway inflation of the time of discourse relative to the time of story, the juxtaposition of a massive proliferation of words on the page and an increasingly narrow, synchronic focus. The last two pages of the story describe many different spatial locations at "the very same instant," the time during which the narrator has been addressing the reader. When the narrator describes one location, we learn that while we've been reading the story "Dave Wallace blinks in the midst of idly scanning class photos from his 1980 Aurora West H.S. yearbook and seeing my photo and trying through the tiny keyhole of himself, to imagine what all must have happened to lead up to my death in the fiery single-car accident he'd read about in 1991" (180). We are informed that the Dave Wallace described in the story is "trying, if only in the second his lids are down, to somehow reconcile what this luminous guy had seemed like from the outside with whatever on the interior must have driven him to kill himself in such a dramatic and doubtlessly painful way" (181). The dramatic focus of the story shifts from the difficulties the narrator has dealing with the "fraudulence paradox" to the fictional Dave Wallace's struggle to deal with "the cliché that you can't ever truly know what's going on inside somebody else," a cliché that strikes Dave Wallace as "hoary and insipid" but unavoidably true (181). The shift in focus is a kind of trick, akin to the ninth pop quiz in "Octet," whereby Wallace pulls away the "fourth" wall of the fictional world of his story, revealing that what readers were led to believe was fiction (and specifically postmodern metafiction) may in fact be a kind of meta-nonfiction. The purpose of this revelation seems to be to cause the reader to experience a form of connection with Wallace as a writer — again, as with "Octet," not "Dave Wallace" the character, but the author. This is also, we should recall, the aim of James O. Incandenza in creating the film cartridge, "Infinite Jest." Incandenza creates "Infinite Jest" as a form of art by means of which to overcome barriers to communication with his son, Hal. If we are to understand how the project I have described as postirony affects the form and content of *Infinite Jest*, we must then turn to "Infinite Jest," the film cartridge around which much of the plot of Wallace's encyclopedic novel revolves.

Infinite Jest and the Avant-Garde

In *Infinite Jest*, Wallace reimagines the terminal nature of avant-garde efforts to end art as an institution and to break down the barricades — for Wallace, as we have seen, these include irony, cynicism, and detachment — that prevent art from changing the consciousness of its consumers. The Entertainment promises to do both. While previous avant-garde practitioners sought to disrupt the culture industry on the supply side of the system, Incandenza's "Infinite Jest" attacks the consumer of art by ending the viewer's ability to consume anything ever again. The historical avant-garde, in contrast, sought to liberate art from the cycle of commodification and bourgeois aestheticism, which had rendered it inert as an agent of social change. It often did so, as in the case of Marcel Duchamp's famous urinal, by trying to reveal the contradictions inherent in the art market. As Peter Bürger famously describes in *Theory of the Avant-garde*, "the European avant-garde movements can be defined as an attack on the status of art in bourgeois society. What is negated is not an early form of art (a style) but art as an institution that is unassociated with the life praxis of men" (49). To fully understand the significance of the Entertainment in *Infinite Jest* we must move beyond a too narrow focus on the status of the film as entertainment, which has understandably dominated critical accounts, and see how James responds to the legacy of the avant-garde. In an interview with Larry McCaffery printed in the same 1993 issue of the *Review of Contemporary Fiction* that his television essay appeared in, Wallace suggests that the avant-garde unleashed something much more destructive than it had realized: "Art's reflection on itself is terminal, is one big reason why the art world saw Duchamp as an Antichrist" (134–5).[11]

One might object to Wallace's characterization of the avant-garde by demonstrating that the historical avant-garde — from the Futurists through Dada up to the Situationists — implicitly or overtly linked its intended projects of institutional destruction to ultimately redemptive Utopian politics. But the outright hostility of the Entertainment toward its viewers, its apocalyptic nature, need not invalidate the cartridge's status as an avant-garde artwork, according to Bürger's definition (which is of course not the only definition, nor necessarily identical to Wallace's). The existence of both Fascist- and Communist-tinged avant-garde movements during the early twentieth century suggests that if it were possible to create an art that again touched the lifeworlds of the bourgeoisie, or of anyone else for that matter, then such an artistic practice could in theory be both socially constructive and destructive. The Entertainment most clearly contradicts Bürger's thesis in the very fact of its existence, in Wallace's implicit claim that such an art is possible in the first place. If indeed the "avant-garde movement can in fact be judged to have failed" because it was "unable to destroy art as an institution," Incandenza's Entertainment should simply not be possible (Bürger 87).

To the degree that Wallace wants to salvage the project of the avant-garde, even in a negative form, he can draw on a postmodernist tradition that came to a conclusion that very much differs with Bürger on the nature of the relationship among institutions, art, and persons. Though Wallace wants to counter what we could call the historical postmodernists, he buys into their aesthetic ontology, their interpretation of how one might extend the project of the avant-garde and the modernists. The historical postmodernists often participated in the symbolic politics of counterculture, on the theory that disruptions of rationality might affect change at the level of what C. Wright Mills called "the cultural apparatus" (203). As Sean McCann and Michael Szalay persuasively argue, the New Left saw power as partly residing in "the symbolic forms that determined how people understood reality" (440). This fact implied, naturally enough, that interrogating and exposing corrupt or authoritarian symbolic forms could do significant political work.

Unlike Bürger, then, postmodernist authors and poststructuralist intellectuals would not claim that the avant-garde is necessarily doomed to fail, so long as it focuses on properly cultural politics. Some postmodernists — like William S. Burroughs, Ishmael Reed, Thomas Pynchon, and Kathy Acker — openly identified with the movement; others merely integrated countercultural assumptions about the efficacy of symbolic political warfare into their fictional experiments. Donald Barthelme, to take one example, emphasizes the ontological status of the book as a thing-in-the-world in his famous essay "After Joyce": "with Stein and Joyce the literary work becomes an object in the world rather than a text or commentary upon the world." The work of art becomes more like "a rock or a refrigerator" than a discursive representation of the world (Barthelme 4). Although Barthelme adjusts his views twenty years later in "Not-Knowing" (1987), allowing that the world still smuggles itself into literary works in the belly of language, the notion of the book as a thing-in-the-world remains a very powerful legacy of modernism and the avant-garde for postmodernist writers. For Barthelme, the material book becomes a thing about which we ponder (*Finnegans Wake* is one of his favorite examples), something we live with and explore. This belief in the "thingness" of the literary text underwrites many of Barthelme's unusual experiments.

Acknowledging its postmodernist forebears, *Infinite Jest* reminds us of its status as a thing by virtue of its girth, its heft, its alleged bloat. More substantively, while the novel itself may not prove to be as massively addictive of a diversion as the Entertainment that it describes, it does self-consciously exhibit the avant-garde aggressiveness toward audience members we have seen associated with the Entertainment itself, not to mention some of Incandenza's earlier films, such as *The Medusa v the Odalisque*, which depicts "mobile holograms of two visually lethal mythologic females" who "duel with reflective surfaces on-stage while a live crowd of spectators turns to stone" (988). Referring to the postmodern novel as a "Hostile Object," Barthelme specifically focuses on Burroughs's cut-up technique, but he might as well be describing *Infinite Jest* when he writes, "The form of the [Hostile Object], in other words, suggests that a chunk of a large building may fall on you at any moment. Burroughs' form is inspired, exactly appropriate to his terroristic purpose" (Barthelme 8). The notion of the artist as a sort of (failed) terrorist —which Don DeLillo ponders in *Mao II* (1992) and, in a different way, in *Falling Man* (2008)—Wallace encodes into both the plot and the form of *Infinite Jest*. The A.F.R., after all, seek to use the Entertainment as a terrorist weapon against American consumers.

By Wallace's own criteria, his novel may constitute outright aggression against his readers. Wallace explains to McCaffery that his hostility toward his readers tends to manifest itself "in the form of sentences that are syntactically not incorrect but still a real bitch to read. Or bludgeoning the reader with data. Or devoting a lot of energy to creating expectations and then taking pleasure in disappointing them" (130). With its massive, syntactically tangled, paragraphs; hundred pages of endnotes in a tiny font; and (for many readers) frustratingly unresolved plotlines, we might find ourselves tempted to consider the novel a Barthelmean "Hostile Object."

Of course, James O. Incandenza never wanted to consider himself an avant-garde artist, although he plays the role of one, often for his own amusement, as a way of laughing at critics who want to impute deep significance to his filmic practical jokes. Let us recall again the original purpose of "Infinite Jest." Incandenza does not make his lethally addictive film in order to shock or destroy his viewing audience; his aim, according to the testimony he offers from beyond the grave to the convalescing Don Gately, is to connect with his troubled son, Hal.

> The wraith . . . says he spent the whole sober last ninety days of his animate life working tirelessly to contrive a medium via which he and the muted son could simply *converse*. To concoct something the gifted boy couldn't simply master and move on from to a new plateau. Something the boy would love enough to induce him to open his mouth and come *out* — even if it was only to ask for more. Games hadn't done it, professionals hadn't done it, impersonation of professionals hadn't done it. His last resort: entertainment. Make something so bloody compelling it would reverse thrust on a young self's fall into the womb of solipsism, anhedonia, death in life. A magically entertaining toy to dangle at the infant still somewhere alive in the boy, to make its eyes light and toothless mouth open unconsciously, to laugh. To bring him "out of himself," as they say. The womb could be used both ways. A way to say I AM SO VERY, VERY SORRY and have it *heard*. A life-long dream. The scholars and Foundations and disseminators never saw that his most serious wish was: *to entertain*. (*IJ* 838–9, emphasis in original)

From the little actual information we learn about the content of the cartridge during Joelle van Dyne's interview with Steeply, the Entertainment during one scene positions its viewers as infants, infantilizing the viewer in very literal, technical ways: "The point of view was from the crib, yes. A crib's-eye view . . . There's something wobbled and weird about [a new-born's] vision, supposedly. I think the newer-born they are, the more the wobble. . . . I don't think there's much doubt the lens was supposed to reproduce an infantile visual field" (939–40). By constructing the Entertainment in this way, Incandenza, and by extension

Wallace, seem to be simultaneously critiquing the hyper-self-involution supposedly characteristic of the avant-garde as well as the infantilizing tendencies of the mass media. The two critiques are in fact inseparable for Wallace.

For Wallace, "Infinite Jest" stages a recursive loop, "a moving right-triangular cycle of interdependence and waste-creation and -utilization," to borrow Ted Schacht's explanation to Idris Arslanian of annular fusion (571). This right triangle brings together the postmodern subject, the avant-garde impulse, and the mass media into a weird web of interdependence. What *Infinite Jest* hopes to reveal is that the logic of the avant-garde is inextricably entangled with the logic of the marketplace; all texts are in a dynamic process of feedback with their myriad paratexts, so much so that the distinction between inside and outside quickly blurs. Inside and outside are, in fact, part of the same circuit, and perhaps have always been, and one has to imagine something like an ultimate entertainment in order to think outside the system, to see its contours, to see how its elements are all tangled together, to imagine what resistance might look like. *Infinite Jest*'s rejection of the ethos of irony is, in this sense, part of the same strategy earlier avant-gardes embraced. Wallace accepts that dismantling or at least resisting the symbolic hegemony of the mainstream is a necessary project and endorses the view that changing one's personal disposition or sensibility can effect such change.

For the postironist, irony must be opposed because it is now part of the established symbolic order. Working against the "bequest from the early postmodernists and the post-structuralist critics" (McCaffery 132), Wallace nonetheless wants not only to imagine a version of postmodern fiction that addresses "reality" to his satisfaction, including mediated hyperreality, but also to imagine the possibility of an ultimate art, one with the power to literally move its consumers and to break down the fundamental barriers that separate the viewer of art from its author. Whereas "Octet" and "Good Old Neon" attempt to achieve this aim on a small scale, using techniques associated with metafiction toward different ends, *Infinite Jest* develops these ideas through its description of the form and purpose of the Entertainment.

Life, Art

In a *LIVE from the NYPL* event held on 17 September 2008 — a conversation among Daniel Mendelsohn, James Wood, and Pico Iyer — an audience member asked the panelists about their views on the death of David Foster Wallace, who had committed suicide only days before. The question: "Does one want to attempt to read the death of David Foster Wallace, a suicide, as a literary gesture, or is that just too distasteful a suggestion?" Wood replies that he feels "sort of wrong even sort of commenting on this," but concludes that Wallace's suicide was not a literary gesture. Mendelsohn is more emphatic in his rejection of the premise behind the question: "I'm so dumbfounded by the question I don't — I'm not sure what to say. The only literary gesture is writing. It's the only — I don't know what it means to be a literary — I just literally don't know what it means . . . I can't comment on it because it seems sort of grotesque, I don't know what to say."

What could it possibly mean to "read" a suicide in the first place? While these reactions are suitably decorous, and predictably enough suggest that life and literature are quite separate spheres indeed — that to read a life as if it were a text or as comprised of "gestures," to treat a text as if it were a person, is simply perverse — at the end of this analysis it seems to me that Mendelsohn's claim that the "only literary gesture is writing" misunderstands the intensity and seriousness with which Wallace approached his work. On the most superficial level, near the end of his life, Wallace found writing to be a difficult struggle, which led to considerable personal pain and suffering and which contributed to his decision to stop taking the drug Nardil.[12] Moreover, Wallace's fiction is studded with suicides and cripplingly depressed characters. In addition to the suicide at the center of "Good Old Neon" and the suicide of James O. Incandenza by microwave oven in *Infinite Jest*, there is the minutely documented suffering of the narrator of "The Depressed Person" and a pantheon of damaged characters in *Brief Interviews with Hideous Men* and *Oblivion*.

Taken as a whole, Wallace's oeuvre might be seen as a single long survey of the different forms individual human suffering can take in a postindustrial or postmodern society. Characters in Wallace's fiction

constantly confront the paradoxes inherent in their suffering, and —
tellingly — usually find psychological and pharmaceutical approaches to
their problems unsatisfying or ineffective, unable to attack the foundation of their discontents, which come to seem intractable. These characters seek philosophical and literary solutions to the problem of personal survival, and more often than not fail to find what they're looking
for. The problem then is not that "reading" a life as literature debases
life, but rather that to assume that one "merely" reads literature without having to take its conceptual commitments seriously — to assume
that writing is merely a gesture — debases literature. Wallace, more than
most contemporary novelists, insists on the necessary link between life
and literature, and in this sense he draws significantly on the legacy of
the historical avant-garde and postmodernism. When Wallace writes,
in his now widely quoted commencement address at Kenyon College,
that "it is not the least bit coincidental that adults who commit suicide
with firearms almost always shoot themselves in the head," he means to
illustrate "the real, no-bull value of your liberal-arts education" ("David
Foster Wallace on Life and Work"). In short, a liberal arts education
can help "keep [you] from going through your comfortable, prosperous,
respectable adult life dead, unconscious, a slave to your head and to your
natural default-setting of being uniquely, completely, imperially alone,
day in and day out" (60). The idea that writing is a means of overcoming
loneliness and the crippling effects of radical individualism/atomism
is, as we've seen, a major theme of Wallace's writing, in both his fiction
and his nonfiction. In these terms, his suicide might be described as a
failure of literature to achieve its promise, its inability to solve problems.

But we have also seen that Wallace's approach to the relationship between life and art differs significantly from the historical avant-garde's.
What separates Wallace from the avant-garde is his lack of interest in re-
making society along any particular institutional lines. Wallace might,
as Paul Giles argues, "mediate . . . the dynamics of globalization, subtly
recording how the mass media impacts upon and interferes jarringly
with the lives of American citizens" (341), but Wallace's idea of politics
— to the degree that he articulates one — rests within a tradition of
symbolic action and countercultural individualism.

Like many members of subcultures and countercultures before them, postironists do of course seek to change social norms, but these changes seem to be squarely (if anxiously) situated within market relations and within the engine of the art-publicity machine, partly because those institutions came to seem to many — including Wallace — to be ubiquitous and fundamentally inescapable. Postironists are more concerned with overthrowing the rule of a particular type of person, the ironist, and have far less to say about changing the institutional relations that give rise to this type. Because of this strategic commitment, Wallace may have been doomed to fail to achieve his aims in strictly literal terms. The means he drew on to untangle the antinomies of the End of History were themselves arguably liberal and individualist in character: put crudely, he sought to defeat bad institutions using a symbolic toolkit. It is perhaps this inattention[13] to the structural causes of postmodernity that leads at least some of those that Wallace inspired — such as Dave Eggers and his associates at *McSweeney's* — to move away from the question of belief in the sincerity (and reality) of other persons as such toward the self-conscious cultivation of personal and literary style as a means of signaling goodness. That is, postironic writers such as Eggers revalued Wallace's more negative orientation and have crafted in its place a relatively optimistic ethos that mixes an offbeat aesthetic with a laudable urge toward philanthropy and the active construction of alternative institutional structures (a publishing house, tutoring centers, a charitable foundation). Both dispositions — the character types constructed by Wallace's and Eggers's writing — can be described as believers, and both authors similarly use metafiction to achieve their respective aims, but where Eggers wants to use nonfiction to make us quirky, to enchant (or more accurately re-enchant) us, to inform us of and involve us in collective projects, Wallace uses fiction in what can often seem like a last desperate effort to make us believe something, to feel anything. Judging by his meteoric literary fame, I would suggest that a great many readers shared his postironic aspirations.

Notes

1. *The End of History and The Last Man*, the book that grew out of Fukuyama's *National Interest* article, presents his account of this new condition in
considerably more detail.

2. Wallace sees Wittgenstein as an early discoverer of the idea that our approach to reality may be fundamentally linguistic in character: "This was
Wittgenstein's double bind: you can either treat language as an infinitely small
dense dot, or you let it become the world — the exterior and everything in it.
The former banishes you from the Garden. The latter seems more promising.
If the world is itself a linguistic construct, there's nothing 'outside' language
for language to have to picture or refer to. This lets you avoid solipsism, but
it leads right to the postmodern, post-structural dilemma of having to deny
yourself an existence independent of language. Heidegger's the guy most
people think got us into this bind, but when I was working on *Broom of the
System* I saw Wittgenstein as the real architect of the postmodern trap. He
died right on the edge of explicitly treating reality as linguistic instead of ontological. This eliminated solipsism, but not the horror. Because we're still
stuck" (McCaffery 144). In terms of these distinctions, we might say that Wallace regards the world as linguistic but nonetheless wants to use language as a
way of reconstructing an extralinguistic reality, specifically the reality of the
existence of other persons.

3. See "E Unibus Pluram," *A Supposedly Fun Thing* 61. For an elaboration
of Wallace's later thinking on the hero best able to oppose American postmodernism, see my discussion of *The Pale King* in the *Los Angeles Review of
Books*.

4. Mary Holland, for instance, claims that Wallace implies that Alcoholics
Anonymous suffers from the same problem of solipsism and narcissism as the
broader American society: "Significantly, the same looping pathology defines
and calls into question the culture of recovery represented in the novel by the
Alcoholics Anonymous program. In equally powerful and less subtle ways
than do the Incandenza family, the novel's drug addicts, recovering and not,
further illustrate the pathological recursivity of narcissism, in which narcissism operates as both the cause and effect of their addictions . . . the AA and
NA programs ultimately ask not that members reach out to empathize with
strangers but that they recognize their own place in this infinitely repeating
sameness, the recursivity of addiction" (232–3).

5. Wood's 2003 novel, *The Book Against God*, provides an intriguing example of his conflation of religion and literature (which he treats as a sort

of secular religion). The novel revolves around Tom's conflicted inability to reveal his atheism to his father, an Anglican minister. Tom — whose name is undoubtedly meant to recall the story of Doubting Thomas, a.k.a. Thomas the Believer — avidly seeks to deny the existence of God, assembling his "Book Against God" instead of writing his Ph.D. thesis, though at one point he is forced to admit that "the cathedral is, after all, a beautiful mistake, a magnificent lie" (173).

6. Note that Wallace suggests that forms of religion (kneeling, prayer) *precede* belief for Don Gately, but that the transition from nonbeliever to believer cannot be willed.

7. See Herbert H. Clark and Richard J. Gerrig, "On the Pretense Theory of Irony."

8. Wood puts the category of plausibility at the center of his theory of fiction in *How Fiction Works* (2008). "Hypothetical plausibility — probability — is the important and neglected idea here: probability involves the defense of the credible *imagination* against the incredible. This is surely why Aristotle writes that a convincing impossibility in mimesis is always preferable to an unconvincing possibility" (238, emphasis in original). This discussion leads Wood to develop his category of "lifeness": "Realism, seen broadly as truthfulness to the way things are, cannot be mere verisimilitude, cannot be mere lifelikeness, or lifesameness, but what I must call *lifeness*: life on the page, life brought to different life by the highest artistry. And it cannot be a genre; instead it makes other forms of fiction seem like genres. For realism of this kind — lifeness — is the origin. It teaches everything else; it schools its own truants; it is what allows magical realism, hysterical realism, fantasy, science fiction, even thrillers, to exist" (247). In other words, "lifeness" has no specific or discernable properties, except of course that it excludes genre fiction, including the hated lifenessless genre of "hysterical realism." As an analytic category, "lifeness" is a bit vague, in my view; one might as well claim that good books have "souls" and that the special ethereal emanations of such soul-filled books expose which of their brethren are soulless, but also hold that — by necessity — there are no particular namable properties we can reference to prove that a book has such a vital spirit. However, understood as a symbolically loaded concept designed to respond to a literary-critical moment desperate to produce new forms of "irreproducible" literary distinction, the quasi-spiritual category of "lifeness" bears considerable interest, mostly as a reflection on the landscape of cultural capital or prestige in the early twenty-first century.

9. Cornel Bonca insightfully observes that "Wallace ... [Rick] Moody, Jeffrey Eugenides, Jonathan Franzen, Donald Antrim, and for good measure, let's throw in that upstart Dave Eggers — have almost had the same trouble.

Schooled in the late '70s and '80s by English departments and creative-writing programs in which narrative deconstruction and paranoid irony was the rage . . . and understandably unwilling to follow the inimitable path of Raymond Carver, these writers find themselves swimming in postmodernism's backwash, not quite sure how to make their own way. It's an old Oedipal story — younger writers trying to write themselves free of their forebears — and so far, Wallace is probably the only one to find his way to shore, and that's because he's the only one who's managed to make postmodern innovation organic to his work, and even that took a while." Bonca identifies the "postmodern innovation" Wallace integrates into his work with "irony." I am arguing against this notion, suggesting that Wallace's project is to fuse postmodernist form with what he regards as the "traditional" moral and emotional concerns of literature. In his essay on Dostoevsky, Wallace writes, "The big thing that makes Dostoevsky invaluable for American readers and writers is that he appears to possess degrees of passion, conviction, and engagement with deep moral issues that we — here, today — cannot or do not permit ourselves. . . . Frank's bio prompts us to ask ourselves why we seem to require of our art an ironic distance from deep convictions or desperate questions, so that contemporary writers have either to make jokes of them or else try to work them in under cover of some formal trick like intertextual quotations or incongruous juxtaposition, sticking the really urgent stuff inside asterisks as part of some multivalent defamiliarization-flourish or some such shit" ("Joseph Frank's Dostoevsky" 271).

10. In his contribution to this volume, Josh Roiland insightfully identifies this systematic denial with Friedrich Nietzsche's description of "oblivion."

11. Unlike conservative critics of postmodernism, Wallace does see some value in postmodernist experimentation in literature: "But I still believe the move to involution had value: it helped writers break free of some long-standing flat-earth-type taboos. It was standing in line to happen. And for a little while, stuff like *Pale Fire* and *The Universal Baseball Association* was valuable as a metaaesthetic breakthrough the same way Duchamp's urinal had been valuable" (McCaffery 134–5).

12. See D. T. Max, "The Unfinished," *New Yorker* 9 March 2009. While struggling to write *The Pale King*, his unfinished last novel, "Wallace had come to suspect that the drug was also interfering with his creative evolution. He worried that it muted his emotions, blocking the leap he was trying to make as a writer. He thought that removing the scrim of Nardil might help him see a way out of his creative impasse. Of course, as he recognized even then, maybe the drug wasn't the problem; maybe he simply was distant, or maybe boredom was too hard a subject. He wondered if the novel was the right

medium for what he was trying to say, and worried that he had lost the passion necessary to complete it."

13. Complicating my argument here, I would quickly note that *The Pale King*, though unfinished, has much more to say about solving the specifically structural and institutional causes of postmodern suffering than does *Infinite Jest*. We can only speculate on what shape the completed novel might have taken.

Works Cited

Barthelme, Donald. *Not-Knowing: The Essays and Interviews of Donald Barthelme*. Ed. Kim Herzinger. New York: Random House, 1997. Print.

Bonca, Cornel. "The Ineluctable Modality of the Marginal." *Orange County Weekly* 15 March 2001. Print.

Boswell, Marshall. *Understanding David Foster Wallace*. Columbia: University of South Carolina Press, 2003. Print.

Bürger, Peter. *Theory of the Avant-garde*. Trans. Michael Shaw. Minneapolis: University of Minnesota Press, 2002. Print.

Clark, Herbert H., and Richard J. Gerrig. "On the Pretense Theory of Irony." In *Irony in Language and Thought: A Cognitive Science Reader*. Ed. Raymond W. Gibbs and Herbert L. Colston. New York: Lawrence Erlbaum, 2007. 25–33. Print.

Eshelman, Raoul. *Performativism, or, the End of Postmodernism*. Aurora, CO: Davies, 2008. Print.

Fukuyama, Francis. "The End of History?" *National Interest* 16 (Summer 1989): 3–18. Print.

———. *The End of History and the Last Man*. New York: Free Press, 2006. Print.

Giles, Paul. "Sentimental Posthumanism: David Foster Wallace." *Twentieth-Century Literature* 53.3 (Fall 2007): 327–44. Print.

Goerlandt, Iannis. "'Put the book down and slowly walk away': Irony and David Foster Wallace's *Infinite Jest*." *Critique: Studies in Contemporary Fiction* 47.3 (2006): 309–28. Print.

Holland, Mary K. "'The Art's Heart's Purpose': Braving the Narcissistic Loop of David Foster Wallace's *Infinite Jest*." *Critique* 47.3 (Spring 2006): 218–42. Print.

Konstantinou, Lee. "Unfinished Form." *Los Angeles Review of Books* 6 July 2011. Web.

Max, D. T. "The Unfinished." *New Yorker* 9 March 2009. Web.

McCaffery, Larry. "An Interview with David Foster Wallace." *Review of Contemporary Fiction* 13.2 (Summer 1993): 127–50. Print.

McCann, Sean, and Michael Szalay. "Do You Believe in Magic? Literary Thinking after the New Left." *Yale Journal of Criticism* 18.2 (Fall 2005): 435–80. Print.

Mendelsohn, Daniel, James Wood, and Pico Iyer. "Reading in a World of Images." *LIVE from the NYPL* 17 September 2008. Web.

Mills, C. Wright. "The Cultural Apparatus." In *The Politics of Truth: Selected Writings of C. Wright Mills*. Ed. John Summers. New York: Oxford University Press, 2008. 203–12. Print.

Rorty, Richard. *Contingency, Irony, and Solidarity*. Cambridge: Cambridge University Press, 1989. Print.

Scott, A. O. "The Panic of Influence." *New York Review of Books* February 2000. Web.

Wallace, David Foster. "David Foster Wallace on Life and Work." *Wall Street Journal*. 19 September 2008. Web.

———. "E Unibus Pluram: Television and U.S. Fiction." In *A Supposedly Fun Thing I'll Never Do Again: Essays and Arguments*. New York: Back Bay Books, 1998. 21–82. Print.

———. "Good Old Neon." In *Oblivion*. New York: Back Bay Books, 2004. 141–81. Print.

———. "Greatly Exaggerated." In *A Supposedly Fun Thing I'll Never Do Again: Essays and Arguments*. Boston: Back Bay Books, 1998. 138–45. Print.

———. *Infinite Jest*. Boston: Little, Brown, 1996. Print.

———. "Joseph Frank's Dostoevsky." In *Consider the Lobster*. New York: Little, Brown and Company, 2006. 255–74. Print.

———. "Octet." In *Brief Interviews with Hideous Men*. New York: Little, Brown and Company, 1999. 131–60. Print.

———. "Westward the Course of Empire Takes Its Way." In *The Girl with Curious Hair*. New York: W. W. Norton, 1996. 231–373. Print.

Waugh, Patricia. *Metafiction: The Theory and Practice of Self-Conscious Fiction*. London: Methuen, 1984. Print.

Wood, James. *The Book Against God*. New York: Farrar, Straus, and Giroux, 2003. Print.

———. "The Color Purple: Toni Morrison's False Magic." In *The Broken Estate: Essays on Literature and Belief*. New York: Random House, 1999. 236–45. Print.

———. *How Fiction Works*. New York: Farrar, Straus, and Giroux, 2008. Print.

———. "Hysterical Realism." In *The Irresponsible Self: On Laughter and the Novel*. New York: Picador, 2005. 167–83. Print.

Young, Toby, and Tom Vanderbilt. "The End of Irony? The Tragedy of the Post-Ironic Condition." *Modern Review* 1.14 (April–May 1994): 6–7. Print.

DAVID LIPSKY

AN INTERVIEW WITH

DAVID FOSTER WALLACE

Do you wonder if books are passé? Do you worry about that? As we were talking about yesterday, Rolling Stone *hasn't covered a writer your age in ten years.*

I think books used to be real important parts of the cultural conversation, in a way that they aren't anymore. And the fact that *Rolling Stone,* which is a pretty important mainstream magazine, doesn't cover them that much anymore says a lot. Not so much about *Rolling Stone.* But about how interested the culture is in books.

For me — and you know this, you get together with writers, and this is a great topic of conversation, 'cause we all just bitch and moan. We'll talk about the decline of education and people's declining attention spans, and the responsibility of TV for this. For me the interesting question is, what's *caused* books to become kind of less important parts of the cultural conversation?

A minority taste?

Yeah, in a certain way. The thing that I think a lot of us forget is, part of the fault of that is books. Is that probably as, you know — you get this sort of cycle, as they become less important commercially and in the mainstream, they've begun protecting their ego by talking more and more to each other. And establishing themselves as this tight kind of cloistered world that doesn't really have anything to do, you know, with real regular readers.

And uh, so, so no, I don't think they're passé. I think they've gotta find fundamentally new ways to do their job. And I don't think for instance we as a generation have done a very good job of this.

Hey, Jeeves — shut that off for a second. [Jeeves whimpers, sits.]

Must find new ways to make books — what new ways?

You know what? I don't know. My guess is, it's gonna involve some way of making some sort of old eternal verities and questions comprehensible — I can't think of a way to say it that isn't academic.

Could you loosen it?

(Silent verbal scowl) Well, it's not just a question of loosening up, it's that it's very hard and complicated, and to try to compress it into a couple of sentences . . .

[Tape off, break]

[We talk it out for a few minutes; then, when he thinks he's ready — and this must be what it's like to watch him go through a few drafts, as he said in the car; he's found a way to do answer drafts on the spot, by regulating the tape flow; clever — he turns the tape back on.]

I'm not sure about "give movies that" [the audience], but you're right, do you want me to just say it over? Yeah, there's stuff that really good fiction can do that other forms of art can't do as well.

And the big thing, the big thing seems to be, sort of leapin' over that wall of self, and portraying inner experience. And setting up, I think, a kind of intimate conversation between two consciences.

And the trick is gonna be finding a way to do it at a time, and for a generation, whose relation to long sustained linear verbal communication is fundamentally different. I mean, one of the reasons why the book is structured strangely is it's at least an *attempt* to be mimetic, structurally, to a kind of inner experience. And I know we disagreed in Monical's about whether experience really feels like that, I mean, I don't know whether I've done it, it's something that I'm interested in, and am trying to do.

Subject matter untackled too?

Yeah, I guess. . . .

[To tape] David is talking about today people watch more MTV and more movies and more TV, and so that the world in which readers move is very different than the world in which, say, you know, our parents moved.

I guess. Yeah, I guess my first inclination would be to say that most of that would be — to create stuff that mirrors sort of neurologically the way the world feels.

[Dogs whimpering]

[Snapping fingers] Hey c'mere! C'mere, Jeeves.

But you're right; and the fact of the matter is —

I was quoting you, actually —

No wonder it sounds so very, very smart.

C'mere! You know what? You're making me nuts. Sit down! Sit down, I can't think when you're doing this.

But I guess part of it is, it also affects the kind of inner experiences. And, you know, the feelings that fiction is about. Today's person spends way more time in front of screens. In fluorescent-lit rooms, in cubicles, being on one end or the other of an electronic data transfer. And what is it to be human and alive and exercise your humanity in that kind of exchange? Versus fifty years ago, when the big thing was, I don't know *what*, havin' a house and a garden and driving ten miles to your light industrial job. And livin' and dyin' in the same town that you're in, and knowing what other towns looked like only from photographs and the occasional movie reel. I mean, there's just so much that seems *different*, and the speed with which it gets different just . . .

The trick, the trick for fiction it seems to me, is gonna be to try to create a kind of texture and a language to show, to create enough mimesis to show that nothing's really changed, I think. [Different position from first interview, five days ago, when I defended the nothing-about-people-has-changed position.] And that what's always been important is still important. And that the job is to find out how to do that stuff, in a world whose texture and sensuous feel is totally different.

And what's important — you've been saying to me — is a certain basic humanity.

Yeah . . . sort of, um, who do I live for? What do I believe in, what do I *want*? I mean, they're the sorts of questions so profound and so deep they sound banal when you say them out loud.

I think every generation finds new excuses for why people behave in such a basically ugly manner. The only constant is the bad behavior. I think our excuse, now, is media and technology.

I think the reason why people behave in an ugly manner is that it's really scary to be alive and to be human, and people are really really afraid. And that the reasons . . .

[As I get closer to the dogs, David likes me better too; has that pet owner's helpless, natural, unavoidable faith in his dog's taste.

The dog keeps whimpering; David jokes he's got "Godfather Cheeks" from chewing the tobacco. Which he's always spitting into things.]

That the fear is the basic condition, and there are all kinds of reasons for why we're so afraid. But the fact of the matter is, is that, is that the job that we're here to do is to learn how to live in a way that we're not terrified all the time. And not in a position of using all kinds of different things, and using *people* to keep that kind of terror at bay. That is my personal opinion.

Well for me, as an American male, the face I'd put on the terror is the dawning realization that nothing's enough, you know? That no pleasure is enough, that no achievement is enough. That there's a kind of queer dissatisfaction or emptiness at the core of the self that is unassuageable by outside stuff. And my guess is that that's been what's going on, ever since people were hitting each other over the head with clubs. Though describable in a number of different words and cultural argots. And that our particular challenge is that there's never been more and better stuff comin' from the outside, that seems temporarily to fill the hole or drown out the hole.

Could it be assuageable by internal means also?

Personally, I believe that if it's assuageable in any way it's by internal means. And I don't know what that means. I think it's fine in some way. [Tape off again; we keep turning it off while he mentally drafts and redrafts answers.] I think it's probably assuageable by internal means. I think those internal means have to be earned and developed, and it has something to do with, um, um, the pop-psych phrase is lovin' yourself.

It's more like, if you can think of times in your life that you've treated people with extraordinary decency and love, and pure uninterested concern, just because they were valuable as human beings. The ability to do that with ourselves. To treat ourselves the way we would treat a really good, precious friend. Or a tiny child of ours that we absolutely loved more than life itself. And I think it's probably possible to achieve that. I think part of the job we're here for is to learn how to do it. [Spits with mouthful voice into cup.] I know that sounds a little pious.

HEATHER HOUSER

INFINITE JEST'S ENVIRONMENTAL
CASE FOR DISGUST

"THE CONTEMPORARY condition is hopelessly shitty, insipid, materialistic, emotionally retarded, sadomasochistic and stupid" (McCaffery 131). In stark terms, David Foster Wallace assesses the bleak condition that he is handed and determines that, in the face of it, the contemporary novelist must cultivate readers' "capacity for joy, charity, genuine connections" (132) by "author[ing] things that both restructure worlds and make living people feel stuff" (quoted in Max 48). The novel, then, is not only an *imaginary* world; it can reconfigure the world beyond its pages by modeling and generating feeling. The outsized scope of *Infinite Jest* (1996) reflects its author's grand hopes for fiction. Read in light of his pronouncements, Wallace's novel raises the question of how aesthetic forms produce feelings that enhance an audience's awareness of "hopelessly shitty" social and material conditions. This query motivates this essay, which contends that, in order to understand *Infinite Jest*'s affective project, we must include the novel's underexamined environmental relations in our interpretive purview.

Like time, space has been radically reconfigured under the political scheme that *Infinite Jest* envisions. The United States, Mexico, and Canada have merged to form the Organization of North American Nations, or O.N.A.N. Because the U.S. is choking on the effluvia of its hyperconsuming society, it annexes additional territory from its impotent northern neighbors to use as a massive dump for discarded waste. From the reshaping of the continent, *Infinite Jest* zooms in on the reshaping of more circumscribed spaces where its dominant plots take place: the Boston conurbation, Phoenix, and the Tortolita foothills in Arizona. In the fictional Enfield neighborhood of Boston, the narration moves between two institutions whose respective locations symbolize their missions. The Enfield Tennis Academy (E.T.A.) occupies a geoengineered site designed by the school's founder, Jim Incandenza, to attract "boys [who] like great perspectival heights and spectacular views encompassing huge swaths of territory" (666). By "balding and shaving flat the top of [a] big abrupt hill," Jim created a setting that offers vistas of Boston's diverse topography: from "the spiky elegance of B[oston] C[ollege]," to the "high-voltage grids and coaxial chokers" of a power plant (241–2). Literally above it all, E.T.A. is a site for lofty ratiocination and abstraction. By contrast, Ennet House Drug and Alcohol Recovery House sits in the shadow of Incandenza's hill and is a refuge for those who have hit a figurative bottom. The halfway house is home to illogic: residents are urged to remain grounded by casting off thought because "most Substance-addicted people are also addicted to thinking" (203). The dilapidated house's open plan discourages the secrecy associated with drug use and facilitates interaction; the doors have no locks, and people and feeling flow unimpeded.

These and other spatial arrangements express and enforce many of the ethical and social concerns that give *Infinite Jest* its thematic heft.[1] If novels are the empathy engines that Wallace wishes for them to be — if they provide "imaginative access to other selves" (McCaffery 127) — their environments are crucial components. *Infinite Jest* makes this argument as it spotlights the environmental injustices that affective and spatial detachment under O.N.A.N. promote. By delineating how social and grammatical detachment motivate the novel's main plots, distinguish its style, and attract Wallace's satirical eye, I will establish that detachment is not only a psychological and ethical problem in *Infinite Jest* but, crucially, also a spatial one. Katherine Hayles first directed needed critical attention to the novel's environmental consciousness by analyzing the text's "recognition that market and individual, civilization and wilderness, coproduce each other" (676). Ultimately, she contends, *Infinite Jest* adopts an ecological perspective that tasks readers with "discover[ing] the text's recursive patterns so we can see it, as well as the world it describes, as a complex system that binds us into its interconnections, thus puncturing the illusion of autonomous self-hood" (695). Hayles recognizes the overlapping spheres of awareness that *Infinite Jest* details, and she helps us begin reading the novel outside of personal trauma. However, she does not adequately elucidate how "real ecologies" crucially figure in the novel's scheme of cultivating connection against detachment. Pursuing this project, this essay argues that Wallace's fiction of social, ecological, and somatic poisoning molds a medicalized environmental consciousness with disgust as its emotional core. Activated by the imbrication of body and environment, disgust is a conduit to engaging with human and nonhuman others as it counteracts forms of detachment that block environmental and social investment. Ultimately, it is through its sick aesthetic that *Infinite Jest* sees a way out of the sicknesses endemic to postmodernity.

Uncritical Distance

The complaint that houses all of the problems that plague the contemporary U.S. in Wallace's fiction is that people and the cultural artifacts that they produce are too self-referential. Solipsism, self-involvement, self-indulgence: conditions in which the individual measures all, these states are psychological analogs to the self-reflexive style of postmodern cultural forms. What troubles Wallace is that, in only looking into the self — or a medium — the person distances, even detaches, herself from the outside world. A psychological disposition with spatial and political dimensions, detachment is the prime mover of *Infinite Jest*'s plots about a failed entertainment and insurgency against U.S. cultural and geopolitical dominance. The novel condemns detachment as a limit on intersubjective relations using distancing grammatical forms — notably, passive voice and prepositional chains — and a logic of emotions that alienates the feeler from the emotions felt. Read together, the thematic, grammatical, and emotional expressions of distancing conduct readers from the personal to the political ramifications of a crippling disposition.

Hal Incandenza is the characterological center for Wallace's critique of detachment. Intellectually and athletically gifted, Hal is impassive to a fault, and he nurses an addiction not so much to marijuana as to the rituals that surround his indulgence in it. Hiding his drug use feeds Hal's habit of emotionally detaching from others but guarantees that he can still excel at E.T.A. To combat the teen's retreat into himself, his father, Jim Incandenza, resorts to entertainment. Before he commits suicide during alcohol withdrawal, Jim conceives and produces the "Infinite Jest" film as an admittedly oblique countermeasure to Hal's transformation into "a steadily more and more *hidden* boy" (838, original italics). He determines to "make something so bloody compelling it would reverse thrust on a young self's fall into the womb of solipsism, anhedonia, death in life. . . . To bring him 'out of himself,' as they say. . . . A way to say I AM SO VERY, VERY SORRY and have it *heard*" (838–9, original italics). Jim's objective, though targeted at only one person, echoes Wallace's program for a new fiction. Rather than get lost in the funhouse of self-reference and metafiction, the responsible novelist should ventriloquize others' voices to "have [them] *heard*." Wallace explains with pathos that "true empathy's impossible. But if a piece of fiction can allow us imaginatively to identify with characters' pain, we might then also more easily conceive of others identifying with our own. This is nourishing, redemptive; we become less alone inside" (McCaffery 127). Wallace's comments to McCaffery for the *Review of Contemporary Fiction* preceded the novelist's essay "E Unibus Pluram: Television and U.S. Fiction," which despairingly critiques two dominant cultural forms, television and advertising, for embracing irony but distorting its ends. In the early postmodern period, Thomas Pynchon and Ken Kesey, among others, employed irony with idealistic intentions, assuming "that etiology and diagnosis pointed toward cure, that a revelation of imprisonment led to freedom" from Americans' image obsession and corporate subservience (*Supposedly* 66–7). Wallace's peer writers must rethink, not recirculate, the stultifying irony that surrounds them amniotically because late twentieth-century irony is the aesthetic corollary to solipsism and cynicism (*Supposedly* 52). The medical diction — "etiology and diagnosis," "cure"— that permeates "E Unibus Pluram" precisely hones the novelist's job description: she can, indeed *must*, be a healer.

In this regard, Jim's efforts fail. The film never reaches Hal to halt his slip into "death in life" and instead misfires, proliferating addicts who, enthralled by the work's pleasures, end up "in exile from reality" (*Infinite Jest* 20). Analogously, Wallace's novel does not escape from that which it critiques. Even as *Infinite Jest* directs its eagle-eyed satire at the social distancing that contemporary culture promotes, its grammatical form and emotional logic inscribe detachment into the narrative. Passive voice, which abounds in Wallace's signature involuted, marathon sentences, speaks volumes in the novel. The description of Joelle van Dyne's overdose provides one example of how passive constructions detach an action from the actor performing it. In a 37-line sentence, Joelle reaches a point where her cocaine high is "so good she can't stand it"; a sign of her ecstasy: "Joelle's limbs have been removed to a distance where their acknowledgement of her commands seems like magic" (240). The cocaine has not only figuratively amputated her limbs, it has severed her agency as well. Her arms move from offstage, as if by "magic." Drug use exemplifies a late modern detached position, and the passive voice here instantiates the limits of this condition: a person's behavior detaches her from her very body. *Infinite Jest*'s psychologically embattled characters also experience feeling as if from afar, insofar as processing "metaresponses"— or emotions about emotions — supplants primary experience. Metaresponses are reactions not to immediate "eliciting conditions" (Oatley 56) — for example, feeling envious of a neighbor's success — but denote "how one feels about and what one thinks about one's responding (directly) in the way one does" (Feagin 97) — feeling ashamed *of* that envy. Across the spectrum of affective content — from the pleasures of smoking a joint to the agonies of wrenching depression — *Infinite Jest* theorizes emotional being as detached in this experiential sense. Ennet House resident Geoffrey Day instances this logic in the text. "[Depression] was a bit like a sail, or a small part of the wing of something far too large to be seen in totality," he describes. "It was total psychic horror: death, decay, dissolution, cold empty black malevolent lonely voided space . . . I understood what people meant by *hell*. They did not mean the black sail. They meant the associated feelings" (650–1, original italics). An expanse opens up between the character and the primary event, and second-order "associated feelings" rush in. To cement this logic, the grammar of these sentences carries detachment into the reading experience. The string of possessive prepositional phrases —"a small part *of* the wing *of* something far too large"— directs the reader's attention from the "thing" to a synecdoche for it.[2]

Grammatical and emotional strategies of detachment thread this disposition into the stylistic and experiential fabric of *Infinite Jest* and amplify the novel's sweeping critique of detachment at the levels of plot and character. Crucial to my analysis of how affective relations might counterpoise environmental and medical injustices, these techniques draw our attention to detachment through the act of reading and attune readers to the literal and figurative spaces that must be traversed in order to escape from disconnection. As I elaborate below, detachment is a psychological disposition that manifests in material policies of environmental reconfiguration and thus conducts readers' awareness from the individual to the geopolitical.

Body Building

Wallace's United States is the apotheosis of the "Cornucopia City" that Vance Packard invented in his iconic *The Waste Makers* (1960). As in Packard's allegory, O.N.A.N.'s "hyperthyroid economy" stimulates excessive consumption that "'deadens sensitivity to other human beings" (6, 238). Unbridled consumption spurs the U.S. government to establish a putatively collaborative alliance with its neighbors, yet this political relationship is just as self-serving as the personal ones that distress Wallace. Under "Interdependence"—"merely rampant nationalism under another guise," as Katherine Hayles aptly notes (685) — the U.S. strong-arms Canada into giving up a portion of its territory for a vast toxic waste dump and energy production site. America is suffocating on "the unpleasant debris of a throw-away past" and must expand its passageways to breathe afresh (*Infinite Jest* 383). It thus enters the business of exporting waste, of "sending from yourself what you hope will not return" (1031n168), by manipulating O.N.A.N. relations. The need to put distance between itself and waste, a source of opprobrium and fear, inspires the U.S.'s reworking of international relations and of space itself. Under the organizing concept of detachment, then, *Infinite Jest*'s psychological climate hooks up with its ecopolitical arrangements.

The U.S. adopts its policy of detachment at a point when "all landfills got full and all grapes were raisins and sometimes in some places the falling rain clunked instead of splatted" (382). With the obsessive compulsive Johnny Gentle at its head, the Clean U.S. Party (C.U.S.P.) capitalizes on environmental decline and rises to power under the motto, "Let's Shoot Our Wastes into Space" for a "Tighter, Tidier Nation" (382). Closer than outer space and politically impotent, Canada presents itself as the ideal site for the nation's waste exports. With this scheme, C.U.S.P. inaugurates a new geopolitical and economic regime: rather than pillage other nations' resources to meet its own industrial demands, as in *im*perialism, the U.S. sends away the byproducts of capitalism under *ex*perialism. In order for this waste export plan to succeed, the American government rigs space and intracontinental relations through a program of spatial reconfiguration and semantic obfuscation. Appealing to Canada's cooperative spirit, Gentle's cabinet relocates residents of the northeastern U.S. and southeastern Canada — the area now known as "the Great Concavity" (or "Convexity" from across the border) — so that it can catapult its unwanted refuse into the nearly vacated territory. Readers learn the history of O.N.A.N.'s creation and the environmental injustices on which it depends through a puppet show created by the second Incandenza son, Mario. Every Interdependence Day (November 8), Mario's characters reenact the cabinet meetings during which the U.S. government reshaped the continent:

> TINE [future head of intelligence services] places two large maps... on Govt.-issue easels. They look both to be of the good old U.S.A. . . . The second North American map looks neither old nor all that good, traditionally speaking. It has a concavity. It looks sort of like some person or persons have taken a deep wicked canine-intensive bite out of its upper right bit, in which an ascending and then descending line has its near-right-angle at what looks to be the historic and now hideously befouled Ticonderoga NY ...

SEC. STATE: A kind of ecological gerrymandering?
TINE: The president invites you gentlemen to conceive these two
visuals as a sort of before-and-after representation of "projected
intra-O.N.A.N. territorial reallocations," or some public term
like that. (403)

Through "ecological gerrymandering," C.U.S.P.'s antiwaste platform
becomes foreign policy. On the map that engenders this policy, the
Concavity is symbolically detached from its home nations: it has been
bitten off. By quarantining contamination, by giving it a designated
place, the U.S. neutralizes "the Menace" of waste and distances itself
from the ugly, globalized consequences of unfettered consumption and
pollution (382). This scheme is also designed to obscure the fact that
displacing waste requires displacing people. *Infinite Jest* thus explores
how ecological gerrymandering is an environmental expression of the
distancing and detachment that corrupts social relations.

Johnny Gentle, "a world-class retentive, the late-Howard-Hughes
kind, . . . the kind with the paralyzing fear of free-floating contamination" (381), successfully transmits his compulsive aversion to waste to
the nation he rules. Under Gentle, *aestheticism* rather than *asceticism*
becomes the point of advocacy for a green-washed political movement
in the twenty-first century. With C.U.S.P., Wallace satirizes the Keep
America Beautiful organization, which formed in 1953 with the mission of "bringing the public and private sectors together to develop
and promote a national cleanliness ethic" (Keep America Beautiful).
Speculating that Keep America Beautiful could become a full-blown
political party, *Infinite Jest* imagines an aesthetic stance generating a perverse environmental politics, one that depends on the same detachment
that compromises social relations and ethical engagement. The nation's
"deaden[ed] sensitivity to other human beings," as expressed through its
territorial and environmental policies, thus results from an individual
pathology but in the end affects entire ecosystems. However, as *Infinite
Jest* makes clear about this environmental policy, environmental despo-
liation isn't simply an aesthetic affair: it has bodily effects and raises
questions about somatic and environmental justice. In fact, Wallace's

fiction establishes that, now more than ever before, the human body is inextricable from the spaces it inhabits, in literature as in life. Ecological gerrymandering is thus one facet of the medicalized environmental consciousness that Wallace's novel promotes. A medical disorder — obsessive compulsion — leads to a disturbed, detached relation to the environment itself that allows for the restructuring of space, of political relations, and, as I establish here, of individual bodies.

In *Infinite Jest*, the human body is the point of application for the unbridled toxification of the landscape that results from overconsumption and ecological detachment. The novel distinguishes two environments: the Great Concavity and everything south of it. Conceiving the former, Wallace flourishes his talent for bleak humor. Because the Concavity is off-limits to civilians, a spirited mythology builds up around it. As E.T.A. students roam the campus's tunnels, they terrorize each other with tales of how the Concavity's mutant rodents have migrated to the campus's trash-strewn underground. The narrator checks the students' wild ideas, assuring readers that "feral hamsters . . . are rarely sighted south of the Lucite walls and ATHSCME'd checkpoints that delimit the Great Concavity" (*Infinite Jest* 670).[3] No one doubts that these creatures, though rare in Enfield, populate Canada, and their terrifying aspect takes hold of the public imagination: "bogey-wise [they are] right up there with mile-high toddlers, skull-deprived wraiths, carnivorous flora, and marsh-gas that melts your face off and leaves you with exposed gray-and-red facial musculature for the rest of your ghoulish-pariah life" (670).

Hal rehearses the most common "late-night hair-raising Concavity narrative" about the region's mutant features when he expounds on why Québec is a hotbed for extremism:

It's Québecers with cloracne [sic] and tremors and olfactory hallucinations and infants born with just one eye in the middle of their forehead. It's eastern Québec that gets green sunsets and indigo rivers and grotesquely asymmetrical snow-crystals and front lawns they have to beat back with a machete to get to their driveways. They get the feral-hamster incursions and the Infant-depredations and the corrosive fogs. . . . Proportionally speaking it's Québec that's borne the brunt of what Canada had to take. (1017n110)

The tone here is playful, yet the allusion to chloracne — which is a breakout of cysts caused by dioxin exposure — undercuts the humor of this fantasy. As this passage already hints with the mention of one-eyed infants, diminished function balances out abundance in the toxic equation that drives U.S. environmental and energy policy.[4] As Québec vacillates between a barren wasteland and an "environment so fertilely lush it's practically unlivable," "Québecers" mutate into disfigured giants (573). As the novel spins out the somatic consequences of O.N.A.N.'s environmental policies, the full import of experialism materializes. Elsewhere in the text, Rémy Marathe, the paraplegic leader of the Québecois separatists Les Assassins des Fauteuils Rollents, further grounds the reality of toxic exposure. Marathe inventories his wife's contaminated body as a way to convince his collaborator in U.S. intelligence of the health injustices of O.N.A.N. policy. In English marked with French grammatical tics, he catalogs his wife's deformities:

> She had no skull, this woman. Later I am learning she had been among the first Swiss children of southwestern Switzerland to become born without a skull, from the toxicities in association of our enemy's invasion. . . . Without the confinement of the metal hat, the head hung from the shoulders like the half-filled balloon or empty bag. . . . Her head it had also neither muscles nor nerves. . . . There was the trouble of the digestive tracking. There were seizures also. There were progressive decays of circulation and vessel, which calls itself restenosis. (779)

The medical blazon spans several more pages. Note that Wallace's proliferative style does not let up in descriptions of lack and deficiency, signaled by "half-filled," "empty," and "restenosis" (the narrowing of blood vessels). As Americans distance themselves from the filthy detritus of consumption, they also jettison the ethical implications of experialism and ecological gerrymandering. Like the waste that's fated to return, American policies come back to haunt it. Marathe's wife's health defects fuel his anger and his rebellion against O.N.A.N. The entanglement of environmental change and somatic sickness therefore partly generates the separatist plot in *Infinite Jest*. The novel's almost Rabelaisian descriptions of poisoned bodies thus highlight not only that the toxification of space expresses itself through bodies but also that the body is the way that we come to understand toxification as a sick practice.

The damages of detachment ramify beyond interpersonal relations. Endemic and systemic, detachment undergirds intracontinental and environmental politics as well. The text makes this toxic state of affairs visible and palpable through human bodies that are inextricably woven into their environments. We can therefore understand Wallace's novel as adding a new dimension to the cultural form of "toxic discourse" that Lawrence Buell delineates. Buell defines this mode as "expressed anxiety arising from perceived threat of environmental hazard due to chemical modification by human agency" (*Writing* 31). He historicizes toxic discourse, continuing, "As such, it is by no means unique to the present day, but never before the late twentieth century has it been so vocal, so intense, so pandemic, and so evidentially grounded" (31). While Buell's account of the cultural forms of toxicity is masterfully wide-ranging, he overlooks one of the representational outcomes of pervasive toxicity: this ubiquitous "irritant" (53) — and the sickness that results from it — shapes a literature in which the medicalized body seeps into environmental consciousness, much like industrial poisons seep into the permeable skin. Buell contends that late twentieth-century environmental culture cannot help *but* account for toxicity; I add that the writers of toxic discourse cannot help but imbricate the mutable human body in its imperiled surroundings, through formal techniques and their correlated effects.

In *Infinite Jest*, environmental manipulation and contamination disrupt ecologies and produce sick bodies through which readers become conscious of the injustices of experialism. This causal relay between body and environment — a degraded form of the latter yields a disfigured form of the former — yields an ecological awareness that the narrative enhances through a conceptual relay between body and environment. That is, *Infinite Jest* expounds its claims for somatic/ecological interdependence by conceiving of urban space *in terms of the medicalized human body*. *Infinite Jest* animates its setting through human forms such that contemporary space and the body are "cobuilt," to borrow from Elizabeth Grosz. Grosz posits that "the body and its environment . . . produce each other as forms . . . which have overtaken and transformed whatever reality each may have had into the image of the other: the city is made and made over into the simulacrum of the body, and the body, in its turn, is transformed" (43). Just as social norms, values, and symbols sediment in built spaces and are taken up by the bodies that move through them, cities take on the evolving forms and norms of the human body.

Fredric Jameson also insists that the condition of postmodernity compels us to examine how space and body are coconstitutive. In *Postmodernism*, he diagnoses a "mutation in built space itself," one that has outpaced our ability to adapt to it. These new spaces "stan[d] as something like an imperative to grow new organs, to expand our sensorium and our body to some new, yet unimaginable, perhaps ultimately impossible, dimensions" (39). In *Infinite Jest*, the imperative to adapt physiologically to such "mutation[s] in . . . space" attains monstrous proportions, as the lurid descriptions of toxic mutants and disfigured bodies attest. As the visible effects of environmental toxicity evince, bodies metamorphose in response to mutations in space, but, crucial to my argument here, space also mutates into the human body. That is, Wallace grows buildings and landforms as "new organs," in the mold of human anatomy.

Enfield Tennis Academy sits on the "cyst" of "the whole flexed Enfield limb [which is] sleeved in a perimeter layer of light residential and mercantile properties" (*Infinite Jest* 241). Protruding from Enfield's growth, E.T.A. is "laid out as a cardioid, with the four main inward-facing bldgs. convexly rounded at the back and sides to yield a cardioid's curve, with the tennis courts and pavilions at the center and the staff and students' parking lots . . . forming the little bashed-in dent that from the air gives the whole facility the Valentine-heart aspect" (983n3). The branching tunnels that snake under E.T.A. form this heart-shaped institution's veins and arteries, which supply the school's Pump Room and "Lung," a polyurethane dome that shelters the tennis courts from winter frost.

If E.T.A. is part of Boston's circulatory system, M.I.T.'s Student Union constitutes its nervous system.[5] The Student Union is "one enormous cerebral cortex of reinforced concrete and polymer compounds" (184). A lexical shift occurs in this and subsequent passages describing M.I.T.: the use of medical jargon kicks into high gear as snippets of Madame Psychosis's broadcast, a list of medical disorders (enuresis, hyperkeratosis, hydrocephalus), interrupt the neurologic depiction of the Student Union. This building takes shape as the narrator tracks the sound engineer's movements through its halls. He "comes in through the south side's acoustic meatus and gets a Millennial Fizzy® out of the vending machine in the sephenoid sinus, then descends creaky back wooden stairs from the Massa Intermedia's Reading Room down to about the Infundibular Recess" (182). This is just one slice of an extensive passage in which human brain anatomy—"sephenoid sinus," "Massa Intermedia," "Infundibular Recess"—provides a heuristic for apprehending the urban environment. The narration carefully avoids the language of metaphor or simile here: the Student Union is not *like* a cerebral cortex, it *is* one. The body is the vehicle for a conceit that generates a medicalized symbolic landscape filled with "abundant sulcus-fissures and gyrus-bulges," a balcony "which curves around the midbrain from the inferior frontal sulcus to the parietooccipital sulcus," and a "venous-blue emergency ladder," among other features (186).

Read in light of my analysis of poisoning under experialism, the medicalized depictions of space not only suggest the degree to which sickness suffuses contemporary experience but also make the case that, in the twenty-first century, it is impossible to conceive of either body or environment without the other. On the one hand, *Infinite Jest*'s corporeal imagination — adduced through Marathe's wife, the Québecer infants, and even, we might argue, Mario's and Marathe's bodies as well — arises from its environmental imagination of toxification. On the other hand, the narrative's spaces would not have their contours without the biomedical body. Environmental critics such as Louise Westling and Stacy Alaimo have argued that the gendered body crucially codes figurations of American landscapes in the twentieth century. Gender, they claim, structures an individual's "environmentality," her way of "thinking environmental belonging and citizenship" (Buell, "Ecoglobalist" 227). *Infinite Jest* introduces a new cultural habit: it establishes that a biomedical conception of the body now performs this structuring function in contemporary narrative. Entangling body and environment conceptually and through causal dependencies, the narrative thus reaches toward an environmental consciousness keyed to the vulnerable, malleable body. Thinking outside of a contemporary politics and culture of detachment and injustice requires this vision. The text not only makes the case that we cannot detach the somatic from the ecological but also vice versa. As the rest of this essay argues, *Infinite Jest* also imbricates the body in its environments to produce a toxic discourse that generates disgust, an affective relation that is an unexpected counterfoil to detachment.

How to Do Things with Disgust

Assigning disgust as the affective correlate to a medicalized environmental consciousness, *Infinite Jest* promotes an unlikely emotion as a conduit to involvement in the world beyond the self. Proffering disgust as an effective means of social and environmental engagement, the novel thus revalues an affect that is often maligned — if addressed at all — in aesthetic thought. Concentrating on *Infinite Jest*'s style and the mechanics of disgust, I will establish that Wallace ultimately approaches a sick world that is out of joint through disgust, which I theorize as a force that balances detachment and excessive attachment to aids to solipsism.

"Balanced" is not an adjective that one customarily assigns to Wallace's fiction. Indeed, excess appears to be the impetus for *Infinite Jest*, and Wallace seems to heed his young character Jim Troeltsch's call for "an inflation-generative grammar" (*Infinite Jest* 100). The novel's heft and proliferative aesthetic suggest that Wallace inflated the novel form to match the content of his story. Reviewing *Infinite Jest*, Michiko Kakutani castigates the author for his overabundant style. The novel is, in her words, "a big psychedelic jumble of characters, anecdotes, jokes, soliloquies, reminiscences and footnotes, uproarious and mind-boggling, but also arbitrary and self-indulgent" (Kakutani). Kakutani slams Wallace for his evident lack of control; the laudable novelist, she intimates, must make measured choices. An ounce of control must counterweigh excess.

Questions of style preoccupied — better, obsessed — Wallace. According to D. T. Max's narrative of Wallace's last years, the writer's struggle to produce a formally distinct follow-up to *Infinite Jest* intensified his severe depression and led him to hang himself on 12 September 2008. Max quotes a letter to Jonathan Franzen in which Wallace identifies himself with his style and confesses his impatience with both: "I am tired of myself, it seems: tired of my thoughts, associations, syntax, various verbal habits that have gone from discovery to technique to tic" (Max 60). Wallace has lost control of a style that is ultimately coextensive with his self. Through the optic of disgust, I contest Wallace's self-assessment and Kakutani's criticisms. *Infinite Jest*'s idiom of disgust, one of the novel's "inflation-generative" features, raises this question: Might excess be a peculiar form of control? Ennet House resident Ken Erdedy suggests as much. He trusts that by hitting bottom he can extricate himself from his addiction. To do this, he travels through the gateway of excess and induces self-disgust. The narrator describes Erdedy's mission:

> He'd smoke his way through thirty high-grade grams [of marijuana] a day . . . an insane and deliberately unpleasant amount. . . . He would smoke it all even if he didn't want it. . . . He would use discipline, persistence and will and make the whole experience so unpleasant, so debased and debauched and unpleasant, that his behavior would be henceforward modified. . . . He'd cure himself by excess. (22)

Erdedy's practice accords with the principle of Alcoholics Anonymous that the addict must reach a personal bottom before he can rehabilitate himself and climb out of his addiction. The final sentence above —"He'd cure himself by excess"— raises a question germane to my analysis: can affective excesses — in particular, the disgusting — effectively reform an individual life as well as reposition us with respect to the systemic afflictions of detachment endemic in Wallace's story world?

Infinite Jest concentrates disgust in descriptions of the somatic effects of environmental reconfiguration and of the drug-poisoned body. In both instances, the text makes damaging ethical and environmental policies visible in human bodies that are entwined with their environments. Only through reading the great number of repulsive vignettes in *Infinite Jest* can the reader fully experience how disgust works. Here, a couple of passages must stand in for total immersion. I begin by returning to and expanding on a passage that I examined above. As Marathe continues to enumerate his wife's medical abnormalities, her body exceeds its bounds and the reader's revulsion intensifies:

> She had no skull, this woman. . . . Without the confinement of the metal hat, the head hung from the shoulders like the half-filled balloon or empty bag, the eyes and oral cavity greatly distended from this hanging. . . . Her head it had also neither muscles nor nerves. . . . There was the trouble of the digestive tracking. There were seizures also. There were progressive decays of circulation and vessel, which calls itself restenosis. There were the more than accepted amounts of eyes and cavities in many different stages of development upon different parts of the body. There were the fugue states and rages and frequency of coma. . . . Worst for choosing to love was the cerebro-and-spinal fluids which dribbled at all times from her distending oral cavity. (779)

Leaking fluids carry us to another passage with similar designs. In this scene, addict Tony Krause's degrading withdrawal from opiates forces him to set up residence first in a new Empire Displacement Co. dumpster and then in the Armenian Foundation Library's bathroom:

> His nose ran like twin spigots and the output had a yellow-green tinge he didn't think looked promising at *all*. There was an uncomely dry-rot smell about him that even he could smell. . . . Fluids of varying consistency began to pour w/o advance notice from several openings. Then of course they stayed there, the fluids, on the summer dumpster's iron floor. . . . Poor Tony Krause sat on the insulated toilet in the domesticated stall all day and night, alternately swilling and gushing. (301–3, original italics)

As this mortifying experience dilates, the reader seeks escape from Krause's private hell. Through these scenes and others like them, characters' bodies serve as vehicles for readers' disgust. Images of flowing and overflowing — Marathe's wife's shapeless head and features hang loose and are indistinct; Tony's bodily fluids run over — materialize the many ways in which we are living in "chemically troubled times" (151). Through these passages, *Infinite Jest* attests that depicting the body in contemporary culture almost demands the aesthetic relation of disgust.[6] Disgust is a primary means of making bodies physical and, moreover, of envisioning how social and environmental conditions produce bodies expressing a full complement of symptoms.

Marathe's wife and Erdedy present cases where poisoning — whether from environmental toxins or drugs — renders the body radically unfamiliar. By making the body strange, Wallace reaches toward one of the goals that he assigns to contemporary fiction. In "E Unibus Pluram" he argues that "today's most ambitious Realist fiction is going about trying to *make the familiar strange*" at a moment when "we can eat Tex-Mex with chopsticks while listening to reggae and watching a Soviet-satellite newscast of the Berlin Wall's fall — i.e., when damn near *everything* presents itself as familiar" (*Supposedly* 52, original italics). The novelist must reverse the trend of excessive familiarization, and render the ordinary strange. Many critics point out *Infinite Jest*'s defamiliarizing techniques, but they largely focus on recognizably postmodern formal strategies of metafiction and multiperspectival narration.[7] While I concur that these narrative techniques challenge readers intellectually, I maintain that Wallace most fully succeeds in his project by deploying disgust, a bodily affect that shatters familiarity. In a sense, sickness practices itself in the novel through Wallace's sick aesthetic of disgust, but this aesthetic is also an approach to remediating detachment. Rather than distance the reader from the outside world, as we might expect, the defamiliarizing affect of disgust reattaches her to it. Examining salient points from theories of disgust will ground my approach to the question of whether a negative emotion like disgust can promote the kind of involvement toward which *Infinite Jest* sincerely aims.

One premise of Erdedy's project to cure his addiction through extreme unpleasantness is that disgust is compelling because it is such a visceral emotion. Directing enough disgust at himself, he cannot help but eradicate that disgust's cause. Legal scholar William Ian Miller backs up this conviction when he argues that the disgust response is unambiguous and undeniable because it is "so much in the gut." Disgust "signals seriousness, commitment, indisputability, presentness and reality. . . . We are surer of our judgments when recognizing the bad and the ugly than the good and the beautiful. And that's at least partly because disgust (which is the means by which we commonly feel the bad and the ugly) has the look of veracity about it. . . . The disgust idiom puts our body behind our words" (180–1). Disgust has a gravity that feelings of attraction lack. Though Miller contrasts it to the beautiful, disgust, like Kant's beautiful, also demands universal assent, but for different reasons. Our reaction is so much in the body that we believe, perhaps naïvely, that prejudice or social norms have not contaminated it, and yet disgust also "seeks to include or draw others *into* its exclusion of its object, enabling a strange kind of sociability" (Ngai 336, original italics). It is for these reasons that Sianne Ngai puts disgust at a threshold point in her account of "ugly feelings." While emotions such as anxiety are anticipatory and suspend agency, disgust's immediacy, intensity, and certainty locate us at the borderline of "more instrumental or politically efficacious emotions" (354). Disgust is politically powerful by Ngai's reckoning because it is unignorable. We must ask, though: Is this always the case? What if we cannot stand to examine the offending source? We may be certain about how we feel and still not want to dwell in that certainty. Architectural critic Mark Cousins's treatise on ugliness introduces this possibility. The disgusting object comes at us as a threat; on this, philosophers from Kant to Derrida agree. Cousins explains that we have two choices in the face of this threat: "to destroy the object, or to abandon the position of the subject. Since the former is rarely within our power, the latter becomes a habit. The confrontation with the ugly object involves a whole scheme of *turning away*" (64, original italics). For that reason, even though the disgust response may be unequivocal, the object also produces the desire to avert our eyes, to put space between ourselves and disgust's threatening object. Given this, disgust would appear to be an emotion of disattention, one that we express through that socially and environmentally corrupting distancing that animates *Infinite Jest*. Our own experience of disgust might substantiate Cousins's observation that we want to turn away from (and in) disgust, but we have also surely experienced the opposite: even after looking away in aversion, we turn back for another look at the offending source, peeking between the fingers shielding our eyes. We waver between repulsion and attraction.

Conflicting drives to attend to and turn away from the repulsive constitute the emotion of disgust. The tension between these responses is particularly important with respect to environmental debates because calls to environmental engagement are so often predicated upon calls to attention. Surveying environmental thought, we find numerous pronouncements of the causal relationship between attention and investment. As one example, environmental educator Mitchell Thomashow advocates a pedagogy of "perceptual ecology," a practice of attending to the details of local ecosystems as a way to grasp global environmental change. A host of environmental thinkers — including Edward Abbey, Rachel Carson, Scott Slovic, and Arnold Berleant — similarly stake their projects in the bedrock of ecological awareness. The alternative of disattending is anathema to environmental ethics, as it arguably is to ethics more generally. *Infinite Jest* voices varied objections to "turning away": Erdedy's trip to the bottom is also a trip away from the world, while experialism and "ecological gerrymandering" pivot on distancing and detachment. Wallace certainly writes from an antidistance platform as he delineates the material, psychological, and social valences of detachment in his fiction and nonfiction. The issue here is that *Infinite Jest*'s prevalent use of the disgusting might be at cross purposes with its condemnation of breaking off and turning away. How can a text that proliferates disgust then ensure that readers do not disengage?

Wallace skirts the danger of inattention by staging the interplay between mimesis — by which I mean commitment to the order of relations outside the text — and hyperbole. Along with its nonlinear narrative, tortuous syntax, and endnotes, the novel revises our reading strategies through this dynamic. In the selections from *Infinite Jest* that I have analyzed thus far, the ugly scenes are based on observable biological phenomena and punctuated with medically, anatomically detailed diction. Grounded in detailed mimesis, these scenes demand readers' attention. They call up our knowledge that something akin to what we are reading could and indeed does occur to our bodies. Marathe's dialogue paints the wide-ranging effects of poisoning from environmental toxins, and Krause's thoughts simulate the phases of heroin withdrawal. That said, *Infinite Jest* is not strictly faithful to evidence from lived experience of these disorders. The narrative hyperbolizes in laying out scenarios of environmental and physiological reconfiguration, and thereby defamiliarizes both bodies and the spaces they inhabit. An excessive number of ailments afflicts Marathe's wife, so many that she obviously could not survive them all. Additionally, the Concavity's vacillations between the extremes of desert and rainforest violate mimetic expectations. Through disgust, *Infinite Jest* toys with degrees of closeness to and distance from threats to bodily integrity that are the emotion's source. The conditions the novel relates are plausible enough that they capture the reader's attention, while the hyperbolized details of these conditions elicit aversion and dare readers to look away. We thus find in *Infinite Jest* a case of what Buell calls the "dislocation of ordinary perception" (*Imagination* 104). He claims for novels the capacity to make worlds, and remarks that some texts also "make the shadow of the actual haunt the reinvention, as a brake on imagined liberties taken, indeed even as a conscience" (*Future* 60). If we take Buell at his word, exercising writerly control is a kind of ethical practice. The author may "dislocate" readers with his imaginings, but the real must leak in to temper the excessive shock.

Measuring mimesis and hyperbolic invention performs another balancing act: between overstimulation and being "divorced from all stimulus" (*Infinite Jest* 142). At either of these two poles, we risk becoming numb to the world outside of the self. Overstimulated, we attend with fixation, often on a damaging object. Within the text, this habit manifests in O.N.A.N. society's absorption in drugs and entertainment as well as in characters' detached solipsism. Understimulated, we are apathetic and affectless, and we cannot invest socially, politically, or environmentally. (Within *Infinite Jest*, overattending to the Entertainment and drugs eventually shades into this second state.) Through a medicalized form of disgust, the novel successfully modulates the actual and the invented as a way to balance these positions. Disgust — with its dual aspect of drawing us in and pushing us away — satisfies the demand for an even attention that can negotiate self-awareness and involvement in the human and nonhuman world. In the final analysis, readers are impelled to reflect on their disgust and its implications. Moreover, the novel genre is the safest home for the play of disgust because this play and the reflection it stimulates require the slow unfolding and recursivity of narrative. That is, all novels to some extent afford readers the time and space to look close, pull back, and then return for another glimpse. A markedly recursive novel such as *Infinite Jest* further advocates this behavior through the nonlinear diegesis, multivocal narration, and endnotes that demand that one read forward and backward at once.[8] Through a kind of reflective reading, the disgusting has the potential to move us from observation to involved response. If the contemporary ethos is to "send from yourself what you hope will not return" (1031n168), temporarily but faithfully tramping through the disgusting offers an alternative in which you release such domination and allow the outside to come streaming in. Wallace thus positions disgust against self-absorption and environmental, psychic, and social detachment as a means of organizing interaction between the self and the world.

AS *INFINITE JEST* gives disgust a place in social, environmental, and aesthetic thought, the novel challenges readers to remain receptive to the curative invasion that characterizes disgust. This is a challenge to open attention, a disposition that Wallace valorizes in comments he made while composing his unfinished last novel, *The Pale King*. On the occasion of Kenyon College's 2005 commencement, he revises his young listeners' understanding of freedom. "The really important kind of freedom," he teaches them, "involves attention and awareness and discipline, and being able truly to care about other people" (*This Is Water* 120). *Infinite Jest*'s idiom of disgust offers ways of cultivating these values: it instills that "the really important kind of freedom" is not detachment from but attachment to other people and our surroundings. As it denigrates the material and interpersonal forms of distancing that manifest in the late twentieth-century U.S., the novel aims to provide the stimuli that prevent you "from going through your comfortable, prosperous, respectable adult life dead, unconscious, a slave to your head and to your natural default setting of being uniquely, completely, imperially alone day in and day out" (*This Is Water* 60). A chorus of thinkers about postmodernity has made similar claims about the solipsism and apathy of contemporary existence. Wallace's unique contribution to this conversation is to elaborate a medicalized environmental consciousness that mobilizes disgust as a way to set our ethical bearing, as solder for social and environmental bonds.

Notes

1. In my analysis, I alternate between the terms *space* and *environment* to collocate two ideas. First is the idea, derived from David Harvey, that *environment* refers to whatever surrounds us but also to "whatever exists in the surroundings of some being that is *relevant to* the state of that being at a particular place and time" (118, original italics), including the emotions that that environment generates. Second, with *space*, I simultaneously evoke the notion that human intervention in the environment results from social relations and historical processes.

2. See also "The Depressed Person" in Wallace's story collection, *Brief Interviews with Hideous Men*.

3. The ATHSCME company produces fans for blowing waste over the U.S.–Canada border.

4. I do not have space here to elaborate on "annular fusion," the energy generation process that Wallace invents to complement ecological gerrymandering. See Hayles's tight summary of this terribly complex reaction (688–9). With annular fusion, Wallace figures a predicament that is acutely familiar to

twenty-first-century Americans: hyperconsumption fuels the need for energy, the production of which alters the environment irremediably.

5. The Student Union figures in the narrative because it houses WYYY, the studio where Joelle van Dyne records her radio program, the Madame Psychosis Hour.

6. Wallace's exhaustively titled short story, "On His Deathbed, Holding Your Hand, the Acclaimed New Young Off-Broadway Playwright's Father Begs a Boon," lends support to this claim (*Brief* 259).

7. See especially Cioffi, LeClair, and Nichols.

8. With respect to this formal requirement, the coexistence of humor and disgust in *Infinite Jest* merits comment. I contend that the humor of the text dissipates over time under pressure of its content. That is, the humor becomes less salient as scenes of pain and anguish aggregate. Flooded by tortuous textual moments, engaged readers reflect on how horrific content had previously seemed so funny and potentially reorient their responses.

Works Cited

Abbey, Edward. *Desert Solitaire: A Season in the Wilderness.* 1968. New York: Random House, 1971. Print.

Alaimo, Stacy. *Undomesticated Ground: Recasting Nature as Feminist Space.* Ithaca, NY: Cornell University Press, 2000. Print.

Berleant, Arnold. *The Aesthetics of Environment.* Philadelphia: Temple University Press, 1992. Print.

Buell, Lawrence. "Ecoglobalist Affects: The Emergence of U.S. Environmental Imagination of a Planetary Scale." In *Shades of the Planet: American Literature as World Literature.* Ed. Wai-chee Dimock and Lawrence Buell. Princeton, NJ: Princeton University Press, 2007. 227–48. Print.

———. *The Environmental Imagination: Thoreau, Nature Writing, and the Formation of American Culture.* Cambridge, MA: Harvard University Press, 1995. Print.

———. *The Future of Environmental Criticism: Environmental Crisis and Literary Imagination.* Malden, MA: Blackwell, 2005. Print.

———. *Writing for an Endangered World: Literature, Culture, and Environment in the U.S. and Beyond.* Cambridge, MA: Belknap Press of Harvard University Press, 2001. Print.

Carson, Rachel. *The Sense of Wonder.* New York: Harper & Row, 1965. Print.

Cioffi, Frank Louis. "'An Anguish Become Thing': Narrative as Performance in David Foster Wallace's *Infinite Jest*." *Narrative* 8.2 (2000): 161–81. Print.

Cousins, Mark. "The Ugly (Part 1)." *AA Files* 28 (1994): 61–4. Print.

Feagin, Susan. "The Pleasure of Tragedy." *American Philosophical Quarterly* 20.1 (1983): 95–104. Print.

Grosz, Elizabeth. "Bodies-Cities." In *Places through the Body*. Ed. Heidi J. Nast and Steve Pile. New York: Routledge, 1998. 42–51. Print.

Harvey, David. *Justice, Nature and the Geography of Difference*. Cambridge, MA: Blackwell, 1996. Print.

Hayles, N. Katherine. "The Illusion of Autonomy and the Fact of Recursivity: Virtual Ecologies, Entertainment, and *Infinite Jest*." *New Literary History* 30.3 (1999): 675–97. Print.

Jameson, Fredric. *Postmodernism or, the Cultural Logic of Late Capitalism*. Durham, NC: Duke University Press, 1991. Print.

Kakutani, Michiko. "A Country Dying of Laughter. In 1,079 Pages." Review of *Infinite Jest*, by David Foster Wallace. *New York Times* 13 February 1996. Web.

Keep America Beautiful. "A Beautiful History." N.p. 2006.

LeClair, Tom. "The Prodigious Fiction of Richard Powers, William Vollmann and David Foster Wallace." *Critique* 38.1 (1996): 12–37. Print.

Max, D. T. "The Unfinished." *New Yorker* 9 March 2009: 48–61. Print.

McCaffery, Larry. "An Interview with David Foster Wallace." *Review of Contemporary Fiction* 13.2 (Summer 1993): 127–50. Print.

Miller, William Ian. *The Anatomy of Disgust*. Cambridge, MA: Harvard University Press, 1997. Print.

Ngai, Sianne. *Ugly Feelings*. Cambridge, MA: Harvard University Press, 2005. Print.

Nichols, Catherine. "Dialogizing Postmodern Carnival: David Foster Wallace's *Infinite Jest*." *Critique* 43.1 (2001): 3–16. Print.

Oatley, Keith. *Best Laid Schemes: The Psychology of the Emotions*. New York: Cambridge University Press, 1992. Print.

Packard, Vance. *The Waste Makers*. New York: David McKay, 1960. Print.

Slovic, Scott. *Seeking Awareness in American Nature Writing: Henry Thoreau, Annie Dillard, Edward Abbey, Wendell Berry, Barry Lopez*. Salt Lake City: University of Utah Press, 1992. Print.

Thomashow, Mitchell. *Bringing the Biosphere Home: Learning to Perceive Global Environmental Change*. Cambridge, MA: MIT Press, 2002. Print.

Wallace, David Foster. *Brief Interviews with Hideous Men*. 1999. New York: Little, Brown, 2007. Print.

———. *Infinite Jest*. Boston: Little, Brown, 1996. Print.

———. *A Supposedly Fun Thing I'll Never Do Again: Essays and Arguments*. New York: Back Bay Books, 1998. Print.

———. *This Is Water: Some Thoughts, Delivered on a Significant Occasion, about Living a Compassionate Life.* New York: Little, Brown and Company, 2009. Print.

Westling, Louise Hutchings. *The Green Breast of the New World: Landscape, Gender, and American Fiction.* Athens: University of Georgia Press, 1996. Print.

DAVE EGGERS

FOREWORD TO TENTH ANNIVERSARY
EDITION OF *INFINITE JEST*

IN RECENT YEARS, there have been a few literary dustups — how insane is it that such a thing exists in a world at war? — about readability in contemporary fiction. In essence, there are some people who feel that fiction should be easy to read, that it's a popular medium that should communicate on a somewhat conversational wavelength. On the other hand, there are those who feel that fiction can be challenging, generally and thematically, and even on a sentence-by-sentence basis — that it's okay if a person needs to work a bit while reading, for the rewards can be that much greater when one's mind has been exercised and thus (presumably) expanded.

Much in the way that would-be civilized debates are polarized by extreme thinkers on either side, this debate has been made to seem like an either/or proposition, that the world has room for only one kind of fiction, and that the other kind should be banned and its proponents hunted down and, why not, dismembered.

But while the polarizers have been going at it, there has existed a silent legion of readers, perhaps the majority of readers of literary fiction, who don't mind a little of both. They believe, though not too vocally, that so-called difficult books can exist next to, can even rub bindings suggestively with, more welcoming fiction. These readers might actually read *both* kinds of fiction themselves, *sometimes in the same week*. There might even be — though it's impossible to prove — readers who find it possible to enjoy Thomas Pynchon one day and Elmore Leonard the next. Or even: readers who can have fun with Jonathan Franzen in the morning while wrestling with William Gaddis at night.

David Foster Wallace has long straddled the worlds of difficult and not-as-difficult, with most readers agreeing that his essays are easier to read than his fiction, and his journalism most accessible of all. But while much of his work is challenging, his tone, in whatever form he's exploring, is rigorously unpretentious. A Wallace reader gets the impression of being in a room with a very talkative and brilliant uncle or cousin who, just when he's about to push it too far, to try our patience with too much detail, has the good sense to throw in a good lowbrow joke. Wallace, like many other writers who could be otherwise considered too smart for their own good — Bellow comes to mind — is, like Bellow, always aware of the reader, of the idea that books are essentially meant to entertain, and so almost unerringly balances his prose to suit. This had been Wallace's hallmark for years before this book, of course. He was already known as a very smart and challenging and funny and preternaturally gifted writer when *Infinite Jest* was released in 1996, and thereafter his reputation included all the adjectives mentioned just now, and also this one: Holy shit.

No, that isn't an adjective in the strictest sense. But you get the idea. The book is 1,079 pages long and there is not one lazy sentence. The book is drum-tight and relentlessly smart, and though it does not wear its heart on its sleeve, it's deeply felt and incredibly moving. That it was written in three years by a writer under thirty-five is very painful to think about. So let's not think about that. The point is that it's for all these reasons — acclaimed, daunting, not-lazy, drum-tight, very funny (we didn't mention that yet but yes) — that you picked up this book. Now the question is this: Will you actually read it?

In commissioning this foreword, the publisher wanted a very brief and breezy essay that might convince a new reader of *Infinite Jest* that the book is approachable, effortless even — a barrel of monkeys' worth of fun to read. Well. It's easy to agree with the former, more difficult to advocate the latter. The book is approachable, yes, because it doesn't include complex scientific or historical content, nor does it require any particular expertise or erudition. As verbose as it is, and as long as it is, it never wants to punish you for some knowledge you lack, nor does it want to send you to the dictionary every few pages. And yet, while it uses a familiar enough vocabulary, make no mistake that *Infinite Jest* is something *other*. That is, it bears little resemblance to anything before it, and comparisons to anything since are desperate and hollow. It appeared in 1996, *sui generis*, very different from virtually anything before it. It defied categorization and thwarted efforts to take it apart and explain it.

It's possible, with most contemporary novels, for astute readers, if they are wont, to break it down into its parts, to take it apart as one would a car or Ikea shelving unit. That is, let's say a reader is a sort of mechanic. And let's say this particular reader-mechanic has worked on lots of books, and after a few hundred contemporary novels, the mechanic feels like he can take apart just about any book and put it back together again. That is, the mechanic recognizes the components of modern fiction and can say, for example, *I've seen this part before, so I know why it's there and what it does. And this one, too — I recognize it. This part connects to this and performs this function. This one usually goes here, and does that. All of this is familiar enough.* That's no knock on the contemporary fiction that is recognizable and breakdownable. This includes about ninety-eight percent of the fiction we know and love.

But this is not possible with *Infinite Jest*. This book is like a spaceship with no recognizable components, no rivets or bolts, no entry points, no way to take it apart. It is very shiny, and it has no discernible flaws. If you could somehow smash it into smaller pieces, there would certainly be no way to put it back together again. It simply *is*. Page by page, line by line, it is probably the strangest, most distinctive, and most involved work of fiction by an American in the last twenty years. At no time while reading *Infinite Jest* are you unaware that this is a work of complete obsession, of a stretching of the mind of a young writer to the point of, we assume, near madness.

Which isn't to say it's madness in the way that Burroughs or even Fred Exley used a type of madness with which to create. Exley, like many writers of his generation and the few before it, drank to excess, and Burroughs ingested every controlled substance he could buy or borrow. But Wallace is a different sort of madman, one in full control of his tools, one who instead of teetering on the edge of this precipice or that, under the influence of drugs or alcohol, seems to be heading ever-inward, into the depths of memory and the relentless conjuring of a certain time and place in a way that evokes — it seems so wrong to type this name but then again, so right! — Marcel Proust. There is the same sort of obsessiveness, the same incredible precision and focus, and the same sense that the writer wanted (and arguably succeeds at) nailing the consciousness of an age.

Let's talk about age, the more pedestrian meaning of the word. It's to be expected that the average age of the new *Infinite Jest* reader would be about twenty-five. There are certainly many collegians among you, probably, and there may be an equal number of thirty-year-olds or fifty-year-olds who have for whatever reason reached a point in their lives where they have determined themselves finally ready to tackle the book, which this or that friend has urged upon them. The point is that the average age is appropriate enough. I was twenty-five myself when I first read it. I had known it was coming for about a year, because the publisher, Little, Brown, had been very clever about building anticipation for it, with monthly postcards, bearing teasing phrases and hints, sent to every media outlet in the country. When the book was finally released, I started in on it almost immediately.

And thus I spent a month of my young life. I did little else. And I can't say it was always a barrel of monkeys. It was occasionally trying. It demands your full attention. It can't be read at a crowded café, or with a child on one's lap. It was frustrating that the footnotes were at the end of the book, rather than on the bottom of the page, as they had been in Wallace's essays and journalism. There were times, reading a very exhaustive account of a tennis match, say, when I thought, well, okay. I like tennis as much as the next guy, but enough already.

And yet the time spent in this book, in this world of language, is absolutely rewarded.

When you exit these pages after that month of reading, you are a better person. It's insane, but also hard to deny. Your brain is stronger because it's been given a monthlong workout, and more importantly, your heart is sturdier, for there has scarcely been written a more moving account of desperation, depression, addiction, generational stasis and yearning, or the obsession with human expectations, with artistic and athletic and intellectual possibility. The themes here are big, and the emotions (guarded as they are) are very real, and the cumulative effect of the book is, you could say, seismic. It would be very unlikely that you would find a reader who, after finishing the book, would shrug and say, "Eh."

Here's a question once posed to me, by a large, baseball cap-wearing English major at a medium-size western college: Is it our duty to read *Infinite Jest*? This is a good question, and one that many people, particularly literary-minded people, ask themselves. The answer is: Maybe. Sort of. Probably, in some way. If we think it's our duty to read this book, it's because we're interested in genius. We're interested in epic writerly ambition. We're fascinated with what can be made by a person with enough time and focus and caffeine and, in Wallace's case, chewing tobacco. If we are drawn to *Infinite Jest*, we're also drawn to the Magnetic Fields' *69 Songs*, for which Stephin Merritt wrote that many songs, all of them about love, in about two years. And we're drawn to the ten thousand paintings of folk artist Howard Finster. Or the work of Sufjan Stevens, who is on a mission to create an album about each state in the union. He's currently at State No. 2, but if he reaches his goal, it will approach what Wallace did with the book in your hands. The point is that if we are interested in human possibility, and we are able to cheer each other on to leaps in science and athletics and art and thought, we must admire the work that our peers have managed to create. We have an obligation, to ourselves, chiefly, to see what a brain, and particularly a brain like our own — that is, using the same effluvium we, too, swim through — is capable of. It's why we watch *Shoah*, or visit the unending scroll on which Jack Kerouac wrote (in a fever of days) *On the Road*, or William T. Vollmann's 3,300-page *Rising Up and Rising Down*, or Michael Apted's *7-Up, 28-Up, 42-Up* series of films, or . . . well, the list goes on.

And now, unfortunately, we're back to the impression that this book is daunting. Which it isn't, really. It's long, but there are pleasures everywhere. There is humor everywhere. There is also a very quiet but very sturdy and constant tragic undercurrent that concerns a people who are completely lost, who are lost within their families and lost within their nation, and lost within their time, and who only want some sort of direction or purpose or sense of community or love. Which is, after all and conveniently enough for the end of this introduction, what an author is seeking when he sets out to write a book — any book, but particularly a book like this, a book that gives so much, that required such sacrifice and dedication. Who would do such a thing if not for want of connection and thus of love?

Last thing: In attempting to persuade you to buy this book, or check it out of your library, it's useful to tell you that the author is a normal person. Dave Wallace — and he is commonly known as such — keeps big sloppy dogs and has never dressed them in taffeta or made them wear raincoats. He has complained often about sweating too much when he gives public readings, so much so that he wears a bandanna to keep the perspiration from soaking the pages below him. He was once a nationally ranked tennis player, and he cares about good government. He is from the Midwest — east-central Illinois, to be specific, which is an intensely normal part of the country (not far, in fact, from a city, no joke, named Normal). So he is normal, and regular, and ordinary, and this is his extraordinary, and irregular, and not-normal achievement, a thing that will outlast him and you and me, but will help future people understand us — how we felt, how we lived, what we gave to each other and why.

PART THREE

COMMUNITY

ED FINN

BECOMING YOURSELF:
THE AFTERLIFE OF RECEPTION

IF THERE IS one thing to be learned from David Foster Wallace, it is that cultural transmission is a tricky game. This was a problem Wallace confronted as a literary professional, a university-based writer during what Mark McGurl has called the Program Era. But it was also a philosophical issue he grappled with on a deep level as he struggled to combat his own loneliness through writing. This fundamental concern with literature as a social, collaborative enterprise has also gained some popularity among scholars of contemporary American literature, particularly McGurl and James English: both critics explore the rules by which prestige or cultural distinction is awarded to authors (English; McGurl). Their approach requires a certain amount of empirical work, since these claims move beyond the individual experience of the text into forms of collective reading and cultural exchange influenced by social class, geographical location, education, ethnicity, and other factors. Yet McGurl and English's groundbreaking work is limited by the very forms of exclusivity they analyze: the protective bubble of creative writing programs in the academy and the elite economy of prestige surrounding literary prizes, respectively. To really study the problem of cultural transmission, we need to look beyond the symbolic markets of prestige to the real market, the site of mass literary consumption, where authors succeed or fail based on their ability to speak to that most diverse and complicated of readerships: the general public. Unless we study what I call the social lives of books, we make the mistake of keeping literature in the same ascetic laboratory that Wallace tried to break out of with his intense authorial focus on popular culture, mass media, and everyday life.

Tracing the social lives of books in the sphere of popular consumption requires extensive empirical research and would probably be impossible to accomplish in any kind of complete way. Instead, what I will offer here is a case study or core sample of Wallace's cultural reception in particular areas of the literary marketplace drawn from a project exploring the changing nature of literary culture in the digital era (Finn). My larger argument is that millions of cultural consumers are now empowered to participate in previously closed literary conversations and to express forms of taste through their purchases and reviews of books. These traces of popular reading choices constitute a fresh perspective on elusive audience reactions to literature, one that reveals distinct networks of conversation that are transforming the relationships between writers and their readers, between the art of fiction and the market for books. Employing network analysis methodologies and "distant reading" of book reviews, recommendations, and other digital traces of cultural distinction, I develop a new model for literary culture in America today. I will explain what this means in practical terms below, but I'd like to begin by offering three conjectures about Wallace that we can explore with empirical data, allowing us to make some grounded claims about Wallace's ongoing literary impact.

1. Wallace is *different*: unlike contemporaries such as Jonathan Franzen, Richard Powers, Jonathan Lethem, or Michael Chabon, Wallace employs a style wildly divergent from that of anyone else on the literary scene. He pioneered a radical new narrative voice so successfully that editors now complain about the endless pitches: "I'd like to do a David Foster Wallace take on _____" (Lipsky 320). As we will soon see, this uniqueness resulted in an oeuvre with a deep interiority to it, a cluster of texts that beckon readers almost invariably to read more Wallace, more of the "literary equivalent of cocaine" that they simply could not find anywhere else (Lipsky 157).

2. Wallace is *postmodern*, not just in his thematic and stylistic approaches to narrative but in a historical sense; his books speak to Pynchon, Barth, and DeLillo in a way that they rarely do to younger novelists. The pointedly difficult style of massive, occasionally antagonistic tomes like *Gravity's Rainbow* is magnified, footnoted, and distilled into Wallace's own particular blend of militant cultural critique and eloquent despair.

3. Wallace is *integral*. Despite being so frequently lost in the funhouse of postmodern prose experiments, his earnest narrative approach aspires to the unity of experience as we perceive it — the ways in which we stitch together mediated fragments and jumbled thoughts into coherent stories of ourselves. This individual, intellectual definition of the word has a collective parallel in the ways that Wallace's work encourages readers to work together on this project of integration. Wallace has been incredibly effective at uniting a diverse readership around his intense fictions of loss, addiction, and pervasive loneliness precisely because he enrolls each of them in the project of his fictional calculus, of approximating the area under the contemporary curve. As Kathleen Fitzpatrick notes in her contribution to this collection, Wallace's fear of loneliness was tempered by his faith in the potential of literature to bridge the gap between each of our consciousnesses. His iterative, splintered, capture-each-detail-under-the-curve-to-describe-the-curve approach has obviously succeeded with readers, who gladly do the work of completing the equation, responding to genuine honesty in his texts in spite of the postmodern distancing that makes such work necessary.

How to Read a Thousand Book Reviews

If these conjectures seem relatively timid for a piece of literary criticism, I hope they become a bit more compelling when I explain how I hope to prove them, or at least support them, empirically. I'll begin this argument with a set of simple observations intended to introduce my methodology and define key terms. My work is influenced by a number of scholars exploring literary production in its interaction with other systems. From Pierre Bourdieu I have adapted the grounding perspective that literary culture operates at the intersection of intellectual or symbolic status and the financial influences of capitalism (*The Field of Cultural Production*; *Distinction*; *The Rules of Art*). Whereas Bourdieu's analyses focus on the production and dissemination of cultural capital, John Guillory notes the fragility of capital as a metaphor for intellectual value, and Guillory's work on canon formation has inspired my own close readings of clustering in the literary marketplace.[1] I am also indebted to English and McGurl for adapting sociological metrics and forms of description that shed light on literary systems as forms of material production; their arguments about the deeply social nature of authorial fame are, I believe, borne out by my results below. My research methodologies combine an attention to popular culture and new collaborative forms of production advanced by media scholars like Henry Jenkins with the distant reading and systemic perspective adopted by Franco Moretti. I use measures from network analysis to analyze my data, particularly those defining the formation and structure of groups.

The digital traces that I will analyze here are drawn from two primary datasets: First, networks of recommendations based on consumer purchases drawn from Amazon; second, a corpus of professional and consumer reviews of Wallace's books collected from nationally prestigious newspapers and magazines along with consumer reviews from Amazon. "Network" here refers to a limited set of nodes and edges, and I will be extracting two basic kinds of networks from this data.[2] The first charts out recommendations on Amazon by defining books as nodes and recommendations as edges or links that point from one text to another. The second visualizes collocations in reviews of Wallace's work, defining author names and book titles as nodes and collocations within the same paragraph as links. I generated both datasets and the attendant visualization files using a combination of Perl scripts (to gather and groom the data), a MySQL database (to store it), and the visualization tool yEd (to create the figures below). By studying these networks side by side, we can explore the two primary spheres of public literary action: conversation and consumption. "Conversation" roughly encompasses the cultural side of the equation, represented here by professional and nonprofessional readers' written reviews of books. The decline of professional book reviewing and the familiar public sphere of literary profiles, blurbs, and other prestige-laden interactions have paralleled the rise of new digital public spaces. Web sites like Amazon have succeeded not just by dint of cost-cutting efficiency but because they have fostered new kinds of community around their products, and book reviewers on their sites often engage in dialogue with other reviews, creating spaces where users can form microcommunities around particular products.[3] This growing digital ecology of voluntary contributions from readers is what makes Amazon an appealing object of study for the "consumption" half of the equation. Amazon's recommendations allow us to observe the world's largest bookseller in its feedback loop with consumer desire and market influences. To be sure, the results are contingent and clearly manipulated to promote various publicity campaigns and new authors. But by considering these recommendation networks over time, we can see how a significant number of readers are associating texts through their shopping carts, and thereby establishing patterns and networks of literary consumption.

These networks can often include hundreds or thousands of nodes and edges, so how can we interpret them? We can engage in a certain amount of close reading, for instance to see what texts are immediately associated with Wallace's oeuvre through recommendations and reviews. But we can also perform distant readings of these findings using metrics drawn from network analysis; one of the most useful and approachable of these is "prestige." Figure 1 introduces the data and the concept of prestige, which I use here both in its Bourdieu-inspired register[4] and in its network-analytic sense of describing nodes that are most central or significant within a network. There are various ways to define centrality, but the simplest is this: in recommendation networks, the more times a text is recommended "by" another text, the higher its prestige value.[5] In review networks, where the links (based on collocations) have no directionality, it is even simpler: nodes with the most links are the most prestigious. Using these networks and prestige analysis, we can compare Wallace conversations and consumption to each other and to our critically grounded notions of his position in contemporary American literature. The value of this methodology is two-fold. First, my results here will allow us to trace the process of canonization for Wallace as he is integrated into a broader constellation of literary stars, offering some proof of his authorial success as well as a characterization of its nature.[6] Second, these results demonstrate the validity of the exercise: everyday readers do, in fact, contextualize Wallace differently from professional critics, and this revelation offers us another way to see the continued growth and evolution of Wallace the literary figure. The first step lies in exploring Wallace's distinct position in the literary marketplace.

Wallace Is Different

Wallace was deeply attuned to his own commercial obligations and the material risks of authorship, airing his concerns about the subject a number of times to interviewers.[7] He also compared himself to his peers several times in print, but my analysis of Amazon recommendations below reveals how different he really was from others of his generation. The images that follow are based on the first ten things that are recommended by the "Customers Who Bought This Item Also Bought" panel on each book page, starting from *Infinite Jest* and fanning out from there to three levels of depth. These networks fluctuate over time, so figure 1 is a synthesis of four different scans of Amazon recommendations conducted over a period from August 2010 to January 2011, showing only those texts that appeared consistently over this period.

The gray oval demarcates what I will call the Wallace subnet — an intricately interconnected zone of texts where buyers of one Wallace book are highly likely to purchase another. In fact, on Amazon, Wallace's recommendations almost invariably point browsers to more Wallace texts (including the criticism, reading guides, and biographical material on the edge of the circle in figure 1). This is very unusual. For comparison, as of 4 February 2011, Jonathan Franzen's *Freedom* linked to nine "external" novels in addition to *The Corrections* — more outgoing links than Wallace's cumulative total for the six-month period represented

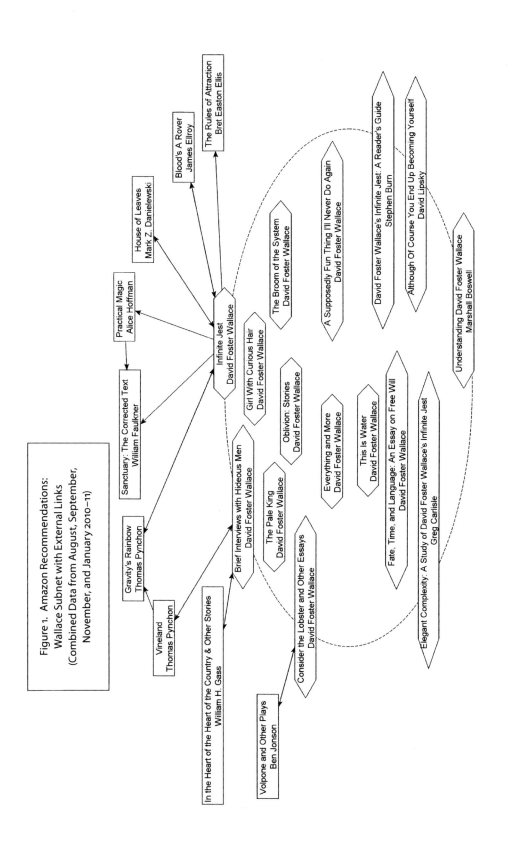

Figure 1. Amazon Recommendations: Wallace Subnet with External Links (Combined Data from August, September, November, and January 2010–11)

here. On the same day, Richard Powers's *Generosity* pointed to seven external books out of ten. My broader research indicates that with better established writers like Toni Morrison, these figures are even higher, as celebrated novels enter into "super-canons" that transcend authorship.[8] But for our purposes here, the point I am illustrating is simple: Wallace is different.

Beyond the glaring absence of links, we can prove this point by taking a closer look at the external texts recommended from the Wallace subnet. These links reflect a cultural marketplace struggling to effectively contextualize Wallace. His idiosyncratic essays in *Consider the Lobster* were connected to *Volpone and Other Plays* by Ben Jonson in the August 2010 data, breaking the genre barrier and linking him to a historical period very different from his own. The connection may be inspired, drawing the two texts together into a synthetic analysis of satire and human observation: perhaps some summer school syllabus asked students to compare Wallace's "Big Red Son" and Jonson's "Bartholemew Fair" as explorations of sexuality in public spectacles. Whatever the origins of this connection, it puts Wallace in rare company, underscoring both his distinction (for being connected to a highbrow, noncontemporary non-novel) and his cultural quirkiness (connecting him not to Shakespeare, for example, but to a writer of second-order canonical status).

This combination of idiosyncrasy and nonstandard links continues around the oval of the Wallace subnet as we consider the novels recommended from *Brief Interviews with Hideous Men*. This, perhaps Wallace's most avant-garde[9] text, leads to classically postmodern writers William Gaddis and Thomas Pynchon. The link from one collection of innovative short stories to another is relatively unsurprising, though the link once again invites browsers of the relatively mainstream Wallace to consider a text significantly farther down the long tail of literary obscurity. As with the Ben Jonson plays, the arrows pointing in toward Wallace here make more economic sense: Amazon's feedback loop with previous shoppers suggests that readers of Renaissance satire or postmodern fiction might be sold on a young writer with similar things to offer. But the proposition is much harder to make in reverse, precisely because it involves a move from the relatively well-understood contemporary scene to the smaller market of the backlist, where editions can easily go out of print and the whole apparatus of professional reviews and interviews has much less sway. The arrows pointing out once again distinguish Wallace from his contemporaries, whom readers almost always link in more obvious ways to recent works and similar genre spaces.

The *Vineland* connection offers another kind of peculiarity, placing as it does one of Wallace's less approachable books in dialogue with one of Pynchon's most approachable. In terms of thematic and temporal distance, this link makes much more taxonomic sense than the leap from Wallace to Jonson, but it also highlights the complex forces inflecting literary culture. *Vineland* seems to be connected to the wrong book here — its focus on media-saturated, television-steeped California life has a great deal in common with *Infinite Jest*. But once again the shopping carts have spoken, and its link with *Brief Interviews* is a double bond of mutual reinforcement. There are no direct mentions of *Vineland* in the customer reviews of *Brief Interviews with Hideous Men*, but Pynchon is a persistent presence. As one Amazon reviewer put it,

> Writers can be divided into two major types: poets and scientists. If poet-writers are your thing — guys like Henry Miller, Gabriel Garcia Marquez, or J. D. Salinger — stay away from this book. Wallace is a mad scientist, a manipulator of storytelling's double helix. Instead of going for the heart he opts for the brain. Some authors paint picures [sic]; this guy makes Rubik's cubes. He out-Pynchons Pynchon. (dgillz)

But why *Vineland*? As two relatively approachable books by postmodern authors, it's possible that this link represents the influence of college syllabi, where professors are often constrained to select authors' shorter works in order to cover more ground. One can easily imagine the "Introduction to Postwar American Fiction" course in which the two books would be assigned.

Far less mysterious are the links between *Vineland* and *Gravity's Rainbow* and the connection between the latter and *Infinite Jest*. These two books seem to have everything in common: sweeping encyclopedic novels widely regarded as their authors' major triumphs, they also address similar themes of individual agency, drug use, psychology, and technology with similar postmodern styles. I will discuss Wallace's larger relationship to Pynchon below in more detail, so for now let us focus instead on the other texts connected to *Infinite Jest*, which exist in surprising tension with one another. Wallace's magnum opus is the only node in his subnet to behave in what I would term a "normal" way, interacting extensively with books by other writers and contextualizing this novelist's work in larger historical and cultural zones. A preoccupation with genre writing also defines the rest of *Infinite Jest*'s connections here, from Ellroy's postmodern crime fiction to Danielewski's and Ellis's complex literary relationships with film. Indeed, perhaps the most surprising link of all here is Alice Hoffman's *Practical Magic*, a text that in other maps of this network immediately spirals off into a Hoffman universe with its own set of interior linkages among her novels, short stories, and young adult fiction. The novel that readers have aligned with *Infinite Jest* is *Practical Magic*, historical fiction with a magical twist that also brings it into dialogue with Pynchon's often fantastical *Gravity's Rainbow*. Yet this, too, is a strange book to put in contact with Wallace; its approachable style is more in line with Oprah's Book Club than Wallace's postmodernist cadre. The only strong connection seems to be through the thematic of film, a major subject for Wallace: *Practical Magic* is the only Hoffman novel to be adapted to the screen, in 1998. This would also explain its connection to *Sanctuary*, which was adapted as *The Story of Temple Drake* in 1933.

Wallace is different: this much we know for certain, based on his unusually introverted network and the unlikely ways in which that clump of texts does connect to outsiders. The rest, and in particular this speculative argument about the role of adaptation and the influence of film on literary production, is guesswork extrapolated from the data presented in figure 1. The focus of his work, particularly *Infinite Jest*, on the relationship between film, television, and the individual is reflected not only in texts that address similar postmodern problems, such as *Vineland*, but on a meta level with narratives of authors who grappled with the same problems in their lives. Cast in this light, Faulkner's *Sanc-*

tuary acts as an anchor that has remained constant over the span of my analysis, grounding an evolving contextual Wallace canon of texts that illuminate the abusive, addictive relationships we have with media and the power those relationships wield over the production of literature itself.[10] Nevertheless the persistence of this theme reveals the significant point that Wallace is contextualized not just along genre lines but in very sophisticated ways, regardless of whether or not I am correct about the thematic details. In the next section I will build on another set of grounded observations to discuss the remarkable difference between this nuanced, wide-ranging contextualization of his work and the much more limited versions of postmodernism that professional reviewers employ to explain Wallace to their readers.

Wallace Is Postmodern

Before most of us contemplate purchasing a novel, we turn to reviews, and literary criticism continues to define Wallace's legacy through the publication of *Fate, Time, and Language* and *The Pale King* in 2010 and 2011, respectively.[11] These reviews impact sales of the latest title as well as the full body of work, adjusting the author's cultural position. This was an evaluative process that Wallace felt keenly, organized, as he described it in "E Unibus Pluram," by "the writerly generation that precedes us, reviews us, and designs our grad-school curricula" (*A Supposedly Fun Thing I'll Never Do Again* 43). The interpretive dialogue of author and critic seemed to haunt Wallace even at the early height of his fame, for instance in the way he kept returning to Sven Birkerts's review of *Infinite Jest* in the *Atlantic* over the course of his long interview with David Lipsky. Only when Birkerts had endorsed the novel did Wallace decree, "yeah, it felt done then" (253). The negative press cut just as deeply, especially Michiko Kakutani's mixed review in the *New York Times* (Lipsky 92).

Applying the same "distant reading" lens to professional reviews allows us to consider these interpretive acts as another body of work, a professional filter built up over years of book reviews and sustained critical engagements. In figure 2, Wallace's books are connected to other texts through collocation in professional reviews: book titles that appear

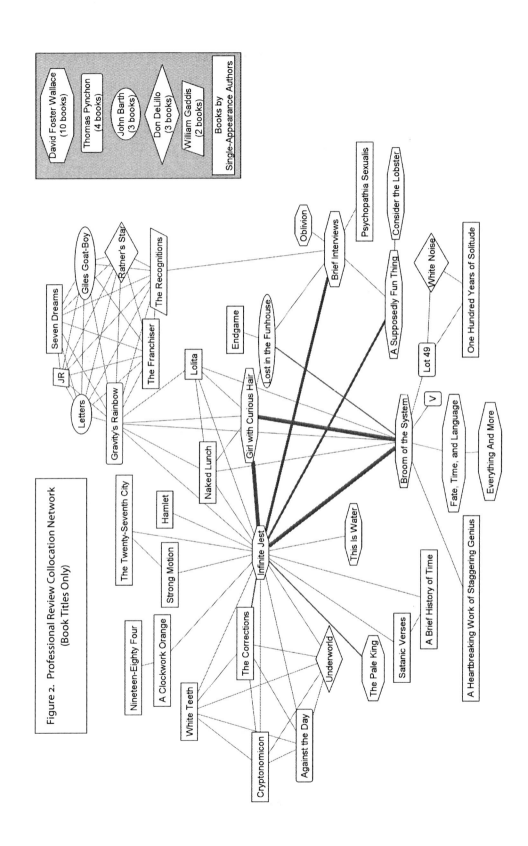

Figure 2. Professional Review Collocation Network
(Book Titles Only)

Books by
Single-Appearance Authors

David Foster Wallace
(10 books)

Thomas Pynchon
(4 books)

John Barth
(3 books)

Don DeLillo
(3 books)

William Gaddis
(2 books)

together in the same paragraph of a particular review are linked, with multiple such collocations indicated by thicker connecting lines. The peculiar connections we just observed in Amazon's recommendations networks are replaced here by a far more predictable set of canonical touchstones. Where Amazon opened strange pathways through Wallace, bridging Elizabethan drama and contemporary experimental fiction, the critics place him squarely in an intellectual tradition of Serious Young Men writing in the shadow of Serious Established Men.[12]

The temporal specificity of the diagram is striking: Wallace is linked primarily to those members of the "preceding writerly generation," the authors against whom he has been measured and contextualized throughout his career. In the eyes of professional reviewers, Wallace is triangulated between Pynchon, Barth, and DeLillo, postmodern not just stylistically but historically: nearly half of the books in figure 2 not penned by Wallace himself were written before 1980. The historical and stylistic senses of the term are conflated here by critics who assign Wallace to a more abstract plane than his contemporaries, thereby distancing him from the present and once again emphasizing his difference by historicizing him with another generation of writers. This critical alignment with the past was often deliberate: Wallace felt his own literary conversation with Barth in *Girl with Curious Hair* was "simultaneously absolutely homicidal and a fawning homage," or exactly the kind of genetic relationship that orients the critical apparatus to literary history instead of to the anxious present (Lipsky 226). Of course, even quick perusal of the reviews indicates that this interpretation is incomplete —Wallace's close attention to the heavily mediated present tense is widely recognized. But this fealty to literary history parallels the more imaginative market reactions we traced in figure 1 that linked Wallace to some of the same postmodern authors as well as to some older literary taproots, such as Jonson.

DeLillo, Barth, Pynchon: of the three, one author truly dominates Wallace's contextual connections in this image, and his iconic novel acts as an anticenter, a competing nexus of prestige to Wallace's network. Pynchon's *Gravity's Rainbow* (connected to fourteen books) is second only to *Infinite Jest* (seventeen books) in terms of prestige, and it works as a gateway to a relatively distinct subnet of classic high post-modernism. This cluster of encyclopedic novels is the result of a single paragraph in a *Chicago Tribune* review of *Infinite Jest* listing each of the texts in the subnet — Gaddis, Barth, Elkin, DeLillo, Vollmann — and concluding with the undisputed centerpiece:

> and especially Thomas Pynchon's magnificent reimagining of the Second World War as the defining event of this century's past and future ("Gravity's Rainbow") — all these daunting (and, to various degrees, brilliant) fictions underlie David Foster Wallace's blackly funny vision of America in the years just ahead. (Allen)

Allen's thoroughness might have exceeded that of his peers, but this critical frame is reiterated several times in Wallace's professional reviews, where his work is linked repeatedly to Pynchon's.[13] Throughout his career as a subject of professional book reviews, Wallace was described by and measured against *Gravity's Rainbow*, but that iconic comparison also sometimes led critics to places removed from Wallace himself, as the quote above implies through its almost overzealous delineation of a canon. The *Tribune* reviewer associates Wallace with "crowded, poly-phonic, loose and baggy monsters of immediately previous postwar literary generations," but ultimately Pynchon "especially" is the yardstick against which his work is most consistently measured.

Of course, there are other postmodern texts all over the diagram. The books that share Pynchon's close alignment with Wallace tell another interesting story about their relative literary positions: *Naked Lunch*, *Lolita*, and *A Clockwork Orange* all connect directly to *Infinite Jest*, placing Wallace squarely within a tradition of writing that is both thematically and formally transgressive. Burroughs and Nabokov are also linked into a subnet of other Wallace fiction, suggesting their value as texts that reviewers have consistently referred to since the publication of Wallace's first novel, *The Broom of the System*. We can contrast this tight interweaving of novels with the more diffuse ways in which Wallace's nonfiction writing is treated: the cultural divide between fiction and nonfiction ends up enforced by professional reviews here, with *Consider the Lobster*, for example, associated only with its essayistic predecessor, *A Supposedly Fun Thing I'll Never Do Again*. Remarkably, Wallace's postmodernity, and particularly his innovations as a stylist, are treated differently depending on genre. According to the critics, his essays and dispatches to magazines like *Harper's* set him apart, but his fiction draws him into comparison with Pynchon, Barth, and the rest.

When Wallace is considered in the context of his contemporaries, his work is still anchored to postmodern mainstays. In the small subnet to the left of *Infinite Jest* in figure 2, reviewers engage younger writers but keep Pynchon's and DeLillo's own most recent encyclopedic novels to hand: *Against the Day* and *Underworld*. Those other texts that are referenced bridge the gulf between "difficult" writing of the Pynchonian variety and more conventional literature: Jonathan Franzen's *The Corrections*, Zadie Smith's *White Teeth*, and Neal Stephenson's *Cryptonomicon*. This subnet also depends on the comments of a single reviewer, and it's worth considering the retrospective Lev Grossman delivered in *Time* more closely:

> It might be just as appropriate to deliver a eulogy for *Infinite Jest* — not to praise it but to bury it. After all, it did not win (nor was it a runner-up for) the National Book Award or the Pulitzer Prize or any other major award. It was hailed as the Novel of the Future, and in fact it kicked off a temporary revival of the maxi-novel, books like *Cryptonomicon* and *The Corrections* and *Underworld* and *White Teeth*. For a moment there, it felt as though novels simply had to get longer and longer to encompass the world's galloping complexity and interconnectedness. Then the fad faded. Now Thomas Pynchon's *Against the Day* (1,085 pages) just seems self-indulgent and stuntish. (Grossman)

This small moment of critical action reveals both the power and the increasingly obvious limits of professional criticism. Grossman employs the list, that most artful and flexible tool for refining distinctions, and he uses it here to tar a major swath of fiction with the same brush. All of these authors are lumped together as "maxi-novel" acolytes trying to recapture the buzz of the ultimately unsuccessful *Infinite Jest*. The charge both draws these novels together in the reader's mind and establishes a chain of fading distinction: *Infinite Jest* inspired imitations, the worst of which is *Against the Day*. Of course my methodology ignores the leap Grossman makes in implying that *Underworld* and *White Teeth* were somehow causally connected to *Infinite Jest*, but I would argue this bug is also a feature: as consumers of criticism, we are trained to accept professional comparisons as valid whether or not they are positive (or legitimated).[14] They form a contextual background, just as the first novels a reviewer chooses to lump together in one analysis develop a mutual bond. Through paragraphs like the *Tribune* and *Time* reviews above, new subnets are born in the history of literary reception.

The larger diagram shows what we already know as literary consumers ourselves: Wallace's books continue to lead active social lives in spite of Grossman and other professional criticism. The most important part of a book review is usually not the critic's final verdict but the context and cultural logic used to get there, the work that Grossman shows here to prove his point about the "maxi-novel." The title of the piece and its hook as a tenth anniversary retrospective overshadow Grossman's argument. These professional reviews also come with limited shelf lives — the following week, *Time*'s book review slots were filled by other authors, and Grossman's status as a reviewer depends not on perfect judgment but on consistency and timeliness. While few people will ever read his review again, except, ironically, as a blurb on a book jacket, thousands might continue to browse consumer reviews of *Infinite Jest* on Amazon, where the cultural logic of relevance is not ordered by temporality but by community.

Wallace Is Integral

At first glance, the same methodology of collocated nodes seems to have created a very similar network map for consumer reviews of Wallace's work on Amazon (figure 3; once again, only books mentioned at least twice are shown). We see many of the same postmodern texts, but where the professional critics clearly peg Wallace as an acolyte in dialogue with Pynchon, Barth, and DeLillo, his everyday readers are much more expansive with their comparisons, bringing *Ulysses*, *Moby-Dick*, and even *Les Misérables* into the conversation. A wider canonical lens

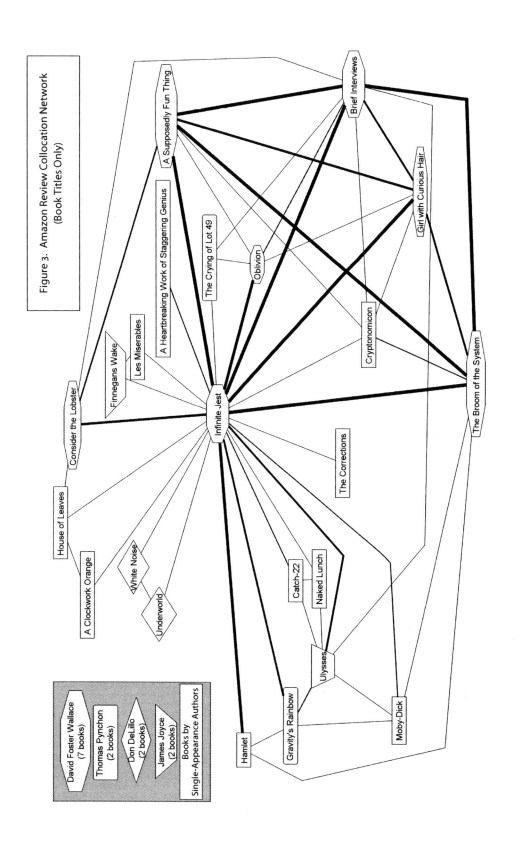

Figure 3. Amazon Review Collocation Network
(Book Titles Only)

Books by
Single-Appearance Authors

David Foster Wallace
(7 books)

Thomas Pynchon
(2 books)

Don DeLillo
(2 books)

James Joyce
(2 books)

A Supposedly Fun Thing

Brief Interviews

Girl with Curious Hair

A Heartbreaking Work of Staggering Genius

The Crying of Lot 49

Oblivion

Les Miserables

Finnegans Wake

Cryptonomicon

Consider the Lobster

The Broom of the System

Infinite Jest

House of Leaves

The Corrections

A Clockwork Orange

White Noise

Underworld

Catch-22

Naked Lunch

Ulysses

Moby-Dick

Hamlet

Gravity's Rainbow

that compares Wallace's texts to what we might call Great Books or familiar literary touchstones supersedes those encyclopedic novels from the 1960s to the 1980s. At the same time, Wallace's distinction from his contemporaries is even more pronounced here, suggesting once again that readers see him more in the context of canonical American literature and less in light of his generational peers. This diagram reflects the extent to which Wallace inspired his readers to integrate his work into their literary lives, encouraging them to think of him not as a Generation X writer but as an aspiring member of a timeless cadre.

In prestige terms Wallace plays a much more prominent role, in part because of the strong links among his own books. In figure 3, two of the top four nodes in the network were by other authors (by decreasing prestige rank: *Infinite Jest, Gravity's Rainbow, The Broom of the System, The Recognitions*), and they were all novels. Amazon reviewers, by contrast, are much more interested in Wallace (their top four: *Infinite Jest, A Supposedly Fun Thing I'll Never Do Again, Brief Interviews with Hideous Men*, and *The Broom of the System*). Even though consumer reviews are much more closely tied to their subjects via paratext (the surrounding Amazon layouts are always intended to draw the eye back to the book title and cover image), their authors mention Wallace's books far more often than professional reviewers did. This reinforces the evidence we saw in Amazon recommendations — Wallace leads on to more Wallace for most readers — but this network is distinct from both the purchase-driven recommendation network, where Wallace was a very distinct subnet, and the professional review network, where he mingled with the postmodernists. There is a balance here between a strong affinity to Wallace in his own right and a diverse contextual network suggesting that readers are working to interpret him on a broader plane. More adventurous than professional critics, these readers cross genre boundaries and compare his fiction and nonfiction alike to an idiosyncratic constellation of literature, drawing together a group of writers who generally share Wallace's concern with capturing the fragmentary nature of contemporary human experience.

As we have already seen, books are associated together in reviews for many reasons. Using some excerpts from Amazon reviews to support my case, I argue here that Wallace establishes a particular kind of challenge-based relationship with many of his readers. The data bears out the dual inflections of *integral* that I began with: the advancement of individual consciousness and the formation of a social or group affinity. The productive difficulty that Wallace creates for his readers has its roots in the postmodern, but everyday readers interpret it as a form of realism instead of a literary exercise, taking his style as a window onto the contemporary. His work is "integral," then, because it presents conflicting, nonlinear narratives and then asks readers to stitch those elements into a multidimensional whole. As one reviewer puts it:

> I for one like the fact that he doesn't feel the need to spell everything out for the reader and makes one mull over his story and possibly even go back and piece together little fragments of seemingly inconsequential lines of dialogue and ambiguous scenes.... I for one like things that remind me that I have a brain and force me to exercise this wonderful organ. Infinite Jest is quite a workout for the brain indeed. (Dr. Gonzo "Hairface")

For some readers, Wallace's influence on the brain offers an explicit stance against the kind of interpretation practiced by the professionals: "Ignore the literary critics and meta-reviews — just indulge in this dystopian world of tennis, drugs, and television that shines the harsh light on how ridiculous we all are. Your brain will expand and your heart will open to the world — it's that kind of a book" (sternj). Amazon reviewers discuss individual experiences, but they are also addressing a very specific audience, a community that has formed around Wallace's work and is distinctly amateur, not caught up in the professional literary game.

This network reveals how Wallace's readers pursue the "workout for the brain," how they exhort each other and, at times, explicitly seek to inform one another's reading. "[Wallace's] concerns are political, spiritual, cultural, and — to me, at least — deeply personal ... like *Ulysses* [*Infinite Jest*] becomes more accessible, touching, and funny as you grow accustomed to it" ("The Greatest American Novel"). Reviewers frequently draw in other canonical texts either to establish a literary connection with their peers or to mark his inferiority with a familiar yardstick. The best argument for this integral impulse is the way in which Wallace's Amazon readers consistently connect his work, particularly *Infinite Jest*, to *Hamlet*. Linking Hal Incandenza to Prince Hamlet highlights Wallace's metaphysical, epistemological, and canonical aspirations as an artist, his desire to interpret the burdens of mortality with an intense focus on language. Consider this reading narrative:

> Then, as I sat looking dully at the last page of the book, it ocurred [sic] to me. This is the last page, but not the end of the story. I had read the story's conclusion a month before, when I first began reading the book. So I went back and started reading again, and my jaw dropped open in awe of the true genius of this book. Sentences that had seemed insignificant or inconsequential when I first began reading were infused with new meaning, providing me with the conclusion to the story, cleverly hinted at by the books [sic] title, which refers to the graveyard scene in *Hamlet*. ("Thinking About Infinity")

This reviewer shares a personal integrative experience, and in doing so offers that experience to others, glossing *Infinite Jest*'s title and explaining his own path to discovering "the true genius of this book."

Hamlet haunts *Infinite Jest*, from its title to its antiheroes, but is rarely mentioned by credentialed book reviewers, for whom it is a relatively superficial feature of a complex novel with inconclusive plots set in a bizarre near-future world, all of which need to be described and contextualized with the book's postmodern antecedents. Everyday readers, however, put *Hamlet* into service as a narratological skeleton key that promises to unlock a basic structure and purpose to *Infinite Jest*'s disjointed story lines: "Modern (post-modern) Hamlet. In structure as well as theme" (Gimpel the Fool). Readers identify Wallace's references to the play, quoting the "infinite jest" line, identifying Hal's debt to Hamlet, and at times making sophisticated arguments about the two: "'We are all dying to give our lives away to something, maybe.' That dangling Hamlet-like doubt — that 'maybe' — calls into question not the quest but its effects — the consequences of surrendering oneself, of being swept away that await the wandering souls at the end of their journey" (Marfin).

Interpretations like these are generative, producing a genuine literary dialogue among reviewers as they do the "work," integrating Wallace into a community and establishing boundaries and classifications of distinction. As both a subtext in need of glossing and a literary comparison, *Hamlet* works as an intertextual space that allows Wallace readers to create new forms of conversation. Another *Infinite Jest* reviewer, Jake Wilson, adopts a more pedagogical route, the kind of opening one might imagine in a college lecture: "In the opening two words of Shakespeare's *Hamlet* (from which *Infinite Jest* derives its title) Bernardo cries Who's there? having seen the ghost of a tragedy; and Wallace answers in the first two words of this epic novel — I am" (Wilson). Wilson moves from this instructive tone into a gradually more intimate voice, closing with "Rest In Peace, DFW — you accomplished more with this one book than most writers ever even imagine." The line is both more poignant and commercial because of Wilson's sign-off in the review, where he offers a link to his own self-published novel. Effectively, Wilson has turned the review into a dialogue with both the Shakespearean past and the literary present, creating a particular kind of public intimacy in the process as he contributes to a wider *Infinite Jest* conversation and builds his own literary link to Wallace.

These readers often embrace the emotional side of this interpretive work in ways that critics never would, and in doing so become characters themselves at the heart of critical comparisons: "It's not that I dislike long or annotated books (I'd just finished the Northwestern University's heavily annotated *Moby Dick* and loved it!), but this almost pointless tome pained me to read in a way not felt since being assigned *The Yearling* in school" ("The Fine Line Between Genius and Inanity (Sic.)"). Wallace is academic in a bad way, reminding the reader of a hated school assignment, yet the review hastens to assure us that *Infinite Jest*'s obviously learned qualities — its length and intimidating footnotes — did not color the decision. Wallace's novel is ranked against Melville's and found wanting, but like *Time*'s Grossman, the reviewer still places them on the same list, and in both cases the reader is confronted with the fact of the comparison as well as its tone. A parenthetical reference establishes Wallace's categorical link to Melville and the perceived difference between the two, once again literally, grammatically writing the reader into the critical act of distinction. This reviewer closes on another intensely personal note: "One Amazon.com reviewer mentioned breaking Wallace's legs. That seems an extreem [sic] and somewhat excessive exercise. I would limit my ministrations to his writing hand."

Such deep involvement becomes familiar, a kind of cliché:

> It's like reading Melville's *Moby Dick*, Joyce's *Ulysses* or Pychon's [sic] *Gravity's Rainbow*. If you are a serious contemporary/postmodern/whatever reader or writer you must read it. Whatever time it takes. Homework. Don't skip the footnotes. You will not regret it. You'll laugh/cry/it will become you/etc. *Infinite Jest* is the book I recommend when I am talking to people who REALLY READ BOOKS." (Roberti)

Here the integral, educational impulse is met head-on: "Homework. Don't skip the footnotes." The breezy slash-concatenated lists belie the earnest imperatives of the review and its elevation of Wallace into a pantheon of encyclopedic novelists. Once again the reviewer is in the middle of the process of integration, calling on others to join the ranks of those who "REALLY READ BOOKS." The lines of reference connecting books in figure 3 exemplify this process of public criticism as it has played out over hundreds of Amazon reviews. In a very real sense, it shows the work of everyday readers as they interpret Wallace and pull him into contact with a popular literary sphere.

I'd like to close by recasting my definition of integral. Over four hundred readers have found *Infinite Jest* sufficiently energizing to write a review of the novel on Amazon, and their verdict emphatically positions the book in a transhistorical American context encompassing postmodernism and expanding beyond it, considering Wallace as stylist, crafter of literary puzzles, and "genius." The work of reading and reviewing inspires many readers to cultivate new kinds of awareness and to share that with a community of fellow readers. In the end, the strange canon that they construct around Wallace, from Victor Hugo to Joseph Heller, is a testament to his success. To call Wallace's fiction "integral" only makes sense in the context of this public readership, which performs the actual work of building his infinite jests into a wider system of cultural meaning.[15] This is the leap that so concerned Wallace himself, the transition from individual to group, from monad to collective, not just in the abstract but in his particular case as a writer and a human being. In this third sense of integrating David Foster Wallace into the world, his literature has largely been a success. His self-questioning entertainments demand challenging acts of reading and interpretation, but they also lead readers to consider the boundaries of personal agency, perception, and mediation that define our cultural landscape.

As the argument above has shown, Wallace occupies a unique position in contemporary literature. His is a distinct literary brand, a *different* author whose style and quirkiness quickly set him apart from his peers in the marketplace. His writing earned critical acclaim for the skill with which he engaged the *postmodern*, though his success among professional reviewers proved only a part of the enthusiastic popular reception that spawned groups like Infinite Summer.[16] He was *integral* in three ways, encouraging his readers to reconstruct the real through his fragmentary prose, getting them to share that experience collectively, and making his own integral leap, leading readers to feel they have "spen[t] time inside his beautiful poetry of a brain" (sternj). These three keywords are all ultimately questions of style, and Wallace was unflagging in his efforts to make his writing a transparent reflection of the perceived contemporary. Wallace is special for this, for his unflinching efforts to address the loneliness of mediation. His fiction lays bare the philosophical foundations of cultural attention, encouraging his audience to rethink their most basic literary acts: reading, contextualizing, enjoying, and judging. As we practice these exercises for the reader on his own body of work, we define new forms of literary culture that amplify and consecrate the voice of the audience. Each review and rating is an act of collective critical trust and another shared experience in which we, and Wallace, become ourselves.

Notes

1. For the relevant discussion on value in *Cultural Capital*, see pp. 325–40.

2. "Limited set" is an important term here — these networks of cultural influence are practically infinite, so the graphs here are subsets defined by reasonable artificial constraints. For example, my network of book recommendations on Amazon begins with *Infinite Jest* and follows links to three levels of depth.

3. I use the term "community" as a way of describing the ill-defined but occasionally powerful associations strangers can form online, a group that might fluctuate between what Guillory calls an "association" and an entity with a more explicit set of shared values and sense of belonging (34–5).

4. In fact the term has evolved for Bourdieu as well, from its original sense as "specific consecration" distinct from capitalistic success (*The Field of Cultural Production* 38) to its more complex contemporary meaning in a world where "the boundary has never been as blurred between the experimental work and the *bestseller*" (*The Rules of Art* 347).

5. For an overview of prestige in network theory, see Wasserman and Faust (174–5).

6. Needless to say, this book is, in another way, also part of that process of canonization.

7. For instance, he brought up the subject of publishers' advance payments five times during his interview with David Lipsky (2, 14–5, 28, 110, 240–2).

8. My work on Morrison, most notably, demonstrates how her fiction transcends an African American canonical space to connect to prominent works from other canonical groups (such as Leslie Marmon Silko's *Ceremony*) as well as a transhistorical "Great American Reading List" ranging from Hawthorne and Twain to Hemingway and Fitzgerald, not to mention Dostoevsky and Joyce. "New Literary Cultures: Mapping The Digital Networks of Toni Morrison," forthcoming in *Transforming Reading: Communities and Practices at the Turn of the Twenty-First Century*, edited by Anouk Lang (Amherst: University of Massachusetts Press, 2012).

9. Readers are encouraged to continue on to Lee Konstantinou's discussion of Wallace and the avant-garde after this essay, if they have not done so already.

10. Faulkner disingenuously claimed he wrote *Sanctuary* as an attempt to make money by appealing to the lowest common denominator of reader appetites ("Faulkner Was Wrong About 'Sanctuary'").

11. This data was assembled before the publication of either of these texts, so the only "review" mentioning *The Pale King* included here is D. T. Max's *New Yorker* essay on Wallace.

12. This network is almost entirely male, with the exception of Zadie Smith

(*White Teeth*). The persistent gender bias of literature perceived as "serious" is a deserving subject too complex to be taken on here.

13. The quote also marks another moment in the history of what Mark Greif, after James Wood, has called "big, ambitious novels" (Greif).

14. This is another version of what Guillory calls the "synecdochic list which is the syllabus"—whether the syllabus positions two texts as antagonistic or complementary, they are nevertheless situated within the same cultural frame (34).

15. Wallace approaches this claim explicitly in *The Pale King* when he claims "the various ways some of the forthcoming §s have had to be distorted, depersonalized, polyphonized, or otherwise jazzed up . . . [have] ended up being integral to the book's whole project" (*The Pale King* 72).

16. See Kathleen Fitzpatrick's chapter in this volume for a discussion of the Infinite Summer group and its blog of the same name.

Works Cited

Allen, Bruce. "Future Imperfect." *Chicago Tribune* 24 March 1996: n. pag. Print.

Birkarts, Sven. "The Alchemist's Retort." *Atlantic* February 1996. Web.

Bourdieu, Pierre. *Distinction: A Social Critique of the Judgement of Taste.* Cambridge, MA: Harvard University Press, 2007. Print.

———. *The Field of Cultural Production.* Ed. Randal Johnson. New York: Columbia University Press, 1993. Print.

———. *The Rules of Art: Genesis and Structure of the Literary Field.* Stanford, CA: Stanford University Press, 1996. Print.

dgillz. "A Little Less Infinite . . ." *Amazon* 31 October 2000. Web.

Dr. Gonzo "Hairface." "Never Ceases to Astonish." *Amazon* 12 April 2005. Web.

English, James F. *The Economy of Prestige: Prizes, Awards, and the Circulation of Cultural Value.* Cambridge, MA: Harvard University Press, 2005. Print.

"Faulkner Was Wrong About 'Sanctuary.'" *New York Times* 22 February 1981. Web.

"The Fine Line Between Genius and Inanity (Sic.)." *Amazon* 22 February 1998. Web.

Finn, Ed. "The Social Lives of Books: Literary Networks in Contemporary American Fiction." Diss., Stanford University, 2011. Print.

Gimpel the Fool. "Who's There?" *Amazon* 28 December 2006. Web.

"The Greatest American Novel." *Amazon* 20 April 1999. Web.

Greif, Mark. "'The Death of the Novel' and Its Afterlives: Toward a History of the 'Big, Ambitious Novel.'" *boundary 2* 36.2 (2009): 11–30. Print.

Grossman, Lev. "Ten Years Beyond Infinite." *Time* 26 November 2006. Web.

Guillory, John. *Cultural Capital: The Problem of Literary Canon Formation.* Chicago: University of Chicago Press, 1995. Print.

Jenkins, Henry. *Convergence Culture: Where Old and New Media Collide.* Revised. New York: New York University Press, 2008. Print.

Lipsky, David. *Although of Course You End Up Becoming Yourself: A Road Trip with David Foster Wallace.* New York: Broadway Books, 2010. Print.

Marfin, Gary C. "A Hypnotic and Remarkable Novel." *Amazon* 1 August 2009. Web.

Max, D. T. "The Unfinished." *New Yorker* 9 March 2009: 48–61. Print.

McGurl, Mark. *The Program Era: Postwar Fiction and the Rise of Creative Writing.* Cambridge, MA: Harvard University Press, 2009. Print.

Moretti, Franco. *Graphs, Maps, Trees: Abstract Models for Literary History.* London: Verso, 2007. Print.

Roberti, J. E. "A Great and Difficult Book (As It Should Be)." *Amazon* 17 February 2008. Web.

sternj. "Literary Everest." *Amazon* 28 February 2008. Web.

"Thinking About Infinity." *Amazon* 29 August 1996. Web.

Wallace, David Foster. *The Pale King.* Boston: Little, Brown and Company, 2011. Print.

———. *A Supposedly Fun Thing I'll Never Do Again: Essays and Arguments.* New York: Back Bay Books, 1998. Print.

Wasserman, Stanley, and Katherine Faust. *Social Network Analysis: Methods and Applications.* Cambridge, UK: Cambridge University Press, 1994. Print.

Wilson, Jake. "*IJ*: An Internal Journey." *Amazon* 4 August 2010. Web.

JONATHAN FRANZEN

INFORMAL REMARKS FROM THE

DAVID FOSTER WALLACE MEMORIAL

SERVICE IN NEW YORK ON

OCTOBER 23, 2008

LIKE A LOT OF WRITERS, but even more than most, Dave loved to be in control of things. He was easily stressed by chaotic social situations. I only ever twice saw him go to a party without Karen. One of them, hosted by Adam Begley, I almost physically had to drag him to, and as soon as we were through the front door and I took my eye off him for one second, he made a U-turn and went back to my apartment to chew tobacco and read a book. The second party he had no choice but to stay for, because it was celebrating the publication of *Infinite Jest*. He survived it by saying thank you, again and again, with painfully exaggerated formality.

One thing that made Dave an extraordinary college teacher was the formal structure of the job. Within those confines, he could safely draw on his enormous native store of kindness and wisdom and expertise. The structure of interviews was safe in a similar way. When Dave was the subject, he could relax into taking care of his interviewer. When he was the journalist himself, he did his best work when he was able to find a technician — a cameraman following John McCain, a board operator on a radio show — who was thrilled to meet somebody genuinely interested in the arcana of his job. Dave loved details for their own sake, but details were also an outlet for the love bottled up in his heart: a way of connecting, on relatively safe middle ground, with another human being.

Which was, approximately, the description of literature that he and I came up with in our conversations and correspondence in the early 1990s. I'd loved Dave from the very first letter I ever got from him, but the first two times I tried to meet him in person, up in Cambridge, he flat-out stood me up. Even after we did start hanging out, our meetings were often stressful and rushed — much *less* intimate than exchanging letters. Having loved him at first sight, I was always straining to prove that I could be funny enough and smart enough, and he had a way of gazing off at a point a few miles distant which made me feel as if I were failing to make my case. Not many things in my life ever gave me a greater sense of achievement than getting a laugh out of Dave.

But that "neutral middle ground on which to make a deep connection with another human being": this, we decided, was what fiction was for. "A way out of loneliness" was the formulation we agreed to agree on. And nowhere was Dave more totally and gorgeously able to maintain control than in his written language. He had the most commanding and exciting and inventive rhetorical virtuosity of any writer alive. Way out at word number 70 or 100 or 140 in a sentence deep into a three-page paragraph of macabre humor or fabulously reticulated self-consciousness, you could smell the ozone from the crackling precision of his sentence structure, his effortless and pitch-perfect shifting among ten different levels of high, low, middle, technical, hipster, nerdy, philosophical, vernacular, vaudevillian, hortatory, tough-guy, broken-hearted, lyrical diction. Those sentences and those pages, when he was able to be producing them, were as true and safe and happy a home as any he had during most of the twenty years I knew him. So I could tell you stories about the bickering little road trip he and I once took, or I could tell you about the wintergreen scent that his chew gave to my little apartment whenever he stayed with me, or I could tell you about the awkward chess games we played and the even more awkward tennis rallying we sometimes did — the comforting structure of the games versus the weird deep fraternal rivalries boiling along underneath — but truly the main thing was the writing. For most of the time I knew Dave, the most intense interaction I had with him was sitting alone in my armchair, night after night, for ten days, and reading the manuscript of *Infinite Jest*. That was the book in which, for the first time, he'd arranged himself and the world the way he wanted them arranged. At the most microscopic level: Dave Wallace was as passionate and precise a punctuator of prose as has ever walked this earth. At the most global level: he produced a thousand pages of world-class jest which, although the mode and quality of the humor never wavered, became less and less and less funny, section by section, until, by the end of the book, you felt the book's title might just as well have been *Infinite Sadness*. Dave nailed it like nobody else ever had.

And so now this handsome, brilliant, funny, kind Midwestern man with an amazing spouse and a great local support network and a great career and a great job at a great school with great students has taken his own life, and the rest of us are left behind to ask (to quote from *Infinite Jest*), "So yo then man what's *your* story?" (17).

One good, simple, modern story would go like this: "A lovely, talented personality fell victim to a severe chemical imbalance in his brain. There was the person of Dave, and then there was the disease, and the disease killed the man as surely as cancer might have." This story is at once sort of true and totally inadequate. If you're satisfied with this story, you don't need the stories that Dave wrote — particularly not those many, many stories in which the duality, the separateness, of person and disease is problematized or outright mocked. One obvious paradox, of course, is that Dave himself, at the end, did become, in a sense, satisfied with this simple story and stopped connecting with any of those more interesting stories he'd written in the past and might have written in the future. His suicidality got the upper hand and made everything in the world of the living irrelevant.

But this doesn't mean there are no more meaningful stories for us to tell. I could tell you ten different versions of how he arrived at the evening of 12 September, some of them very dark, some of them very angering to me, and most of them taking into account Dave's many adjustments, as an adult, in response to his near-death of suicide as a late adolescent. But there is one particular not-so-dark story that I know to be true and that I want to tell now, because it's been such a great happiness and privilege and endlessly interesting challenge to be Dave's friend.

People who like to be in control of things can have a hard time with intimacy. Intimacy is anarchic and mutual and definitionally incompatible with control. You seek to control things because you're afraid, and about five years ago, very noticeably, Dave stopped being so afraid. Part of this came of having settled into a good, stable situation here at Pomona. Another really huge part of it was his finally meeting a woman who was right for him and, for the first time, opened up the possibility of his having a fuller and less rigidly structured life. I noticed, when we spoke on the phone, that he'd begun to tell me he loved me, and I suddenly felt, on my side, that I didn't have to work so hard to make him laugh or to prove that I was smart. Karen and I managed to get him to Italy for a week, and instead of spending his days in his hotel room, watching TV, as he might have done a few years earlier, he was having lunch on the terrace and eating octopus and trudging along to dinner parties in the evening and actually enjoying hanging out with other writers casually. He surprised everyone, maybe most of all himself. Here was a genuinely fun thing he might well have done again.

About a year later, he decided to get himself off the medication that had lent stability to his life for more than twenty years. Again, there are a lot of different stories about why exactly he decided to this. But one thing he made very clear to me, when we talked about it, was that he wanted a chance at a more ordinary life, with less freakish control and more ordinary pleasure. It was a decision that grew out his love for Karen, out of his wish to produce a new and more mature kind of writing, and out of having glimpsed a different kind of future. It was an incredibly scary and brave thing for him to try, because Dave was full of love, but he was also full of fear — he had all too ready access to those depths of infinite sadness.

So the year was up and down, and he had a crisis in June, and a very hard summer. When I saw him in July he was skinny again, like the late adolescent he'd been during his first big crisis. One of the last times I talked to him after that, in August, on the phone, he asked me to tell him a story of how things would get better. I repeated back to him a lot of what he'd been saying to me in our conversations over the previous year. I said he was in a terrible and dangerous place because he was trying to make real changes as a person and as a writer. I said that the last time he'd been through near-death experiences, he'd emerged and written, very quickly, a book that was light-years beyond what he'd been doing before his collapse. I said he was a stubborn control freak and know-it-all—"So are you!" he shot back at me—and I said that people like us are so afraid to relinquish control that sometimes the only way we can force ourselves to open up and change is to bring ourselves to an access of misery and the brink of self-destruction. I said he'd undertaken his change in medication because he wanted to grow up and have a better life. I said I thought his best writing was ahead of him. And he said: "I like that story. Could you do me a favor and call me up every four or five days and tell me another story like it?"

Unfortunately I only had one more chance to tell him the story, and by then he wasn't hearing it. He was in horrible, minute-by-minute anxiety and pain. The next times I tried to call him after that, he wasn't picking up the phone or returning messages. He'd gone down into the well of infinite sadness, beyond the reach of story, and he didn't make it out. But he had a beautiful, yearning innocence, and he was trying.

KATHLEEN FITZPATRICK

INFINITE SUMMER:
READING, EMPATHY, AND
THE SOCIAL NETWORK

One need not simply dissociate affect or empathy from intellectual, cognitive, and stylistic or rhetorical concerns, and one may ask whether empathy is on some level necessary for even limited understanding. One may even contend that there can be no durable ethical and political change without the reeducation of affect in its relation to normative judgment.—Dominick LaCapra

I am describing here a utopian dream, a dream in which ethics and politics converge.—Alison Landsberg

SOME YEARS AGO, in the conclusion to *The Anxiety of Obsolescence*, I wrote about David Foster Wallace's representations of television in *Infinite Jest*. Throughout the book, I'd focused on the ways that earlier postmodern novelists such as Pynchon and DeLillo had conveyed a sense of anxiety about the novel's future through their representations of the damage television was producing in contemporary culture, transforming a once active reading public into a passive, de-individualized, manipulable mass neither capable nor desirous of democratic action. *Infinite Jest* certainly seems to bear a similar kind of anxiety about television, focused as it is on a nation that has come to mistake the freedom to choose what it watches for more robust forms of freedom, and on the ability of a terrorist group to make use of that relationship to the tube in spreading a perfect, and perfectly debilitating, Entertainment.

However, reading *Infinite Jest* against the work of writers such as Pynchon and DeLillo reveals key differences. While those earlier novelists seem to see in television a direct threat to the culture that created and sustained the novel's hegemony, Wallace understands television not as being responsible for the decline of western culture but instead as a symptom of the damage wrought by that culture.[1] The dominance of television, in *Infinite Jest*, is not the force producing the early twenty-first century sense of anomie but rather is produced *by* it.[2] Television, in this later novel, derives its power from a particularly American sense of loneliness, a condition that it winds up exacerbating precisely as it promises a cure. We seek in television the kind of relationship that the twentieth century's alienation has rendered all but impossible, a human connection that we have lost the knowledge of how to make. And as the television gives way to the teleputer in *Infinite Jest*, and as the public's access to entertainment on demand becomes ever more individually tailored, viewers find themselves increasingly alone with the screen, unable to pull themselves away in order to find the contact they're seeking.

Enabling a more authentic human connection, or at least creating its imaginative possibility, was a significant component of Wallace's sense of the role of the novel in contemporary culture. If the novel were able "to give the reader, who like all of us is sort of marooned in her own skull, to give her imaginative access to other selves," it opens the potential that she might, as a result, feel "less alone inside" (McCaffery 127), and therefore more open to the possibility of real human interactions and relationships. In what follows, I explore the ability of the novel to create such connections through a consideration of *Infinite Summer*, an online group reading project that, I argue, instantiates this potential in the act of reading by creating pathways for ethical, empathic connection not just between reader and writer, or between reader and text, but among readers.

Wallace's work thus presents the opportunity to develop an understanding of the relationship between the novel and mediation profoundly different from that manifested in the work of earlier postmodernists. While Wallace did express a great deal of caution about television, a concern he explored at length in "E Unibus Pluram: Television and U.S. Fiction," the risk that he saw for contemporary fiction was not that its audience would become so narcotized that it would lose its attention span or its ability to consume the long text-based narrative. Instead, the danger lay in the facile sneer that television's uncritical deployment of irony would produce in the novelist, redirecting his attention from the others around him to himself, and distancing him from the real human problems that others face. The failure to engage with the real muck of being human, and thus the failure to create an empathic connection with the reader, posed in Wallace's view the most serious threat to the novel's future. *Infinite Summer*, as I will demonstrate, indicates the success of Wallace's work in connecting with the reader, while at the same time suggesting that changes in the nature of mediation since *Infinite Jest* have given the lie to some of that novel's fears, as contemporary communication networks bear the potential to enable substantive human connections, including those among readers.

That the connections between reader, writer, and text that Wallace desired were so inescapably personal requires me to stop here and consider my own situation within this essay. David Wallace was a colleague and a friend, and I have a difficult time writing about his work without considering that relationship and how it affects my reading. This was true throughout his time at Pomona College, but this difficulty has become even more pressing in the aftermath of his death; the personal loss that I felt has been highlighted for me in all of my engagements with his work since then, making clear the degree to which my relationship with his writing and my relationship with him were tangled up in one another.[3] As Dominick LaCapra reminds me, transference resulting from an affective connection between the scholar and her object of study can result in "the tendency to repeat in one's own discourse or practice tendencies active in, or projected into, the other or object" (74). The reader, and particularly the critic, must thus remain attuned to the transferential tendencies in her engagement with the materials, and particularly the individuals, that she studies, remaining aware of the dangers that overidentification presents to understanding.

The risks of such overidentification are particularly clear with respect to Wallace's work; many of his readers experience a sense of intimate connection with his writing, a connection that can very easily bleed over into a relationship, however imagined, with the man himself. A cursory look at the numerous articles and blog posts written after his death reveals both the range and the depth of the impact that his writing has had on contemporary readers, an impact at once salutary and uncomfortable. The public outpouring of grief in the wake of Wallace's death, for instance, was worryingly reminiscent of the spectacle surrounding Kurt Cobain's death — on the one hand, a clear indication of the deep relationship that his fans felt, through his work, to Wallace himself; on the other, an unhealthy transformation of artist into celebrity fetish object, and of a private tragedy into some kind of public performance. If there is a difference in these two cases, it might lie in the sense that, whatever Cobain's actual, personal feelings, his work repeatedly enacted the most intensive form of ironic distance, the complete refusal of any human connection other than a sense of mutual alienation.[4] However his fans may have identified with his work, and through it with Cobain himself, that identification ran the risk of intensifying the fans' alienation by focusing on their failures to connect. Wallace's writing, by contrast, deploys irony not as a gesture designed to protect the author or his readers from the pain of connection but rather as a means of allowing those readers a safe enough space within which they can explore their own feelings of loneliness, of inadequacy, of duplicity, of failure. The novels and short stories make this exploration possible precisely because, as Wallace told Larry McCaffery, "if a piece of fiction can allow us imaginatively to identify with characters' pain, we might then also more easily conceive of others identifying with our own" (127).

There are dangers, however, in this mode of identification, when applied uncritically, and when the tendency toward transference on the part of deeply invested readers is overlooked. As LaCapra has noted, uncritical identification can result in "the derivation of one's identity from others in ways that deny their otherness" (83). This mode of identification not only promotes an essentialist model of selfhood — assuming an identity between self and Other — but it runs the risk of colonizing the Other's experience as one's own, whether by taking over the Other's perspective or by projecting one's own perspective onto the Other. The reader engaging with work such as Wallace's, work that actively courts an affective response, must remain critically aware of the effects of transference, in order to avoid simplistic modes of identification, acknowledging, as LaCapra suggests, "one's own opacities and gaps that prevent full identity or self-knowledge" (77). In so doing, the reader can enact a more ethical form of empathic identification, remaining open to the otherness of the Other while nonetheless benefiting from the affective connection.

What made Wallace's work so phenomenally powerful for so many readers, I would argue, is precisely the combination of factors that enabled it to promote a mode of identification that transcends essentialist notions of identity, producing instead more thoughtful forms of empathy. That ability was created by the work's connection of three consistent impulses in contemporary fiction, wedding, in a way that no other writer has managed quite so well, high-modern and postmodern experimental pyrotechnics with an incisive cultural critique and a deep concern for quotidian human suffering. That is to say that Wallace's fiction combines rich investments in form, in ideas, and in emotion. Any number of writers of the last fifty years can be read as bringing together two of these strains in contemporary fiction, but hardly anyone else has managed all three in a way that feels to the reader not simply sincere but unflinchingly honest. And it's the third factor in particular, I would argue, that leads Wallace's work to stand out from much postmodernist writing that disavows the affective, as it recognizes that affect and political or critical potential are not mutually exclusive but may in fact be mutually dependent. LaCapra has described empathy's affective response as "a virtual but not vicarious experience" in which the historian "puts him- or herself in the other's position without taking the other's place or becoming a surrogate for the other who is authorized to speak in the other's voice" (65). This combination of such affective response with critical analysis works to create in the historian — or, in our case, in the reader — what he refers to as "empathic unsettlement," a feeling for but acknowledgment of the irreconcilable otherness of the Other. Such empathic unsettlement produces the degree of connection that readers have felt with Wallace's writing, deriving not only from the sense that the writing is serious enough to make the reader work nontrivially in its apprehension, and not only from the ways it causes the reader to think seriously about the world in which she lives, but also from its desire to help the reader, on some too often devalued level, to understand her own position within that world.

This focus on the affective, the empathic, and the reader's self-understanding may begin to sound a good bit more self-helpy and a good deal less literary than one might wish to associate with an author as evidently "serious" as Wallace. While such "seriousness" has been almost exclusively encoded as masculine, at least on the U.S. literary scene, as indicated by the September 2010 outburst of "Franzenfreude,"[5] the seriousness of Wallace's fiction is not just a matter of the work's narratological experimentalism or linguistic difficulty, or of its rigorous insights into contemporary culture. It is also, I would argue, driven by the work's recognition of the life-and-death stakes of the emotional terrain that it explores and the radical intimacy of the questions with which it asks the reader to grapple. And it's in his willingness to allow these texts to be the work of what Wallace described as an "anti-rebel," one who has "the childish gall actually to endorse single-entendre values ... [to] treat old untrendy human troubles and emotions in U.S. life with reverence and conviction" ("E Unibus" 192–3), that Wallace's writing encourages an empathic connection within its readers' lives, leading finally to the outpouring of grief upon the news of his death.

Building this kind of intimate relationship between reader and text has long been the motivating force of popular reading groups, perhaps most famously among them, Oprah's Book Club. As Ted Striphas has argued in his exploration of the unlikely relationship between the television empire and the publishing world, the success of Oprah's Book Club derived in no small degree from its practice of tailoring the reading experience to the actual audience that the show hoped to reach, a pragmatic approach that "engages actual and potential readers at the level of the everyday" (Striphas 138). In order to reach its audience, to engage them in the discussions about books that the show's producers wished to have, Oprah's Book Club was required not just to select *good* books, but to find the *right* books for its readers — and, even more, to find clear, compelling ways to communicate to those readers that the book selected was the right book for them. This mode of fulfilling the audience's desire, Wallace has noted, is something "TV is extremely good at . . . discerning what large numbers of people think they want, and supplying it" (McCaffery 128).[6] And yet the explicitly educational goals of the book club resulted in a far more complex sense of "what large numbers of people think they want" than we might ordinarily be willing to give television credit for. What the book club's audience thought they wanted, by and large, was a compelling reading experience within which they felt some personal involvement; these readers were not demanding entertainment so much as they were connection. As Oprah indicated in an interview given in the last days of her show, the program's overarching objective was "to let the viewer know that whatever you're going through, you're not alone" (Stelter). The book club, as one means of achieving that goal — a goal with clear echoes of Wallace's desire to help the reader feel "less alone inside"— worked by forging strong links between readers and books, by finding the right books for those readers, and by communicating that rightness.

The rightness of these books, as Striphas demonstrates, has in the case of Oprah's Book Club less to do with any critical means of assessing a text's "quality" than it does with the ability of the reader to achieve some form of imaginative identification with a novel's characters and their dilemmas. Scholars often dismiss the sort of identification promoted by Oprah's Book Club as being "undertheorized"; this claim in turn produces a response by defenders of mainstream reading practices dismissing scholarly modes of reading as jargon-filled and obscurantist. And so back and forth: philosopher Robert Pippin, for instance, in his *New York Times Opinionator* column, "In Defense of Naïve Reading," calls for a return to a mode of literary study that he characterizes as "an appreciation and discussion not mediated by a theoretical research question recognizable as such by the modern academy" (Pippin). Rather than opening a frank discussion about the importance of different modes of readerly connections to texts, however, Pippin's provocation winds up devaluing the serious work done by literary scholars, resulting in those scholars similarly dismissing Pippin's defense of naïve reading as, well, naïve.

The problem with this kind of mutual accusation across the borders between so-called professional and amateur readers, however, is that its concerns with a specific form of critical vocabulary distract us from larger ethical questions. Scholars are right to be wary of the particular mode of identification promoted by Oprah's Book Club, but not simply because of the appeal to identification *tout court*; rather, the *kind* of engagement with characters and situations espoused by the book club is too often grounded in sympathy rather than empathy, resulting in a romantic, narcissistic notion of identification predicated on the obliteration of difference and working toward the ultimate goal of producing self-acceptance. As Alison Landsberg has argued,

> Sympathy, a feeling that arises out of simple identification, often takes the form of wallowing in someone else's pain. Although it presumes sameness between the sympathizer and her object, whether or not there is actually a "sameness" between them, an actual shared experience, matters little, for in the act of sympathizing, one projects one's own feelings onto another. This act can be imperializing and colonizing, taking over, rather than making space for, the other person's feelings. (Landsberg 149)

This is a mode of reading that desires what contemporary students increasingly refer to as a "relatable" text, one that can be simply incorporated into one's worldview without requiring a change in response. Empathy, by contrast with sympathy, can be a painful process, one that should not "be conflated with an incorporation of the other into one's own (narcissistic) self or understood instrumentally as a means of discovering one's own 'authentic' identity. On the contrary, it induces one to recognize one's internal alterity or difference from oneself. . . . It is not a facile passe-partout but an affect crucial for a possible ethical relation to the other and hence for one's responsibility or answerability"

(LaCapra 76–7). Where Oprah's Book Club falls short is in this tendency to promote personal growth rather than more complex modes of ethical engagement with the world.

This kind of ethical engagement with a text—a mode of engagement that encourages a critical awareness of the unresolvable alterity of self and Other, an understanding, rather than an erasure, of difference —can be a hallmark of academic modes of reading, but only where those modes of reading open themselves to permit a thorough consideration of affect and of the role that complex forms of identification might play in reading. As I've explored elsewhere, one key value shared by a wide variety of scholarly modes of reading has to do with their ability to make what seems to be obvious instead appear strange, to require the reader to step back from something that seems familiar and look at it from a new angle. The point of this kind of theorizing is less to get the reader to think in some particular different way about the object than it is to get her to think differently about *her own perspective* with respect to that object.[7] The value of literary theory has been in helping scholars and students tease out not *how to read*, but rather how they *do* read, how a lifetime of encounters with particular kinds of representations guides us in understanding future texts. And, not incidentally, in helping us think about other potential readings and what they might reveal about the default positions of our culture, and in translating our engagements with texts into engagements with the world. For these reasons, literary scholars should of course resist an unquestioning embrace of naïve, untheorized reading, but at the same time, we must also resist automatic dismissals of popular modes of reading. As Wallace himself noted in *This Is Water*, "the fact is that, in the day-to-day trenches of adult existence, banal platitudes can have a life-or-death importance" (9). Respecting the potential importance of what might appear mere platitude to us must become part of our scholarly ethics; our own empathic engagements with the ways that popular readers read require that we think carefully about the uses they make of the texts they encounter and the ways that we might better connect our readings to theirs.

Certainly Oprah's Book Club, existing as part of the show's larger focus on often treacly notions of personal redemption and the overcoming of obstacles — a focus that, let it be said, sells — has a deep investment in cultivating a form of reading that privileges romantic, and even narcissistic, forms of imaginative identification, in encouraging its audience to understand the narratives of others as object lessons for themselves. But for all its questionable motives and uncritical practices, Oprah's Book Club was in a key regard an unmitigated triumph: it got people to buy books, and to read them, and to care deeply about them. And there is perhaps a question to be raised, given that many of the participants in Oprah's Book Club found themselves caring about books for the first time in their lives, about whether the mode of sympathy that Oprah's readings of these novels elicit might be a step along the way toward developing the more critically aware mode of empathy. For this reason, the form of identification promoted by the book club should not be dismissed as mere bad faith. Moreover, in the deep concern for the books they read, and in the ways they put those books to use in their everyday lives, the readers who participated in Oprah's Book Club are not so far removed from David Foster Wallace's readers, many of whom feel a connection to the work that fruitfully combines aesthetic appreciation, cultural critique, and emotional engagement. *Infinite Jest* in particular has drawn readers in not just due to the intricate puzzles posed by its narrative structure or its trenchant observations about the state of the contemporary world but also due to its willingness to treat some of the most painful aspects of contemporary life — loneliness, isolation, depression, addiction — with respect and concern.

When it became evident after his death that Wallace had spent much of his own life battling depression, and that this depression had led to his suicide, many of his readers felt the loss in surprisingly personal ways. Wallace had explored throughout his work the connection between "angst about death, the recognition that I'm going to die, and die very much alone, and the rest of the world is going to go merrily on without me" (McCaffery 136) and contemporary fears of loneliness, of being trapped in a self that is unable to form genuine connections with another. For many readers, discovering that Wallace, who had helped them understand and overcome the pain produced by their loneliness and isolation via the imaginative identifications he had fostered within them, seemed to have been lost to the very pain that he had helped them through — unable or unwilling to communicate what he was suffering — was an irony of a most acute sort.

Many of these readers tried to soothe that hurt by rereading the texts they cared about, returning to the Wallace who was still working through his own pain and who was helping them do so as well. They also reached out to share those texts with one another, as a means of forging connections in the face of this loss. Evidence of this desire to work through a shared sense of grief by talking about Wallace's writing — the fiction and the nonfiction alike — can be seen in many articles, memorials, blog posts, and the like dating from the months after his death, but perhaps no example has been more fruitful than *Infinite Summer.*

Seattle blogger Matthew Baldwin launched *Infinite Summer* on 1 June 2009, a project he'd conceived earlier that spring as a means of supporting his own plan to read *Infinite Jest*, which he'd owned for some years but had never managed to finish.[8] By setting a disciplined reading schedule (seventy-five pages per week between 21 June and 22 September), by recruiting friends and fellow bloggers to read along with him, and by creating a public forum within which their collective reading process would be shared, both with one another and with anyone else who happened upon the blog, Baldwin hoped that he and other determined readers would be able to make it through what otherwise appeared to be an overwhelming reading task. Baldwin announced the project on infinitesummer.org on 1 June, immediately inviting participation: "You've been meaning to do it for over a decade. Now join endurance bibliophiles from around the web as we tackle and comment upon David Foster Wallace's masterwork over the summer of 2009" ("The List"). He introduced himself and his fellow guides two days later: "Four writers who have never before read *Infinite Jest* will do so for the duration of Infinite Summer. And each will be posting here weekly, not only to report on their thoughts and progress, but also to promote and facilitate discussion" ("The Guides").

Baldwin expected the usual uphill climb in recruiting busy people to take on this project. As he noted in his concluding post on the site, he'd initially created a lengthy list of folks to approach, hoping to persuade three to join *Infinite Summer* as guides, but to his surprise, "the first three people I asked accepted" (Acknowledgments). In fact, the project took off in ways that might appear unexpected: other bloggers wrote about *Infinite Summer*, leading their readers to the project; the first few days after the project's launch saw posts on Ezra Klein's blog at the *Washington Post*, *Entertainment Weekly*'s *PopWatch* blog, the *Guardian*'s *Books Blog* (Flood), and *Discover* magazine's *Cosmic Variance* (Carroll), as well as on a wide range of personal blogs such as the *Daily Splash* and *harikari.com* ("Read . . . this Summer"). These highly visible authors adopted the project, as did their readers, drawn to the idea of taking on a novel many of them had been putting off but doing so with support from a larger group of readers. When Margaret Lyons asked on *PopWatch*, "Am I alone on [sic] liking this sort of communal reading experience that's not quite a book club so I don't have to make small talk?," the answer was apparently a resounding "no."

The spread of this reading network bears that answer out. As Baldwin noted in his 4 June post, "The Community," by that date the *Infinite Summer* group on Facebook had nearly 2,000 members, #infsum had become an active hashtag on Twitter, an *Infinite Summer* community had been created on LiveJournal, as had an *Infinite Summer* group on Shelfari and an *Infinite Summer* page on Goodreads. And the eighty-two comments that follow Baldwin's post are a chorus of "I'm in," a growing manifestation of the connections that the project inspired. Through dozens of posts at *Infinite Summer* and perhaps hundreds more linked posts elsewhere, written by individual bloggers all commonly engaged in the project of reading and writing together, something that begins to resemble a community formed.

Infinite Summer has many precursors, of course, not only in the offline world of book clubs and other forms of reading groups but also in the many online group readings that have been held of *Gravity's Rainbow*, for instance, on the pynchon-l listserv, and of course of *Infinite Jest* itself on the wallace-l list. But there are some key differences between these e-mail based discussions and *Infinite Summer*, some of which have to do with the affordances of the blog form itself. The blog contains and makes accessible its own archive, allowing the gradual growth of a community, as latecomers are able to catch up on what they've missed with ease. By contrast, the communication on listservs is ordinarily archived, and those archives are usually searchable, but they're not generally published in a way that makes them conducive to "catching up." Moreover, though both the listserv and the blog facilitate discussion within a community, the individual voice can at times be lost in the e-mail chatter; the blog, by contrast, highlights the individual voice within its community. Blog posts, as I've argued elsewhere, are an authorial medium in a way that e-mail messages and discussion board postings often conceal.[9] As a result, a group blog such as *Infinite Summer* both highlights those individual voices and puts them in conversation with one another.

The writerly nature of the blog was particularly important for many of the participants in *Infinite Summer*, who used reading and discussing *Infinite Jest* as a pretext for their own writing, about their lives, their thoughts, their struggles. One pseudonymous participant, for instance, published a guest post on the site about a month into the project, beginning "My name is infinitedetox and I am an addict" (Infinitedetox, "Waving"). The author then told the story of a relationship with "pharmaceutical opiates" that quickly trended from "an experiment" to "a recreation" to clear "dependency," a relationship that a first encounter with *Infinite Jest* helped to change:

> Somehow the book — and now brace yourself for one of those clichés that Wallace seems so interested in in *IJ* — *made me want to be a better person.* And it inspired me to stop taking drugs immediately, to Kick the Bird, via a mechanism which I've had a hard time articulating. But let me give it a stab anyway. (Infinitedetox, "Waving")

Infinitedetox then goes on to connect the kind of self-surrender that Wallace suggests makes twelve-step programs like Alcoholics Anonymous work to that required of the reader of a big novel such as *Infinite Jest.* This mode of self-surrender is not a passive submission but an active engagement of reader with the text's perspective, a giving over of the self to the preoccupations of another mind. This kind of reading-assurrender requires the reader not simply to take the text in, Infinitedetox suggests, but to care about its concerns as much as its author did, thus laying the groundwork for an empathic engagement with the text.

> You can probably see where I'm going with this. What happened to me, on December 26, 2008, is that I surrendered myself completely to *Infinite Jest*. I signed some sort of metaphorical blood-oath committing myself to looking at the world through David Foster Wallace's eyes. And what happened then was that I saw myself as DFW would have seen me, refracted through the wobbly nystagmic lens of *Infinite Jest*. Wallace's judgments on addicts and addictions fell upon me with great force, and something about the ferocity of his critique, coupled with his profound compassion and humaneness toward the subject, compelled me to waste absolutely zero time in booting the pills and Getting My Shit Together. (Infinitedetox, "Waving")

Perhaps unsurprisingly, *Infinite Jest* as a cure for actual opiate addiction only holds for a little while; in enacting such a literal form of self-surrender, Infinitedetox gives the impression of having mistaken a text about the struggle with addiction for the struggle itself. This failure to recognize the power of transference in engaging with the novel's perspective seems to have produced a certain naïveté about the novel's power.[10] *Infinite Summer*, however, provided Infinitedetox with both the impetus for a return to the novel and its perspective, as well as a venue for the kind of safe, anonymous sharing that AA inspires. In addition to this guest post on *Infinite Summer*, Infinitedetox also maintained an individual blog detailing both the reading and the recovery processes. Many other participants in the group blog's comments sections similarly posted on their own blogs, and read and commented on one another's entries. All of this new work reveals the degree to which the desire among the readers was not simply to spend a summer working through the novel itself, though that was the starting point for their interactions; they were also driven to work through the text in a way that was productive of more new writing.

But the writing that was produced on and around *Infinite Summer* wasn't just shouting into the void, and it wasn't just the kinds of self-absorbed rambling critics often associate with personal blogs. The public, open nature of the group and the kinds of sharing that it produced reveal the degree to which AA, blogs, and *Infinite Jest* all present an opportunity to build empathic relations with others, transforming self-expression into a generous mode of Giving It Away that, like Wallace's novel, creates the possibility of connection for other readers. For many participants, that engagement could only come through the mediating safety of the Internet, where they could discuss their own personal experiences with an openness and honesty not possible in face-to-face interactions. For others, the desire for connection in and around the text led to the development of in-person reading groups and meetups, and culminated in a number of events marking the conclusion of *Infinite Summer*, held at bookstores and libraries around the country.

That all of this energy was being poured into reading and discussing a novel — and an extremely difficult one at that — seems highly unusual in such a hypermediated age. We've all of course heard it said with quite convincing authority that no one reads novels anymore, and certainly that literary fiction is a form in decline. The National Endowment for the Arts famously warned the country about the devastating prognosis for literary fiction in their recent reports, *Reading at Risk* (2004) and *To Read or Not to Read* (2007), indicating that rates of leisure-oriented reading of poetry and fiction were dropping in every demographic group surveyed. It's a head-scratcher: the conventional wisdom insists that people aren't supposed to be reading books, and yet here were hundreds of them spending their summer reading an exceptionally difficult one.[11]

Moreover, the Internet is frequently imagined to be one of the causes of reading's decline, a key factor in so diminishing our attention spans that we can no longer sustain ourselves through the long-form narrative, and yet here is a reading group inspired and sustained by its Internet context. Clearly, as in the case of Oprah's Book Club, the relationship between the newer medium and the more traditional form of the novel is more complex than we've acknowledged. And as in Oprah's Book Club, one of the successes of *Infinite Summer* lies in its savvy connection of the right text with the right readers — readers seeking a gamelike challenge in the novel's narrative structure, readers critical of the direction of contemporary culture, readers turning to a book for solace in the wake of grief, readers open to the possibilities of empathic connection mediated through the book's perspective. Beyond connecting the right text with the right readers, however, *Infinite Summer* succeeded by connecting the right readers with one another.

All of this reflects what might now be seen to be a profound misunderstanding in *Infinite Jest* of the future development of mediation. The novel, perhaps needless to say, explores that future from its own vantage point in the early to mid 1990s, a point when the Internet was only beginning to break into the popular consciousness. That Internet of course was strikingly different from the network of networks with which we now engage. Though the novel was being completed contemporaneously with the earliest of what we now think of as blogs, which began to appear in 1994, the term "weblog" was used for the first time in late 1997; Wikipedia was launched five years after *Infinite Jest*, in 2001; Facebook appeared eight years after the novel's publication, in 2004; YouTube emerged the following year, in 2005. Given the influence that these projects have had not just on how the Internet has developed but on our very conceptions of how it operates, it's not terribly surprising that *Infinite Jest* imagined a very different networked future, one that would take much the same course as the then-dominant medium, television.

Infinite Jest was prescient in understanding that some form of convergence between the computer and television was in the offing, and in foreseeing that more and more of the entertainment we consume would be delivered on demand through the network to which this hybrid device would be connected. But the novel did not have the opportunity to fully consider the radically different technical possibilities and affordances of the computer and the television, or of the networks that tie them together. The television is by design only a receiver of signals; without the addition of video recording devices, it cannot produce new programs, and even with those devices, it cannot publish what it produces. Accordingly, the network that the television is connected to is a centralized, unidirectional, one-to-many broadcast network; signals come in, but they don't go out. The teleputer of *Infinite Jest* similarly receives signals from a centralized agency through a one-way network; it is capable of generating some signals of its own, but those seem limited to the ability to request more information or entertainment.

The computer, by contrast, is at its core a read/write device, and the Internet is a distributed, multidirectional, many-to-many network. These technological differences have given rise to a profound shift in the function of mediation over the last ten years, a shift that *Infinite Jest* was simply too early to be able to recognize: the social connections produced in a media environment governed by a logic of many-to-many networks, rather than one of one-to-many broadcast or one-to-one cartridge distribution, can produce precisely the kinds of human relationship, the kinds of conversation, that Wallace's vision of the novel meant to foster.[12]

Those human interconnections, as we see in the case of Infinite detox, are bound up in the need to understand something about one's life by engaging with the stories told by others. The impulse toward identification can, as we have seen, be grounded in a narcissistic or even imperialistic assumption of identity between the self and the story-telling Other, but it can also lay the groundwork for a more critical, empathic recognition of the irresolvable difference between self and Other. While the novel, as Wallace suggests, fosters a kind of imaginative identification in the reader, the Internet, by virtue of its two-way channels, which lend themselves to mutual communication *with actual human beings* rather than fictional characters, has the potential to produce modes of identification that exceed merely "relating" to another's story, instead becoming part of a deeply ethical process of grappling with the very otherness of the Other. The tension produced by such ethical engagement — the simultaneous necessity and impossibility of achieving some kind of mutual comprehension[13]— was one of Wallace's concerns throughout his career, surfacing in numerous aspects of his writing from *The Broom of the System* forward, but it's given the most focus, perhaps for obvious reasons, in the AA sections of *Infinite Jest*. Ennet House residents, for instance, are encouraged to sit close to the speakers at meetings in order to "try to Identify instead of Compare,"

INFINITE SUMMER | KATHLEEN FITZPATRICK

with "Identify" immediately glossed as "empathize" (345). This gloss, as it plays out through the AA scenes, makes clear that the mode of identification here being promoted is not merely aimed at understanding one's own situation, or simply relating to the situation another is in, but is instead part of a necessary, and necessarily painful, process of opening oneself to the utterly unimaginable situation of another by genuinely *listening* to what they share.

It is perhaps not accidental, then, that Maurice Blanchot describes the basis for ethical community, the obligation that we owe one another, as "an infinite attention to the other" (quoted in Readings 161). Nor is it accidental that this formulation becomes the seed for Bill Readings's reconception of teaching and learning "as sites of *obligation*, as loci of *ethical practices*" (154), in which our primary obligation is to listen: "The other speaks, and we owe the other respect. To be hailed as an addressee is to be commanded to listen, and the ethical nature of this relation cannot be justified. We have to listen, without knowing why, before we know what it is that we are to listen to" (162). In each of these visions, our membership in a voluntary community and our participation in the processes of education, as either teachers or students, require us not to focus on our own stories but instead to grapple with our exposure to the stories that others tell us.

Processes of social reading, moreover, require us to engage not just with the stories of others but with others' *interpretations* of those stories. Striphas suggests that the success of Oprah's Book Club lay not simply in its ability to create a "talking life" for books themselves but instead in the program's "remarkable willingness to listen" (138) to what its participants have to say about their reading processes. In this sense, the "ethic of active listening" espoused by Oprah's Book Club "underscores the degree to which people's everyday lives and their actual concerns form a creative basis for the book club's ways of operating" (Striphas 139). Despite its commercial determination, the book club thus becomes, in its concern not simply with getting people to read but also with helping them to discover through discussion the potential that reading holds for their whole lives, a site that reveals the profound interconnections among narrative, education, and ethical community. This is not intended to suggest that we overlook the shortcomings of Oprah's Book Club: as did the rest of the program, the book club's tendency to fall back onto individualistic, narcissistic notions of self-improvement tended to produce readings that relied on sympathy rather than empathy, on a mode of relating to narratives that confirmed rather than expanded readers' worldviews. It is, however, to suggest that this mode of reading may be a crucial first step along the path toward more complex, diverse, critically engaged reading communities.

As Kuisma Korhonen points out, literature has always created communities, some of which have been voluntary and ethical, and others of which have fostered exclusions and violence: "We need communities, textual and non-textual, in order to love and stay alive. But the need for protection also harbors the fear of the other within it" (Korhonen). Communities that are built around literary texts, however, "create a challenge for all homogenized communities" (Korhonen), as their texts escape their initial contexts and are read by groups that cannot be homogenized, whose differences remain visible and important:

> The unstable character of institutionalized textual communities can be seen as an indicator revealing the existence of an invisible textual community, perhaps the most radical community of all: those who do not know each other, who are not reading for any clearly determined purpose, who open themselves to the otherness of literary texts beyond all socially shared conventions of reading and interpretation. (Korhonen)

Korhonen means us to understand the "community of solitary readers" to be that most radical invisible textual community, but the experience of *Infinite Summer* suggests that connecting those solitary readers through the Internet's social networks has the potential, if obviously not the certainty, of producing bonds among them that amplify their openness, not just to the otherness of the text but also to the otherness of one another's readings of those texts.

While television, then, is critiqued, justly or unjustly, for pretending to soothe our need for human contact while instead exacerbating our loneliness, networked culture has the potential to help those who participate in it forge real human connections, if at a distance. There are of course all sorts of negative examples of networked interactions to be found and all sorts of cautions against overidealizing online social networks to be raised. As my epigraph from Alison Landsberg reminds me, what I am describing here is a "utopian dream," in which ethics and social engagement converge. If we seek to create spaces for ethical engagement, for public manifestations of empathy as the foundation of social and intellectual life, we must not overlook the examples that can be found in some online communities. That so much of this form of engagement is produced in the very act of reading and writing together as a group is not incidental; reading in the social network presents the potential to transform widely dispersed individuals into a community, by giving them the opportunity to share their thoughts, to listen to one another, and to be listened to. These networked experiences of reading, of entering into a discussion that is not just between author and reader but among readers, can help those readers not just to feel "less alone inside" but in fact to *be* less alone in the world as well.[14]

The question remains, of course, whether *Infinite Summer* is an extensible model for social reading in the network age or whether it was an isolated instance. A core group of the participants in *Infinite Summer* conducted a group reading and discussion of Bram Stoker's *Dracula* in October 2009, but the discussion thinned out fairly quickly, and even Matthew Baldwin noted that despite "diligently keeping up with the *Infinite Jest* reading schedule for three months straight, *Dracula* somehow got the better of me" ("Nobody"), forcing him to struggle to keep going. After *Dracula*, the group decided to take on Roberto Bolaño's mammoth *2666*; that reading, which took place on its own dedicated site, gained a bit less attention, but a number of the *Infinite Summer* readers participated, and those who read along rave about the experience. Moreover, the blog *Infinite Zombies*, spun off from the *Infinite Summer* project, has since led group readings of *Moby-Dick* and *Ulysses*, and as of November 2010 is proposing a reading of *Gravity's Rainbow*.[15] While there is thus reason to suggest that the scale of *Infinite Summer* was so thoroughly determined by the specifics of its situation — the particular connections of *this* text with *these* readers; the emotional circumstances of its author's death; the Internet savvy of the project's organizer — that it could not be repeated, there is equal evidence that such social reading projects are growing online.

Moreover, social networks that are built around books and reading are flourishing: LibraryThing boasts "a community of 1,000,000 book lovers" and the ability to make connections among them ("Library-Thing"); Goodreads claims that "more than 4,200,000 members . . . have added more than 110,000,000 books to their shelves" and that the site helps them to "recommend books, compare what they are reading, keep track of what they've read and would like to read, form book clubs and much more" ("About Goodreads"). While *Infinite Summer* may have been an outlier phenomenon, there's certainly reason to believe that a desire exists for community in and through reading.

THOUGH I HAVE focused here on a mode of reading and discussion primarily engaged in by book clubs and online communities — and thus a mode of reading too often dismissed as unsophisticated or naïve by scholars — there is much for scholars to learn from these modes of engagement. There's a vital importance for our work in developing a genuine — even *empathic* — understanding of the ways that popular readers read, and why. As we learned from Janice Radway, and relearned from Ted Striphas, there is crucial work to be done in exploring how a book connects with its readers, why those readers form an affective relationship with that book, and how those readers connect with one another through the medium of the book. Exploring how these connections are formed and what readers draw from them is crucial to the future of literary culture, particularly as literature itself increasingly becomes part of the mediated world from which it historically held itself apart.[16] There is also work for scholars in thinking about our contributions to this culture — what a literary education adds to readers' experiences of texts and engagements with one another.

There are encouraging signs in projects like *Infinite Summer* that the conventional wisdom of recent years may be wrong: television and the Internet do not seem to be driving reading into obsolescence. But they are undoubtedly changing what and how we read, and perhaps even why. Understanding those changes — and understanding that, as Kor-honen indicates, the "literary community" extends far beyond the "spa-tially and temporally determined group of authors, readers, translators, editors, publishers, booksellers, critics, [and] students" with which we have conventionally associated the term — presents a profound ethical imperative for the future of literary studies. Given that this mode of open reading and discussion can and will go on without us, we schol-ars ignore those possibilities — holding ourselves at precisely the kind of safe distance from the Other that Wallace's novel insists we must overcome — at our own risk.[17]

Notes

1. This is obviously an oversimplification of both positions; see Fitzpatrick, *The Anxiety of Obsolescence*, for a more nuanced argument.

2. I make this argument in opposition to McLaughlin, who understands Wallace to be suggesting that television is "both the biggest challenge to seri-ous fiction's relevance in today's society and the cause of contemporary Ameri-cans' isolation and loneliness" (63).

3. The result of this tangling, and the reason for my determination to un-tangle these relationships in my writing, is that "Wallace" has become in some sense an imagined figure for me, the author as known solely through his tex-tual traces, a figure quite separate from David, who was my colleague. Any-thing I write in this essay about "Wallace" should be understood as referring to that author function, and not to the actual human being I knew.

4. See Dettmar 129–38 for a far more nuanced reading of Cobain's suicide and the complex responses it provoked.

5. See Katha Pollitt: "We have different expectations of male and female writers; we put them in different categories and different frames — and Great American Novelist is a frame that is coded male."

6. Wallace in this interview misjudges the television audience's desire for pleasure; while it's undoubtedly true that some television programming has historically fed a very unchallenging sense of pleasure, not all of it has catered to the "couch potato," not even in the early 1990s. In fact, that much of the audience craves the more challenging pleasures of a text that requires interpre-tive work might account for the success of recent, post-*Sopranos* HBO series, as well as of complex network series such as *Lost*. What undoubtedly is true is that this more "sophisticated" sense of pleasure is produced in no small part through education; the genius of Oprah's Book Club was in encouraging a

part of its audience that hadn't benefitted from such an education to learn along with others. For his part, Wallace goes on to indicate that the distance between television and fiction may not be all that great, when it comes to giving the people what they want: "TV's real agenda is to be liked, because if you like what you're seeing, you'll stay tuned. TV is completely unabashed about this; it's its sole raison. And sometimes when I look at my own stuff I feel like I absorbed too much of this raison" (McCaffery 130).

7. See Fitzpatrick, "On the Impossibility of Naïve Reading."

8. As he told reporter James Cowan, he'd read the first 120 pages on a flight six years before, and then didn't pick the book up again: "'Once I wasn't on an eight-hour plane flight with nothing to do but devote myself to the book, it just seemed like a monumental thing to go through,' said Baldwin, a freelance writer who lives outside Seattle, Washington. 'I didn't revisit it, but at the back of my mind, I always wanted to read it, because I enjoyed what I had read'" (Cowan). Moreover, as he noted in his first "guide" post, "In addition to *Infinite Jest*, here is a list of other David Foster Wallace works that I have somehow failed to read: all of them. Or at least that was the case two month [sic] ago, when I first envisioned this crazy event" ("Mountaineering").

9. See Fitzpatrick, "The Pleasure of the Blog."

10. In fact, as George Carr reminds me, the ultimate lesson of *Infinite Jest* may well be that the kind of commitment to the text that Infinitedetox embraces is a trap; the novel's final injunction to the reader is, as Carr says, "to put down the book and go live your life." In this sense, moving beyond an individualized, transferential relationship to the novel toward the kinds of social engagements produced by *Infinite Summer* may provide a necessary step in that direction.

11. Obviously the singular case of *Infinite Summer* does not give the lie to the NEA's studies all by itself, but it's a useful example of the kinds of phenomena these reports missed in the narrowness with which they defined "reading" (the consumption of book-length printed and bound fiction and poetry solely for pleasure) and in their failure to explore the increase in writing that these studies uncovered. The little hyped follow-up report, *Reading on the Rise* (2009), takes a more expansive view of reading in the contemporary moment, and accordingly presents a much more optimistic portrait of the role of literary reading today.

12. Wallace's annotated copy of George Gilder's 1990 *Life After Television* makes clear that he was thinking about the relationship between television and what Gilder refers to as the "telecomputer, a personal computer adapted for video processing and connected by fiber-optic threads to other telecomputers all around the world" (17). Wallace's marginalia indicate that he recognized

the individualized potential of the computer network, but he nonetheless seems to have missed the implications its many-to-many architecture presents for online community; written in the margin next to Gilder's description of the potential for niche-based programming is the note, "So where is community? Everyone stays home, everyone does his own thing" (35). Many thanks to Molly Schwartzburg of the Harry Ransom Center for drawing my attention to this annotation.

13. Enormous thanks to Jim Brown for helping me clarify this point.

14. As Jason Mittell notes, the ultimate irony might be that television, with its scheduled, serialized dissemination strategies, has proven in certain ways more conducive to creating these sorts of reading communities. It's perhaps in that sense important that *Infinite Summer*'s 75-pages-per-week schedule resembled television's timed-release mechanism, giving the community new fodder for discussion at regular intervals.

15. Interestingly, Daryl Houston, one of the bloggers from *Infinite Zombies*, draws my attention to some of the tensions and conflicts across different spin-off reading groups participating in *Infinite Summer*; this kind of factionalized subgroup creation might provide a fruitful avenue for further research.

16. On the interpolation of literature into popular culture, see Collins.

17. As a final note, I would like to thank all of the readers who participated in the online review of the draft of this article; some of those readers are cited in this final, published version, but all of them pressed me to rethink my argument in productive ways. Moreover, their open, rigorous engagement with my essay draft indicates the potential that online networked reading experiences might benefit scholarly communities, both in their internal engagements as well as in their encounters with the broader community of readers.

Works Cited

"About Goodreads." *Goodreads*. Web.

Baldwin, Matthew. "Acknowledgements." *Infinite Summer* 26 September 2009. Web.

———. "Mountaineering." *Infinite Summer* 22 June 2009. Web.

———. "Nobody Likes a Freeloader." *Dracula* 16 October 2009. Web.

———. "The Guides." *Infinite Summer* 3 June 2009. Web.

———. "The List." *Infinite Summer* 1 June 2009. Web.

Brown, Jim. "Untitled comment." *Infinite Summer: Reading in the Social Network*. 3 December 2010.

Carr, George. "Untitled comment." *Infinite Summer: Reading in the Social Network*. 3 December 2010.

Carroll, Sean. "Putting the Internet to Infinitely Good Use." *Cosmic Variance, Discover* 3 June 2009. Web.

Collins, Jim. *Bring on the Books for Everybody: How Literary Culture Became Popular Culture.* Durham, NC: Duke University Press, 2010. Print.

Cowan, James. "An interview with Infinite Summer creator Matthew Baldwin." *Afterword, National Post* 22 June 2009. Web.

Dettmar, Kevin J. H. *Is Rock Dead?* New York: Routledge, 2006. Print.

Fitzpatrick, Kathleen. *The Anxiety of Obsolescence: The American Novel in the Age of Television.* Nashville: Vanderbilt University Press, 2006. Print.

———. "On the Impossibility of Naïve Reading." *Planned Obsolescence* 20 October 2010. Web.

———. "The Pleasure of the Blog: The Early Novel, the Serial, and the Narrative Archive." In *Blogtalks Reloaded: Social Software Research and Cases.* Ed. Thomas N. Burg and Jan Schmidt. Vienna, Austria: Auflage, 2007. 167–86. Print.

Flood, Alison. "Who's up for a summer of *Infinite Jest*?" *Books Blog, Guardian* 2 June 2009. Web.

Gilder, George F. *Life After Television.* Knoxville: Whittle Direct Books, 1990. Print. Annotated copy housed as part of the David Foster Wallace library, Harry Ransom Center, University of Texas at Austin.

Houston, Daryl. Untitled comment. *Infinite Summer: Reading in the Social Network* 3 December 2010. Web.

"Infinite Summer." *Daily Splash* 3 June 2009. Web.

Infinitedetox. "Infinite Detox." Web.

———. "Waving the White Flag: Reading as Rehabilitation." *Infinite Summer* 22 July 2009. Web.

Klein, Ezra. "A Supposedly Fun Thing I Plan to Do This Summer." *Voices, Washington Post* 3 June 2009. Web.

Korhonen, Kuisma. "Textual Communities: Nancy, Blanchot, Derrida." *Culture Machine* 8 (2006): n. pag. Web.

LaCapra, Dominick. *History in Transit: Experience, Identity, Critical Theory.* Ithaca, NY: Cornell University Press, 2004. Print.

Landsberg, Alison. *Prosthetic Memory: The Transformation of American Remembrance in the Age of Mass Culture.* New York: Columbia University Press, 2004. Print.

"LibraryThing." Web.

Lyons, Margaret. "To 'Infinite' . . . and beyond!" *PopWatch, Entertainment Weekly* 1 June 2009. Web.

McCaffery, Larry. "An Interview with David Foster Wallace." *Review of Contemporary Fiction* 13.2 (Summer 1993): 127–50. Print.

McLaughlin, Robert L. "Post-Postmodern Discontent: Contemporary Fiction and the Social World." *Symploke* 12.1/2 (2004): 53–68. Print.

Mittell, Jason. "Untitled comment." *Infinite Summer: Reading in the Social Network* 4 December 2010. Web.

National Endowment for the Arts. *Reading at Risk: A Survey of Literary Reading in America.* National Endowment for the Arts, 2004. Web.

———. *Reading on the Rise: A New Chapter In American Literacy.* National Endowment for the Arts, 2009. Web.

———. *To Read or Not to Read: A Question of National Consequence.* National Endowment for the Arts, 2007. Web.

Pippin, Robert. "In Defense of Naïve Reading." *Opinionator, New York Times* 10 October 2010. Web.

Pollitt, Katha. "Franzenfreude, Continued." *Nation* 15 September 2010. Web.

Radway, Janice A. *Reading the Romance: Women, Patriarchy, and Popular Literature.* Chapel Hill: University of North Carolina Press, 1984. Print.

"Read David Foster Wallace's *Infinite Jest* this Summer." *harikari.com* 10 June 2009. Web.

Readings, Bill. *The University in Ruins.* Cambridge, MA: Harvard University Press, 1996. Print.

Stelter, Brian. "Oprah Calls and Reflects on 25 Years." *Media Decoder, New York Times* 24 May 2011. Web.

Striphas, Ted. *The Late Age of Print: Everyday Book Culture from Consumerism to Control.* New York: Columbia University Press, 2009. Print.

Wallace, David Foster. "E Unibus Pluram: Television and U.S. Fiction." *Review of Contemporary Fiction* 13.2 (1993): 151–94. Print.

———. *Infinite Jest.* Boston: Little, Brown, 1996. Print.

———. *This Is Water: Some Thoughts, Delivered on a Significant Occasion, about Living a Compassionate Life.* New York: Little, Brown, 2009. Print.

MICHAEL PIETSCH

EDITING WALLACE:

AN INTERVIEW WITH MICHAEL PIETSCH

BY RICK MOODY

I first met Michael Pietsch when he was working at Harmony Books, a division of Crown Publishing Group. It was about 1990, and I was a junior editor at a rival publisher. Michael already had a reputation (about which he is too modest below) as someone with genuinely interesting taste in fiction. He liked rock and roll books, and he liked fiction that other publishers found too risky. He was blond and incredibly enthusiastic, and he looked ten years younger than he was. Pietsch grew up in the South, in a military family, and attended Harvard, and started work in publishing not long after. But he didn't (doesn't) exude business. He's the kind of guy you'd expect to give you a lecture about various iterations of the Modern Lovers, or on why the Telecaster was superior to other Fender Products. When I needed a publisher, after the indie publication of my first novel, he was at the top of my list. By then, Michael had made the jump to Little, Brown. David Foster Wallace, the subject of these ruminations, left W. W. Norton for Little, Brown in 1992 (about the same time I did) and was published by Michael, excepting Everything and More: A Compact History of ∞, *thereafter. In 2001, Michael became publisher of Little, Brown, itself a now very successful division of the Hachette Book Group. This exchange took place by e-mail from late October until early December 2008.*
—Rick Moody

Q: When did you first become aware of David Wallace's work? And what was your experience of it?

A: The first piece of David's that I read was the story "Lyndon" in *Arrivals* magazine. Someone must have told me to check it out, it's not a magazine that I read regularly. Probably it was his agent, Bonnie Nadell, who had advised me that this was a writer I should pay attention to.

What I remember is being stunned by its audacity. In the story's final scene, LBJ's not-very-secretly-gay amanuensis finds his missing partner sharing a deathbed with LBJ, dying of AIDS before AIDS had a name. How did we get here? It started as a story that made use of real history and real public figures — sketching a completely believable LBJ as boss and philosopher — and turned into a wild meditation on compassion and love. I felt like I'd been knocked off my horse completely.

Other writers had used public figures in fiction but this felt like a different order of magnitude, so wildly weird and full of intimacy and tenderness. Even though it was political it didn't feel didactic.

Q: When was that? Before The Broom of the System *or between there and* Girl With Curious Hair? *Was it* Girl *that moved you to want to work with David?*

A: This was late 1987, after *Broom of the System* had been published (January '87) and before *Girl with Curious Hair.*

It was the stories that bowled me over. Bonnie invited me to have dinner with David when he was in New York at some point that fall, and I read *The Broom of the System* before meeting him. We ate Mexican food and I drank a beer, not knowing what an issue substances were for him at the time. I'd read *Broom* in preparation for the meeting and told him how knocked out I was by his ability to write in a woman's voice. Also that I didn't think I'd have been able to sign the book up and I respected Gerry Howard for having done so.

David told me later that he'd always remembered a conversation we had at dinner about smoking. I said I'd quit because I'd noticed that just about every time I got deep into some piece of work I would reward myself with a cigarette, which completely vaporized my focus.

I felt honored later that Bonnie showed me the story "Westward the Course of Empire Makes Its Way." She and David and Gerry were debating whether to include it in the collection. I learned later that I was the representative numbnuts since I'd never read John Barth's *Lost in the Funhouse* and didn't have a clue that the story was based on that novel. I loved the story even not knowing its origins so maybe I helped it make its way into the book.

Q: Can you talk a little bit about some of the other fiction writers you were interested in at that time? I'm wondering if it's possible to see David as having some context in terms of other things you were doing, like Mark Leyner and Stephen Wright.

A: My early correspondence with David is all about writers I was reading and editing. The first books I sent him were Stephen Wright's *Meditations in Green* and Mark Leyner's *My Cousin, My Gastroenterologist*, which he said blew his footwear off. He gave a lovely quote to that book, comparing Leyner to Acker/Burroughs/Coover. Later he said that he admired Stephen Wright's *M31* but had a reflexive distaste as an Illinois boy for anything that seemed to mock Midwestern life.

He claimed to have loved Chuck Berry's memoir and given it to various folks at Syracuse. I got him a copy of Brian Eno's UK-published *More Dark Than Shark* after he mentioned that he liked listening to Eno's atmospheric music while writing. I didn't have a lot of accomplished fiction on my list but I think he responded to the adventurousness of what little I'd taken on and to my advocacy of those writers.

Q: So you come into the story, in terms of active participation, at Infinite Jest. *How did you come to acquire that book? What did you see of it at first? And how did you manage to get Little, Brown to go along for the ride?*

A: My first letter to David is dated September 87. In April 92 I received around 150 pages of *Infinite Jest*, the opening section. Do you remember reading that raucous, wildly detailed, brilliant and convoluted opening? It was smarter, funnier, and more adventurous than any manuscript pages I'd ever held in my hands. The transvestite breakdown on the subway, the kid in the doctor's office. The Year of the Depend Adult Undergarment — I'm crying again as I write this — The Lung. Young Hal with his little brass one-hitter. Gately, Troelsch, Schacht. The names! Erdedy, Wardine, Madame Psychosis.

I just reread my memo to the publishing board, in which I did everything I could to sound restrained and mature while mentioning that "the young people in the office"— ha! — were wild about it.

"The option publisher's offer has been declined and we now have Wallace's second novel exclusively. Samples from the draft partial manuscript are attached. . . ."

"He's a young visionary with a huge future . . . He's one of the most talented young writers around, and it would make a good statement about Little, Brown, that in addition to publishing the established generation of literary grandmasters like Pynchon, Barth, and Fowles, we're developing the next generation." I attached excerpts from reviews and a p&l heavy on the paperback sales.

What I remember is that David knew this book was going to be very, very long, and he wanted to work with someone whose suggestions for restraint he would trust. From our letters and conversations he had decided that I could fill those elbow patches.

I didn't get an okay at the publishing board meeting, and remember our editor in chief, Bill Phillips, going into the office of the president, Charlie Hayward, and closing the door. When he came out he gave me the okay for the offer I'd proposed with a little bit of a lecture that this was a lot of money and an extraordinary circumstance. But he'd gone to bat for me and the book and I've always been grateful to him for that.

Q: I do remember reading that opening and being amazed and delighted by it, yes. Very amazed and very delighted. I didn't know you were allowed to be that showoffy about being brilliant. In fact, I didn't know you were allowed to be brilliant at all. So once you had the offer in hand and it had been accepted, how did you proceed with David? How much input did he want initially?

A: He asked for editorial notes about two-thirds through. You can imagine how hard it was to make sense of the pages without having the whole novel in hand. I did my best, protesting that it was impossible to know what the whole story was and therefore what ultimately mattered. But I did my best to give him an accounting of when I found it impossibly confusing or slow or just hard to make sense of what was happening.

He asked me to tell him what I thought the book was about. After talking about the shardlike structure I wrote, "The most important thing these pieces seem to be getting at is Hal's sadness. For me the emotional core of the novel is this smart, funny, talented, frightened young guy who's likeable but at the same time withholds himself from the reader and those around him. I'm hoping that we're going to see lots more of Hal in extremis and that the worlds of ETA and Ennet House will collide as Hal gets farther into his difficulties with giving up dope.

"But of course his story is just part of this huge roiling story about addiction and recovery, their culture and language and characters, the hidden world that's revealed when people come in and tell their stories.

"And it's also about communication within a family, and the ways people try to rewire their lines to the outside world. And about art and entertainment as forms of communication. And about Boston, and adolescence, and tennis.

". . . But it's way way too long. Not just in reading-hours and retail-price ways but in how long it takes before it gets to the point that it takes the reader over."

The biggest challenges I pointed out were how long it took the pieces to begin to make sense as a story, and "how little connection there is between the ornately-bizarre-to-goofy future superstructure — President Gentle, the Great Concavity, giant babies, feral hamsters, radical Canadians — and the stories of Hal and Gately."

Q: How about the footnotes? As I recall it that innovation really first emerged in IJ. Am I remembering properly? That there were none in Girl with Curious Hair? *What did you think of them then, and what did they add to the project? They must have increased the level of editorial difficulty significantly . . .*

A: My recollection about the notes is that I suggested all kinds of in retrospect completely lame and shortsighted ways of dealing with them. Make them available in a separate volume for people who really wanted them. Incorporate as many as possible into the text and cut the rest completely. (I know! Heresy!) At first I was having so much trouble keeping just the main body of the story in my head that this extra layer of complexity felt overwhelming. David made it completely clear that the notes were there to stay and that they should be endnotes, not footnotes, so readers could find it easy to not read them if they didn't want to, and so the main body of the text wouldn't look intimidatingly multilevel and complex. I took a freer hand in suggesting cuts to the footnotes than to the body of the story.

Did I already say what we'd agreed early on? That our job together was to subject every section of the book to the brutal question: can the book live without this? Knowing how much this book would demand of readers, and how easy it would be to put it down or never pick it up simply because of its daunting size, we agreed that many passages should come out, no matter how beautiful, funny, brilliant or fascinating they were of themselves, simply because the novel did not absolutely require them. Given that the notes were almost by definition secondary, I invited a lot of them to leave. Of course to David they were not secondary. They were further evidence of the many separate levels of life and thought we're all carrying on at all times. And he insisted that many of them stay that I thought could well have come out.

Every decision was David's. I made suggestions and recommendations and tried to make the reasons for them as clear as possible. But every change was his. He accepted many cuts — my recollection is around 250 manuscript pages, though in an interview he said he thought it was 400. But he said no to many more. There's a math proof there in one of the footnotes that I said would be understood by only maybe three readers in the world. And he said it was important to him that those three readers saw that the math in the book was real, and that the character actually had the capabilities he said he had. It stayed.

Here are a few of David's responses to some of my requests for cuts. They give a tiny sense of how engaged he was in this process and how much fun it was to work with him:

> *p. 52 — This is one of my personal favorite Swiftian lines in the whole manuscript, which I will cut, you rotter.*
>
> *p. 82 — I cut this and have now come back an hour later and put it back.*
>
> *p. 133 — Poor old FN 33 about the grammar exam is cut. I'll also erase it from the back-up disc so I can't come back in an hour and put it back in (an enduring hazard, I'm finding.)*
>
> *pp. 327–330. Michael, have mercy. Pending an almost Horacianly persuasive rationale on your part, my canines are bared on this one.*
>
> *Pp. 739–748. I've rewritten it — for about the 11ᵗʰ time — for clarity, but I bare teeth all the way back to the 2ⁿᵈ molar on cutting it.*
>
> *p. 785ff — I can give you 5000 words of theoretico-structural arguments for this, but let's spare one another, shall we?*

Q: I'm still wondering if you think the innovation of the notes originated in this book, IJ? *And what do you think the technique netted him, compositionally? Did he ever speak to that with you?*

A: I flipped back through *Broom* and *Girl* and found nary a footnote or endnote. So *IJ* seems like the efflorescence of his weaving second and third and fourth thoughts into a narrative.

We never talked directly that I can recall about his reason for all the notes. They were so clearly a big part of his intent for the book, and they seemed to me to connect with the midsentence ending of *The Broom of the System* — an insistence that standard notions of plot missed the point that so much more was going on in life at every moment that there was never a single resolution to anything. He pointed out somewhere that the apparently central plot question of *IJ* — what became of the deadly entertainment — is answered, insofar as it's answered, in an endnote or a footnote to an endnote. And the real question that is answered at the end of the novel's main thread is whether Gately can survive being hit all at once with all the sadness that he's staved off through years of narcotics use now that he's sober. Like so much of his work it seems directly connected now to David's own death and his decision to stop using antidepressants.

Q: How did David take the overwhelming response to IJ? *Was there a sense immediately that you had published one of the generation-changing books?*

A: I'll have to plow the letters to see if I have evidence of David's response. At the publication party — how abashed he was to have a publication party! — he hid out and lay low. It was his birthday that day too — 36? — and I had the sense that if I mentioned that fact in my toast he would not survive the mortification.

The day M. Kakutani's review ran in the *Times* I wore a sticker reading OUCH! (She'd lambasted the editor, an attack that I still feel reveals a patronizing view of writers which I hope to discuss with her one day.) But aside from that the acclaim was so universal and exuberant it felt like the book was being noticed in a way that provoked public discussions of fiction's role in our times. David told me that he had a "gloat room" where he put all the great reviews and posters and blowups and such that we'd sent him, and that he only let himself go in there once a week or so because letting the praise in was deranging.

Later he asked us not to send reviews at all, just to leave a message if a hideous one ran in a very public place so he could know why people were looking at him with pity.

In a nutshell, yes: it felt as if we'd published a book that mattered, and that would last, and it was one of the great thrills of my working life. In the decade following, the number of editorial assistant candidates who wanted to talk about *IJ* (and *The Ice Storm*, it's true, it was almost always both) gladdened my heart.

Q: I remember hearing about the gloat room at the time and thinking that was an incredibly graceful response. There was an "It Boy" article in the New York Times Magazine, *if I'm recalling it correctly, and after that I remember hearing about the gloat room, probably from you. Just another one of many moments when he seemed like the kind of guy you always hoped would become the voice of the generation: a humble one.*

Okay, let's talk about the work that came after Infinite Jest. *Was* Supposedly Fun Thing *next? Did your editing relationship change as you moved into the next years? And did he talk about upcoming projects, or did he keep the ideas to himself until a given manuscript was delivered?*

A: *Infinite Jest* was the only substantial editing work I did with David. We published two collections of essays (*A Supposedly Fun Thing I'll Never Do Again* and *Consider the Lobster*) and two story collections (*Brief Interviews with Hideous Men* and *Oblivion*). Nearly all the stories and essays had been published previously in magazines and had been edited there. David often restored for the book the full versions of pieces that had had to be trimmed for magazine publication. My work on these collections mostly involved suggesting a sequence, or suggesting which pieces should be included.

David spoke occasionally about the difficulty of writing a novel again. Once he said it was like trying to carry sheets of plywood in a strong wind. In a letter a couple years ago he said he had written 400 pages of which he thought maybe 60 would survive.

In 2006 we mounted a tenth-anniversary celebration for *Infinite Jest*, with events in New York and LA. I asked him to come speak at the New York event and he said he really really didn't want to, that he would come if I asked him, but I should know he was deep into "something long" and that when he pulled himself out of it it was hard to get back in. We held the event without him and I was thrilled to see the Housing Works bookstore absolutely packed with people for whom *IJ* was an important and meaningful book.

I'm feeling very sad these days as grieving fades and I feel David moving further into the past. He was such an enormous vital force, someone whose every visit and communication so many people anticipated with delight. I miss him.

Q: Any last feelings on the work, how it looks now, what kind of impact you imagine it is likely to have among writers in the future?

A: I can only hope, judging by the fervor expressed by writers after his death, that his work will be appreciated more and more.

I keep trying to imagine David's books alone, separate from this tall, goofy, athletic, brilliant, sweet, funny guy I knew. The way I've encountered most of the writing I've read in my life — Chaucer and Shakespeare and Yeats and Faulkner — bodies of work that were complete long before I encountered them. A human being who arrives only through the words he placed in sequence. It is one of the great miracles of life, our ability to apprehend a human spirit through the words they leave behind. And I have to say that the David who we encounter in his words is pretty amazingly close to the David I knew. And when for a moment I manage to imagine myself as a reader opening up a copy of *Infinite Jest* for the first time, the way I opened *V.* or *Soldier's Pay* or *Suttree* or *A Handful of Dust* or *The Canterbury Tales*, I think *Yeah. Wow. Yeah.*

IRA B. NADEL

CONSIDER THE FOOTNOTE

> I felt best physically enwebbed in sharp angles, acute bisections, shaved corners.— David Foster Wallace, "Derivative Sport in Tornado Alley"

DAVID FOSTER WALLACE loved and battled over footnotes. Throughout his writing, he relied on them as metanarratives, employing footnotes for commentary, criticism, cultural history, autobiography, formulas, digressions, bibliographies, and humor. He defended their use as a window for hyperfocused detail and, more conventionally, as a means to substantiate information, confirm research, and ensure accuracy.[1] But they also confirmed and justified his fractured consciousness, offering a visual display of his multiple consciousnesses. Disrupting the surface of his text, motivated by his own constant self-questioning, his footnotes unleashed additional vectors of thought at the same time they corroborated a statement. Wallace's prose, overabundant and lavish, found in footnotes a grounding, frequently through reference, page number, or commentary. But they also allowed for discursive riffs that could not be contained in the primary text.

The footnote for Wallace alternately anchored his statements and allowed him the freedom to further an idea or secondary thought. But at times the form of the footnote itself was inhibiting. "Host," the final essay in *Consider the Lobster*, where arrows and boxes replace superscript numbers, often intruding on the text and obliterating page numbers, is one experiment. The extended footnote 4, in "The Depressed Person" from *Brief Interviews with Hideous Men*, which becomes a competing narrative running eight pages, is another. For Wallace, the footnote was organic and an extension, as well as a critique, of the text beyond the documentation of an idea or fact. It not only confirmed but expanded his statements, functioning as a kind of aggressive knowledge system or episteme.[2]

Wallace's addiction to footnotes extended beyond the page to his personal life: On his arm was a footnoted tattoo.[3] For Wallace, the footnote, with its digressions, repetitions, detail, and wit, became a physical as well as textual trademark. Editors naturally resisted. During the copyediting of *Infinite Jest*, Wallace argued for endnotes as a way of shortening the text. In April 1994, he presented the idea to his editor, Michael Pietsch, adding, "I've become intensely attached to this strategy and will fight w/all 20 claws to preserve it." The endnotes, he believed, made the primary text easier to read, while mimicking "the information-flood and data triage I expct'd [to] be an even bigger part of US life." Allowing the reader to go back and forth in the text would also "mimic some of the story's thematic concerns" (quoted in Max). Pietsch objected, preferring footnotes at the bottom of the page, which readers would find easier to use, but eventually he agreed. The 388 endnotes, however, created an awkward rhythm of reading and referencing throughout the novel. Wallace continued to use footnotes in several of his short stories, such as "Mr. Squishy" in *Oblivion*. But do the footnotes or endnotes function to elaborate or to contain his thought and imagination? Are they forms of digression, information, disruption, political statement, comedy, self-critique? For Wallace, the footnote is the visual expression and confirmation of his nonlinear thinking. Footnotes or endnotes demonstrate the active intellectual and creative energy of Wallace on and off the page while also exhibiting the double consciousness of the text.

One might begin with Wallace's comments on the footnote made on 27 March 1997 in his television interview with Charlie Rose, who asked, in reference to *Infinite Jest*, "What are the footnotes about? Where did it come from? 304 [sic] footnotes?"

Wallace explained that he inserted ninety-six pages of footnotes to "fracture" his writing, to make it more like reality, which he understood to be ruptured. Texts are linear and unified. The addition of endnotes conveys something of the disorienting, nonlinear world. But their number and length (some with extensive mathematical formulas) made them too difficult to appear at the bottom of the page in such a large book. Yet they become addictive for both the reader and writer. The alternative, he explained, would be to jumble the sentences, but obviously you couldn't do that and expect the reader to make sense of the text. The reality he knew was constantly being disrupted; he wanted to convey that through the endnotes of the novel, adding that there were originally many more than the number retained in the finished work. His editor forced him to pare them down to the absolute essential. They may slow the reader down, perhaps drawing him in, perhaps repelling him, but in any case forcing the reader to refocus again and again, to reconsider what might be important and to think more deeply, even when the endnotes seemed inserted solely for amusement.

And sometimes they are just that: amusement. In his well-known 1996 essay originally titled "Shipping Out: On the (Nearly Lethal) Comforts of a Luxury Cruise" and later reprinted as "A Supposedly Fun Thing I'll Never Do Again," he wrote about developing a "lifelong grudge" against the cruise ship's hotel manager. He explained this in a footnote:

> Somewhere he'd gotten the impression that I was an investigative journalist and wouldn't let me see the galley, Bridge, staff decks, *anything*, or interview any of the crew or staff in an on-the-record way, and he wore sunglasses inside, and epaulets, and kept talking on the phone for long stretches of time in Greek when I was in his office after I'd skipped the karaoke semifinals in the Rendez-Vous Lounge to make a special appointment to see him; I wish him ill.[4]

Wallace then expounds on his fascination with sharks, sharing in a subsequent footnote that during the first cruise ship dinner gathering he asked one of the wait staff of the onboard five-star restaurant if they could donate "a spare bucket of *au jus* drippings from supper so I could try chumming for sharks off the back rail of the top deck" (ASF 263).

He quickly second-guesses this odd request and wonders if it may have been "a serious journalistic faux pas," one perhaps so repulsively disturbing to everyone who learned of it that they treated him differently, with the management reflexively barring his access to the ship's behind-the-scenes workings (ASF 262). Of course, despite the author's stated remorse about his subsequent lack of access, his essay doesn't suffer; in fact, the conceit of nautical isolation and his self-reported bumbling anchors the story.

In a 1998 interview, part of which appeared in the *Boston Phoenix*, Wallace revealed more of his ideas on the footnote. To Tom Scocca, who asked the questions, he attempted to be clear:

Q: How hard do you want the reader to have to work?

DFW: You know what? To be honest with you, it's not something that I — I don't really think that way, and I don't think that way because I just don't, I don't want to go down that path of trying to anticipate, like a chess player, every reader's reaction.

The footnotes, the honest thing is, is the footnotes were an intentional, programmatic part of *Infinite Jest*, and they get to be kind of — you get sort of addicted to 'em. And for me, a lot of those pieces [in *A Supposedly Fun Thing*] were written around the time that I was typing and working on *Infinite Jest*, and so it's just, it's a kind of loopy way of thinking, that it seems to me is in some ways mimetic.

I don't know you, but certainly the way I think about things and experience things is not particularly linear, and it's not orderly, and it's not pyramidical, and there are a lot of loops. Most of the nonfiction pieces are basically, just, look, I'm not a great journalist, and I can't interview anybody, but what I can do is kind of, I will slice open my head for you. And let you see a cross-section of just a kind of average, averagely bright person's head at this thing.

And in a way, the footnotes, I think, are better representations of, not really stream-of-consciousness, but thought patterns and fact patterns. How exactly different readers read them — I mean, I've talked to people who wait and read the footnotes at the end, or who do them absolutely the way they're numbered.

I think the only thing for me, the tricky thing with the footnotes, is that they are an irritant, and they require a little extra work, and so they either have to be really germane or they have to be kind of fun to read. (Wallace, "'I'm Not a Journalist'")[5]

Here, Wallace again links his nonlinear way of thinking and writing to the footnote, emphasizing that they allow or reveal "thought patterns and fact patterns." They may actually be, as Patricia Duncker has stated, "the unconscious of the text. It's buried there producing all its dreams because the footnote sometimes contains the text that the author didn't dare to write and those are the best. It's always the nether regions that give you away" (quoted in Jackson 154–5). Rather than act as a chorus to the text, footnotes are often soloists with their own scores and voice.

D. T. Max's *New Yorker* essay of 9 March 2009, "The Unfinished," quotes Wallace as telling his editor that the endnotes satisfy "your request for compression of text without sacrificing enormous amounts of stuff," while adding "a lot more technical/medical verisimilitude." Max then comments that Wallace "was known for endlessly fracturing narratives and for stem-winding sentences adorned with footnotes that were themselves stem-winders. Such techniques originally had been his way of reclaiming language from banality, while at the same time representing all the caveats, micro-thoughts, meta-moments, and other flickers of his hyperactive mind" (Max).

Wallace's fascination with the footnote may have started with his philosophical and mathematical studies. His 1985 senior thesis at Amherst, "Richard Taylor's 'Fatalism' and the Semantics of Physical Modality," plus a seminar on Wittgenstein, introduced him to the philosophical footnote or, more accurately, the footnote in philosophy.[6] Wittgenstein's *Tractatus* may have stimulated his ideas on the value of footnotes as examples of "atomic fact," sharing Wittgenstein's idea that "the world is a mosaic of atomic facts embedded in logical space" (Black 72) which Wallace would elucidate in his work. Wittgenstein's idea that "philosophy is not a body of doctrine but an activity" (4.112) also likely appealed to him.[7] Additionally, Gottlob Frege, one of the pre-Wittgenstein figures studied in Wallace's seminar and a logician as well as mathematician (and cited in *Infinite Jest*), also freely used footnotes that substantiated his arguments or offered self-criticism. Footnote 13, for example, in his essay "On the Foundations of Geometry," soundly criticizes Bertrand Russell (34), while footnote 4 in a later essay with the same title confronts objections to his argument, while simultaneously providing self-criticism (84).[8]

Wallace's concern with clarity is nowhere illustrated more clearly than in his senior thesis on fatalism and the semantics of physical modality, which itself contains forty-seven footnotes. The majority of them are source based, documenting his argument, but several suggest the direction his later footnotes will take: in notes 23 and 31, for example, he apostrophizes, beginning with, "The especially observant and picky reader might eventually notice that many of the formal and semi-formal 'propositions' . . . turn out strictly speaking to be ill-formed under the rules of system J," his own theory.[9] He then becomes self-critical, declaring that he should have introduced his "system J" earlier in the essay but because it is "itself so very new, different, and potentially weird-looking, I have elected to build up to its introduction gradually" (*FTL* 215). The insouciance that came to dominate his later notes is already apparent here. The philosophical footnote, as observed and practiced, offered the opportunity to challenge, explore, and even refute.

Wallace's study of mathematics and symbolic logic, including his history of infinity, published in 2003, provides further context for his use of the footnote. His interest in math at Amherst, more particularly in mathematical logic, initially recalled home: it repeated the vectors, lines, and grids of the Midwest, which he describes in "Derivative Sport in Tornado Alley." Even his athleticism, particularly tennis —"I was extremely comfortable inside straight lines" (8) — he attributed to a "weird proclivity for intuitive math" (4). His detailed, precise thinking allowed him to "induct trends in percentage, thrust, and retaliatory angle" (9) brought about by the wind, which made him a Midwest junior tennis winner.

Wallace's later analysis of mathematical concepts, summarized in *Everything and More: A Compact History of* ∞, actually contains a partial explanation of his footnoting practice. This takes the form of the Axiom of Choice, a mathematical concept discussed late in the book. The idea is part of Set Theory, explained by Wallace in this way: "from any S you can construct a subset S' with a particular property even if you can't specify a procedure for choosing the individual members of S'."[10] This may explain the free-wheeling nature of his footnotes, which follow no set procedures or rules. The Axiom of Choice allows for the digression, divergence, and even humor in his notes. Wittgenstein said of philosophy that "it will signify what cannot be said, by presenting clearly what can be said" (4.115). This applies as well to Wallace and his footnotes, which are analogous to the relationship between a Set S and its Subset S'. His footnotes are subsets of the reality or events he depicts in his primary text, although not necessarily the logical extension of Set S.

Footnote 1 in *Everything and More* encapsulates the Wallace style. It begins with his new sign or sigla IYI, meaning "if you're interested." The note in its entirety conveys the distinctive Wallace method:

> IYI Here's a good example of an IYI factoid. Your author here is someone with a medium-strong amateur interest in math and formal systems. He is also someone who disliked and did poorly in every math course he ever took, save one, which wasn't even in college, but which was taught by one of those rare specialists who can make the abstract alive and urgent, and who actually really talks to you when he's lecturing, and of whom anything that's good about this booklet is a pale and well-meant imitation. (*EM* 2)

The informality and tone immediately ease the reader into complicated ideas. And the IYI designation becomes an aid for the reader because, as Wallace writes, the sign designates "bits of material that can be perused, glanced at, or skipped altogether if the reader wants." Over half the document's footnotes, he adds, "are probably IYI" (*EM* 2). This allows the reader to disregard or study or even laugh at his notes. Footnote 46 in section 2d, for example, reads: "A bit of drollery among math historians is that killing Archimedes was the only truly significant mathematical thing the Romans ever did" (*EM* 87). And he prefers the direct address. Writing that Indian math introduced zero as the tenth numeral and used the familiar goose egg as its symbol, his footnote reads "if you learned in school that the symbol came from the Greek omicron, you got lied to" (*EM* 91).

Wallace's goal is to make math beautiful as he explains the history and concept of infinity with characteristic panache and yet self-criticism. Footnote 4 in section 4 reads: "Sorry about the hideous syntax here; there's no nice way to compress [G. P. de] Roberval" (*EM* 127). Roberval discovered that the tangent of a curve could be "expressed as a function of the velocity of a moving point whose path composed the curve" (*EM* 127). Of Leibniz, who was a lawyer, diplomat, courtier, and philosopher "for whom math was sort of an offshoot hobby," Wallace's note reads "surely we all hate people like this" (*EM* 129). And after a particularly complex sentence explaining differential equations and problems that pertain to the Fourier Series, his note reads: "There's really nothing to be done about the preceding sentence except apologize" (*EM* 164). This engaging, personal tone, almost a dialogue with the reader, runs through most of the 408 footnotes in the 319-page book, contributing to its dazzling and inviting style and suggesting a kind of double consciousness at work: one a high-level articulate exposition of dense mathematical ideas, the other a self-commentary on the very manner of the primary statements.

The footnote for Wallace revises usability theory, replacing an information-based functionality, represented through the standardization of the footnote, with an emotional design that creates an affective reading stemming from a purposeful, if at times confusing, navigation (the unexpected in content and design of his footnotes).[11] An interactive exchange between the note and text often occurs, which incorporates the reader. The unexpected nature of Wallace's footnotes revises their operation while creating a double consciousness for the author or a hypertext for the reader (although Wallace later denied consciously thinking of hypertext in his use of footnotes). Nonetheless, systems logic and rhetoric combine in the footnote. Wallace's interest and study of mathematical logic and the philosophy of language carries over, of course, to his fiction represented in his short stories, *The Broom of the System*, and *Infinite Jest*. The source of his appreciation and application of the footnote derives from his encounters with philosophical writings and math.[12]

Wallace felt that his generation was disconnected from its surroundings. Imagining his readers after *Infinite Jest* appeared, he explained to David Lipsky that the novel reproduced a lot of feelings he and others shared "that *nothing* was connected to anything else."[13] Footnotes confirm or at least illustrate this by (a) not always connecting to the text or (b) sometimes having connections that make sense, although they may not at first be evident. The parallel may be to information systems and their seeming randomness, but they have actual linkage. The footnotes represent entity relationships in systems theory, a kind of neural network that provides a cognitive mapping of the text that simultaneously reconfirms and contrasts with the nonlinear experience of reading and life. This fulfills Wallace's goal in teaching the reader "that he's way smarter than he thought he was" and illustrating that "a good book teaches the reader how to read it" (*ART* 71–2). Footnotes reconnect, in imaginative ways, the reader to the text and the world.

Realizing that his generation's relation to long sustained, linear verbal communication was different and no longer supportable, Wallace structured *Infinite Jest* as an "*attempt* to be mimetic, structurally, to a kind of inner experience" seeking to "create stuff that mirrors sort of neurologically the way the world feels" (*ART* 290).

The footnote for Wallace corroborates, corrects, or criticizes material in the body of the text, whether nonfiction or fiction. And a brief history of the footnote in Wallace's work shows that from its earliest presentation in his first published essay to his last, it possesses a playful if not original role, debating the very content it was meant to confirm as well as questioning the very truthfulness of the claims it was meant to support. One among many examples is footnote 29 in his essay "Big Red Son," the opening essay in the collection *Consider the Lobster*, on the Adult Video News awards in Las Vegas in 1998. Describing the relentless egoism of porn producers, Wallace focuses first on Max Hardcore, a.k.a. Max Steiner, a.k.a. Paul Steiner, né Paul Little. Joining Dick Filth and Harold Hecuba, two experienced porn journalists, in Hardcore's hospitality suite, Wallace overhears how a photo feature of Hardcore might take place on the Las Vegas Strip. Commenting on the absence of irony as Max inflates his ego while describing the nature of the shoot, Wallace footnotes this comment: "He's in the kind of earnest that one imagines Irving Thalberg was always in." Footnote 29 begins with "Yes, this is it: What's so unbelievable is not the extent or relentlessness of porn people's egotism. . . . It's the *obtuseness* of it" (32). The note continues for another two pages.

At other times, the footnotes display an inherent intellectuality that reveals Wallace's blend of knowledge and play, underscored by his love of analytical reasoning. Footnote 6 in his long review of David Markson's *Wittgenstein's Mistress* (thirty-nine footnotes in all), one of Wallace's favorite books, shows that intelligence reigns. The footnote responds to this statement: "The novel's end involves the use, not the mention, of such a message." It reads: "A distinction of Frege, a Wittgenstein-era titan: to mention a word or phrase is to speak about it, w/ at least implicit quotation marks: eg 'Kate' is a four-letter name; to use a word or phrase is to mention its referent: eg Kate is, by default, the main character of *Wittgenstein's Mistress*." [14] Other footnotes in the review quote advertising slogans, reference Beckett, and define words. Commenting on the fact that Wittgenstein never had a mistress because he was gay, Wallace offers this distinction in footnote 10: "Too, 'mistress' conveys the exquisite loneliness of being the linguistic beloved of a man who could not, in emotional practice, confer identity on a woman via 'love'" (*WM* 222).

In the same review, Wallace uses the footnotes to record discoveries and offer literary judgments. In footnote 18, he remarks that tennis balls bouncing all over the place "are about the best macroscopic symbol there is for the flux of atomistic fact" (*WM* 227). In footnote 20, he writes:

> Since I can't find any more graceful place to stick it in, let me invite you, with this line as exemplar, to see another cool formal horizon-expansion Markson effects in *WM* — the mode of presentation is less "stream of consciousness" than "stream of conscious *utterance*"; Markson's technique here shares the associate qualities of Joycean s.o.c. but differs in being "*directed*": at what or whom it's directed becomes the novel's implicit, or anti-, plot, & accounts for a "narrative movement" that's less linear or even circular than spiral. (*WM* 227)

The personal voice again dominates, often self-critical and complaining: footnote 26 begins "this is not my analogy, but I can't think of a better one, even though this isn't all that good, but I see the point & trust you do — it's one of those alarm-bell issues where the narrative voice is clearly communicating to a reader while pretending not to" (*WM* 231). A long, involved, colorful example of such writing concerning a tattoo and the attempt to outrun a 74-car grain train in Decatur, Illinois, follows. The penultimate footnote condenses the energy and liveliness of Wallace's voice. After quoting this passage from *Wittgenstein's Mistress*,

> If I exist, nothing exists outside me
>> But
> If something exists outside me, I do not exist

he comments in footnote 38: "I won't waste anybody's time shouting about what a marvelous inversion of the *Cogito* & Ontological Argument this is" (*WM* 239).

Footnotes on language and grammar also appear in almost every essay. For the son of an English composition teacher, this is not surprising. Footnotes appear that not only define terms but also comment on usage and grammar. His lengthy essay "Authority and American Usage" is a tour de force of what we might call the linguistic-historical footnote. Originally published in 1999 in *Harper's Magazine*, the essay's various and lengthy notes gained as much notoriety as praise. The essay begins with a page-length set of faux pas taken from everyday usage in print and conversation. The unsuspecting reader locates the title of the essay in a forest of microtype. The seventy-two lines of text hardly make sense until Wallace explains that the block of type contains "contemporary boners and clunkers and oxymorons and solecistic howlers and bursts of voguish linguistic methane" (71n7).

The variety of footnotes in this essay provides a microcosm of Wallace's practice. They range from the personal and autobiographical to the self-critical. Footnote 8 is one of the most personal and confessional as he outlines the sources for his obsession with grammar and language. Declaring his bona fide identity as a SNOOT —"SNOOTS know when and how to hyphenate phrasal adjectives and to keep participles from dangling" (70) — he explains that his mother, a teacher of English Composition, is a SNOOT "of the most rabid and intractable sort" and for years she brainwashed him in subtle ways, coughing at dinner when he or his sister made a usage error. He then interpolates his footnote, citing a song on linguistic error that his family would sing on trips. And *then* he provides an asterisk to reveal a further source for the song, writing that surely his note for the note (again in microtype) will be cut by the editor (71n7). It wasn't.

In the preceding footnote, Wallace identifies his role as a college English teacher, mostly lit, but who, when he reads his first set of student papers, turns fanatical, offering a three-week "Emergency Remedial Usage and Grammar Unit, during which my demeanor is basically that of somebody teaching HIV prevention to intravenous-drug users" (70n6). With self-deprecating humor, characteristic of many of his footnotes in general, he writes, "Every August I vow silently to *chill about usage* this year, and then by Labor Day there's foam on my chin. I can't seem to help it" (70n6). But he also admits that any person, especially an adolescent interested in language "is going to be at best marginalized and at worst savagely and repeatedly Wedgied — see *sub*" (74n12).

The footnotes in this extended essay are also historical. Footnote 10, for example, clarifies the importance of Samuel Johnson's dictionary — "the Shakespeare of English usage"— while Henry Fowler's *Dictionary of Modern English Usage* is "the Eliot or Joyce" (73n10). And they are also grammatical, offering details on the correct representation of numbers, when to spell them out or use cardinals (73n11). Mixing grammar with individual anecdote, however, is the best teaching method, he suggests, and Wallace does this in footnote 14. Commenting on how "regular citizens" go to the dictionary "for authoritative guidance," he writes: "There is no better indication of The Dictionary's authority than that we use it to settle wagers. My own father is still to this day living down the outcome of a high-stakes bet on the correct spelling of *meringue*, a bet made on 14 September 1978" (75n14). Citing the date provides an authenticity to the footnote that balances the anecdotal element.

Footnotes in "Authority and American Usage" also critique rhetoric, which, again in microtype, Wallace explains is being used "in its strict traditional sense, something like 'the persuasive use of language to influence the thought and actions of an audience'" (76n15). And Wallace is unabashed in entering some of the more esoteric thickets of linguistics. Explaining the Descriptivists' revolution (language changes constantly, spoken language *is* the language), he says that this is an old claim, at least as old as Plato's *Phaedrus*, and it's specious. He then adds that the "infamous Deconstructionists" have at least debunked the idea that speech is "language's primary instantiation" and follows this with footnote 27, which reads, "(Q.v. the 'Pharmakon' stuff in Derrida's *La dissemination* — but you'd probably be better off just trusting me.)" (84n27). Again, the personal voice joins the critical.

His self-deprecating humor reaches a wonderful crescendo in footnote 32 where, in preparation for a two-page note on the proposition that language is public and that no private language exists, he advises that although the proposition is true "as is interpolatively demonstrated just below, and although the demonstration is persuasive it is also, as you can see from the size of this FN, lengthy and involved and rather, umm, dense, so that once again you'd maybe be better off simply granting the truth of the proposition and forging on with the main text" (87n32). At times, Wallace's enthusiasm for commenting on his own statements is so strong that his interpolations appear in the body of his text, as on page 99. He titles the interpolation "POTENTIALLY DESCRIPTIVIST-

LOOKING EXAMPLE OF SOME GRAMMATICAL ADVAN-
TAGES OF A NON-STANDARD DIALECT THAT THIS
REVIEWER ACTUALLY KNOWS ABOUT FIRSTHAND"
(99). In the commentary, he addresses his own double dialect, the first
SWE, Standard Written English, the product of his "hyper-educated
parents," and the second the "hard-earned Rural Midwestern of most
of my peers" (99). For good measure, a footnote clarifies a point in the
passage.

Eighty-one footnotes supplement "Authority and American Usage,"
followed by three pages of sources "OF CERTAIN STUFF THAT
DOES OR SHOULD APPEAR INSIDE QUOTATION MARKS
IN THIS ARTICLE" (125–6). But what resonates most strongly
throughout the article, in addition to his pointed criticisms, is, again, the
personal, confessional nature of his footnotes. Footnote 42 is particularly revealing because Wallace admits that he has always had difficulty
in ending conversations or asking someone to leave. On occasion, the
situation becomes so "fraught with social complexity" that he gets overwhelmed by trying to sort out "all the different ways of saying it" (97).
What he will do, then, is blank out and say it straight. One consequence
is that he appears rude and abrupt and actually terminates friendships
by his actions. But in this self-commentary and his many footnotes,
Wallace's honesty and personality come through.

Works dealing with philosophy or language are not the only places
where Wallace relies on the footnote. They appear in essays on food,
television, film, and sports. His article on Roger Federer appearing in
the *New York Times* on 20 August 2006 is a case in point. In exciting
narrative prose that contains the history of modern power-baseline tennis, the innate skill of Roger Federer, and the natural power of Rafael
Nadal, there are also references to Aquinas and Leni Reifenstahl. The
seventeen footnotes expand, correct, and modify the various displays of
tennis knowledge. They range from philosophical remarks on the body
to narratives of Roger Federer's relationship with the press and detailed
tennis history.

There are also technical notes dealing with the speed of the top serv-
ers (125–30 mph) and the physics of the topspin. One of the most in-

triguing is footnote 9, an analysis of the math of a speeding serve, with Wallace chiding the reader not to send in corrections to his formula: "If you want to factor in the serve's bounce and so compute the total distance traveled by the ball as the sum of an oblique triangle's two shorter legs, then by all means go ahead — you'll end up with between two and five additional hundredths of a second which is not significant."[15] And there is that constant sense of wonder both in the main article and in the footnotes. The final note, in fact, ponders the randomness of a deity who afflicts a child with cancer (7-year-old William Caines, who conducted the ceremonial coin toss at Wimbledon) *and* creates a gifted Roger Federer playing on center court.

But of course it was the 388 endnotes of *Infinite Jest* that caused the greatest debate, if not furor, over the importance of his annotations.[16] From the beginning Wallace was insistent they remain, winning the battle with his editor over their placement. The first draft of the novel, however, had scattered notes at the bottom of the page; many were added later and soon took the form of endnotes, a breakthrough in his thinking because the integrity of the primary text remained while all additions and discursive sections appeared separately at the back. The transformed footnotes became endnotes of such magnitude that they could not attach themselves to the page. Nonetheless, his editor preferred them as footnotes, although he finally acquiesced.[17]

The endnotes of *Infinite Jest*, headed "Notes and Errata," vary from short, single statements to the extensive filmography of James O. Incandenza (985n24).[18] Some are comic: endnote 41 reads "Intra-O.N.A.N. sobriquet for 'acting as a double agent': similarly w/ 'tripling', and so on" (995). Several are long narratives involving the characters as in endnote 109, which runs for eighteen pages with notes within the note. Inset narratives in endnote 109 include a letter from Avril Incandenza to her eldest child, Orin, and a lengthy set piece of Orin reading old letters and talking to Hallie, offering definitions of words like *samizdat* and postulating, among other things, about the separation of Québec (1011, 1020).

Among the most complex notes is 123, which deals with the calculations and nuances of Eschaton, the complicated game played at the Enfield Tennis Academy involving 400 tennis balls and eight to twelve players. The sentence leading to the note begins: "Practical distribution of total megatonnage requires a working knowledge of the Mean-Value Theorem for Integrals" and ends with the need to understand regressive ratios and "stratego-tactical expenditures" of combatants' military budgets (323). Various formulas and coefficients, supported by graphs, calculus, and ratio theory work together with the narrator — here Pemulis dictates to Inc, declaring, after presenting the illustrated "Halsadick" diagram, that "this fucking *works*. You don't have to crunch out a whole new ratio each time for each Combatant to dole out the ordinance. . . . This is *wicked*. This is fucking *elegant*" (1024n123). He then adds that you can use the Mean-Value time saver "with anything that varies within a (*definable*) set of boundaries and whatnot — like any line, or a tennis court's boundaries, or like maybe say a certain drug's urine-level range" (1024n123), these images of order and measure marking major tensions in the novel.

The range of endnotes in *Infinite Jest* includes the informative, the interpretative, and the narrative. No single format dominates as they record social identity (n131), cultural change (n150), translation (n170), international relations (n177), food labeling (n197), tennis court etiquette (n213), science (n232), transcripts (n234), correspondence (n269, an endnote with its own footnotes), term papers (n304), manifestoes (n324), drugs (notes 355–62), quips (n326), and pronunciation (n374). The final note reads "Talwin-NX —®Sanofi Winthrop U.S." and relates to the last line of page 979, two pages from the end, identifying a drug. Endnotes in *Infinite Jest* fracture, intimidate, layer, expand, frustrate, revise, critique, and support the text. A few provide only bibliographic information: endnote 122 gives details for a Rand McNally map; endnote 317 refers to an actual book that is "wildly expensive" and "not on disk" (1063). Reviewers were overcome, while critics were less than overjoyed.[19]

Brief Interviews with Hideous Men, a collection of footnoted short stories, appeared three years later. They carry forward the method of *Infinite Jest*, footnote 4 in "The Depressed Person," for example, running two-and-a-half pages, footnote 5 occupying six pages. The most abstruse treatment of the footnote appears in the short story entitled

"Datum Centurio," more accurately a series of descriptive entries for a pseudo lexicon of contemporary usage. The narrative is a series of increasingly more complex definitions of the words "date" and "dating" taken from a 600gb DVD produced in 2096. A parody of dictionary-speak, the story expands the language of a dictionary page, updating Borges's "Tlön, Uqbar, Orbis Tertius." The future dictionary's entry on "date" incorporates footnotes and at the bottom of the page a series of usage guides to the pronunciation of words. Semiotic signs substitute for superscript numbers relying on the asterisk, the dagger, and the double dagger. Here, the footnote is abstracted into more symbolic expressions in a story that traces the contextual, etymological, and historical roots of the word "date" as used in the twentieth and twenty-first centuries. The footnotes and usage guide are reproduced identically on all the pages.[20]

The graphic element of Wallace's footnotes suggests a constant, implied reference to scholarly or academic work. The appearance of the page with its visually demanding footnotes generates a vibrant spatial dimension that physically embodies the complexity of the prose, creating what one might label the *mise-en-page*. The visual impact of the page has meaning, although the "academic" is often invested with comedy, wit, or irony. The placement of the footnote either at the bottom of the page or as an endnote affects the reading experience, interrupting one's reading practice to slow the pace and allow time to process ideas.

But did Wallace envision a future for the footnote? "Host," his 2005 article for the *Atlantic Monthly* dealing with California radio host John Ziegler, suggests that he did. Striking in its visual presentation is the uplifting of the footnotes into the text, separated by boxes and referenced by arrows to the margin. This geometric presentation suggests a Cubist rendering of citation and interpretation. The result is an intrusive reading experience where the eye jumps about the text following arrows that lead to one box and then to another. Page 278 illustrates this clearly as the reader finds his eye moving in new directions almost every two or three lines. One box defines a term, while another provides a further definition (re: "mike processing") or offers an additional interpretation. Another box is completely (and enjoyably) procedural, describing the "technical path" Mr. Ziegler's voice travels from the studio to the airways, including the height of the station's main antenna and the monthly electrical bill.

"Host" carries on two levels of discourse, one Wallace's critique of Ziegler's jingoistic and inflammatory attitudes, the other a more nuanced and often technical commentary on the nature of producing and transmitting a talk radio show. What is absorbing is the growing inclusiveness of the box notes and their encroachment on the text. Graphic design seems to overwhelm content: two pages are actually submerged by boxes when three large box notes appear on pages 288 and 289. Page numbers themselves are obliterated by the scale of the boxes, which bleed out into the now reduced or nonexistent margins. One box has the heading "VERY EDITORIAL" as Wallace confronts the question "why is conservatism so hot right now?" (288). He labels another "CONTAINS EDITORAL ELEMENTS" to alert readers.

As late as November 2007, Wallace continued to incorporate footnotes in his nonfiction. A short piece, "Just Asking" in the *Atlantic*, part of a series entitled "The American Idea" with contributions by John Updike, Joyce Carol Oates, Anna Deavere Smith, and others, contains two. "Deciderization 2007 — A Special Report" contains more characteristic annotations. The nine discursive notes are critical and instructive as Wallace outlines his role and reaction as guest editor of *The Best American Essays 2007*. He begins by criticizing his own selection and the assumption that because one might be a good writer, he or she might be a good reader. He quickly shifts to the technical, claiming that acting as "the Decider" is, from the perspective of Information Theory, like Maxwell's Demon or "any other kind of entropy-reducing info processor, since the really expensive, energy-intensive part of such processing is always deleting/discarding/resetting" (xv). Early in the introduction he even admits that he doesn't know what an essay is, a claim footnote 4 expands upon when Wallace outlines the actual process of selection and the role of the in-house Houghton Mifflin series editor: no matter how much I "strutted around in my aviator suit and codpiece calling myself the Decider for BAE '07, I knew it was Mr. Atwan [HM editor] who delimited the field of possibilities" (xvi). Footnotes for Wallace even continue posthumously: they are present in his unfinished novel *Pale King*, including one offering a long history of Lake James in Illinois, where Wallace went for IRS training in May 1985 (Max, "The Unfinished").

Wallace's introduction of the expansive footnote, the footnote as its own recursive discourse, encouraged others to experiment with their use. Mark Danielewski's *House of Leaves* (2000) is a prime example. In that novel, Danielewski actually assigns different typefaces to the different footnotes, each typeface signaling a different character from the novel. Other writers have also recently employed the footnote as narrator, notably Mark Dunn in *Ibid: A Life* (2004, a novel told entirely in footnotes), Junot Díaz in *The Brief Wonderful Life of Oscar Wao* (2007), and the Filipino Canadian novelist Miguel Syjuco in *Illustrado* (2010).

What Wallace revised — Joyce, Nabokov, and O'Brien preceded him — others have continued, although often without his volume or voice. His 2006 article on Roger Federer summarized these features in a single word. Writing about Federer's intelligence as a player, Wallace claimed it "often manifests as angle. Federer is able to see, or create, gaps and angles for winners that no one else can envision" ("Federer").[21] His use of the footnote constantly opened new angles and unexpected "proofs" for the reader, as well as the writer, which are always sources of discovery. Or as Wallace succinctly stated in summarizing his tennis game, "I could think and play octacally" ("Derivative Sport" 9).[22]

Notes

1. His first published footnote appears in his first published essay, "Fictional Futures" (1988). It notes that "C.Y." will be the abbreviation for Conspicuously Young Writers throughout the piece (Wallace, "Fictional Futures" 36).

2. An episteme (*Gr.* for knowledge) is an accepted mode of acquiring and arranging knowledge in a given period uniting various discourses. Foucault in *The Order of Things* showed how a seventeenth-century episteme based on resemblance was replaced by one based on difference in the nineteenth century. He also believed an episteme was the historical a priori ground of knowledge. Wallace's footnotes repeatedly revise or question existing epistemes.

3. Wallace had a heart tattooed with the name "Mary" in it when he was in love with Mary Karr at Syracuse but put a strikeout through it and an asterisk under the heart. Further down he added another asterisk and the name

"Karen," that of Karen Green, the visual artist he married in 2004. A satirical article in the *Onion* describes a (fictional) footnoted, 67-page, seven-chapter "Dear John" breakup letter to his girlfriend of two years, Claire Thompson. Dated 3 February 2003, the letter contained sections with such headings as "Why We Could Never Grow Old Together" and "Ways It — US, The World, And Everything — Has All Changed."

On the history of the footnote see Anthony Grafton, *The Footnote*, and Chuck Zenby, *The Devil's Details*. There is also a chapter on the footnote in Kevin Jackson, *Invisible Forms.*

4. In the spirit of full disclosure, I write this essay in Cabo San Lucas, Mexico, in full view of the cruise ships Wallace criticized. The essay originally appeared in *Harper's Magazine* in January 1996. The passage is from "A Supposedly Fun Thing I'll Never Do Again" 259. Hereafter ASF.

5. Math by contrast was "pyramidical." See Wallace, *Everything and More* 43.

6. Wallace's thesis has recently been published by Columbia University Press as *Fate, Time, and Language: An Essay on Free Will.*

7. Wittgenstein writes that "one name stands for one thing, and another for another thing, and they are connected together. And so the whole, like a living picture, presents the atomic fact" (4.0311). Wallace admired the *Tractatus*, writing to a friend that he thought the first sentence "the most beautiful opening line in western lit." (Ryerson 24). The sentence reads: "The world is everything that is the case." Wittgenstein forms the backdrop to *The Broom of the System* and is partly the focus in Wallace's essay "Authority and American Usage."

8. Wallace cites Frege on page 1072 of *Infinite Jest* at the end of note 324.

9. Wallace, *Fate, Time, and Language* 215. Hereafter *FTL*.

10. Wallace, *Everything and More* 288. Hereafter *EM*.

11. On information based usability theory see Nielsen. On emotional design and the importance of visceral and affective responses see Norman.

12. James Ryerson notes in his introduction to Wallace's republished senior thesis that "philosophy [was] the source of his academic identity" (3). Also see James Ryerson, "Consider the Philosopher," *New York Times* 14 December 2008.

13. Lipsky 273. Hereafter *ART*.

14. Wallace, "The Empty Plenum" 221. Hereafter *WM*.

15. Wallace, "Federer as Religious Experience," *Play Magazine, New York Times* 20 August 2006: 46–51, 80–83. The date of the magazine is September 2006.

16. Of course, Wallace was not the first to use footnotes in fiction. Pope,

Swift, and Sterne used them in their eighteenth-century satires and fiction, and Melville used them in *Moby-Dick*. More recently they appear (in alphabetical order) in Paul Auster's *Oracle Night*, Nicholson Baker's *The Mezzanine*, Beckett's *Watt*, Borges's *Ficciones*, Michael Chabon's *Amazing Adventures of Kavalier and Clay*, John Fowles's *The French Lieutenant's Woman*, Vladimir Nabokov's *Pale Fire*, Laurence Norfolk's *In the Shape of a Boar*, Flann O'Brien's *The Third Policeman*, Manuel Puig's *The Kiss of the Spiderwoman*, and Jose Carlos Somoza's *The Athenian Murders*, to cite only a sample. J. G. Ballard's short story "Notes Toward a Mental Breakdown," collected in *War Fever*, consists of only one sentence in which every word is footnoted.

17. See Steven Moore, "The First Draft Version of *Infinite Jest*," where he writes that the first version was "a patchwork of different fonts and point sizes, with numerous handwritten corrections/additions on most pages, and paginated in a nesting pattern (e.g., p. 22 is followed by 22A–J before resuming with p. 23, which is followed by 23A–D, etc). Much of it is single-spaced, and what footnotes existed at this stage appear at the bottom of pages. (Most of those in the published book were added later.) Several states of revision are present: some pages are early versions, heavily overwritten with changes, while others are clean final drafts. Throughout there are notes in the margins, reminders to fix something or other, adjustments to chronology (which seems to have given Wallace quite a bit of trouble), even a few drawings and doodles. Merely flipping through the 4-inch-high manuscript would give even a seasoned editor the howling fantods."

18. On the filmography see Schwartzburg. The article shows his reliance on Pamela Cook's edited volume *The Cinema Book*, including the format of the filmography itself.

19. A single example is this passage from the *Los Angeles Times* review: "What keeps it [the novel] fresh is Wallace's prose style, a compulsively footnoted amalgam of stupendously high-toned vocabulary and gleeful low-comedy diction, coupled with a sense of syntax so elongated that he can seem to go for days without surfacing.... A Wallace sentence finally draws to a close amid reluctance and relief, like a hitting streak. Half the time you'll want to pitch the damn book clear into the next room, with or without benefit of doorway, but the other half you can actually feel your attention span stretching back out to where it belongs" (Kipen).

20. Wallace, *Brief Interviews* 125–30.

21. Wallace also writes, this time about Ivan Lendl the Czech player, that "he could pull off radical, extraordinary angles on hard-hit groundstrokes" ("Federer"), exactly what Wallace does when he footnotes extremely well-written passages in his essays and fiction. Wallace's footnotes are, in fact the

"hard-hit groundstrokes" of his writing, often unexpected and dazzling. Furthermore, Wallace especially stresses that the surprising angles and shots in top tennis are set up early and planned. Similarly, every footnote is prepared by the text, just as every successful shot of Federer's or Nadal's is set up three, four, or even five shots earlier.

22. Octacally — a mathematical term meaning using the base-8 system as opposed to a binary system. Also, the eight regions into which three-dimensional space is divided by the x-, y-, and z-axes. For Wallace, it was his uncanny ability of admitting the differential complications of wind into his calculations "for the wind put curves in the lines and transformed the game into 3-space" ("Derivative Sport" 9).

Works Cited

Black, Max. *A Companion to Wittgenstein's* Tractatus. Cambridge, UK: Cambridge University Press, 1964. Print.

Cook, Pamela. *The Cinema Book*. New York: Pantheon, 1985. Print.

Frege, Gottlob. *On the Foundations of Geometry and Formal Theories of Arithmetic*. Trans. Eike-Henner W. Kluge. New Haven, CT: Yale University Press, 1971. Print.

Grafton, Anthony. *The Footnote: A Curious History*. Cambridge, MA: Harvard University Press, 1999. Print.

Jackson, Kevin. *Invisible Forms: A Guide to Literary Curiosities*. London: Picador, 1999. Print.

Kipen, David. "Terminal Entertainment." *Los Angeles Times* 11 February 1996. Web.

Lipsky, David. *Although of Course You End Up Becoming Yourself: A Road Trip with David Foster Wallace*. New York: Broadway Books, 2010. Print.

Max, D. T. "The Unfinished." *New Yorker* 9 March 2009. Web.

Moore, Steven. "The First Draft Version of *Infinite Jest*." *The Howling Fantods!* 16 July 2009. Web.

Nielson, Jakob. *Designing Web Usability*. Berkeley, CA: Peachpit Press, 1999. Print.

Norman, Donald. *Emotional Design: Why We Love (or Hate) Everyday Things*. New York: Basie Books, 2004. Print.

Rose, Charlie. "Charlie Rose Interviews David Foster Wallace." *The Charlie Rose Show* 27 March 1997. Web.

Ryerson, James. "A Head that Throbbed Heartlike: The Philosophical Mind of David Foster Wallace." In Wallace, *Fate* 1–35. Print.

Schwartzburg, Molly. "Infinite Possibilities: A first glimpse into David Foster Wallace's library." *Cultural Compass* 8 March 2010. Web.

Wallace, David Foster. "Authority and American Usage." In *Consider the Lobster* 66–127. Print.

———. "Big Red Son." In *Consider the Lobster* 3–50. Print.

———. *Brief Interviews with Hideous Men*. New York: Little, Brown, 2007. Print.

———. *Consider the Lobster and Other Essays*. New York: Little, Brown and Company, 2005. Print.

———. "Deciderization 2007 — A Special Report." In *The Best American Essays 2007*. Series Ed. Robert Atwan. New York: Houghton Mifflin Company, 2007. xii–xxiv. Print.

———"Derivative Sport in Tornado Alley." In *A Supposedly Funny* 3–20. Print.

———. "The Empty Plenum: David Markson's *Wittgenstein's Mistress*." *Review of Contemporary Fiction* 10.2 (1990): 217–39. Print.

———. *Everything and More: A Compact History of* ∞. New York: Norton, 2003. Print.

———. *Fate, Time, and Language: An Essay on Free Will*. Ed. Steven M. Cahn and Maureen Eckert. New York: Columbia University Press, 2010. Print.

———. "Federer as Religious Experience." *New York Times* 20 August 2006. Web.

———. "Fictional Futures and the Conspicuously Young." *Review of Contemporary Fiction* 8.3 (1988): 36–53. Print.

———. "Host." *Atlantic Monthly* April 2005: 51–77. Print.

———. "'I'm Not a Journalist, and I Don't Pretend to Be One': David Foster Wallace on Nonfiction, 1998, Part 1." Interview by Tom Scocca. *Slate* 22 November 2010. Web.

———. *Infinite Jest*. New York: Little, Brown and Company. 2006. Print.

———. "Just Asking." *Atlantic Monthly* November 2007. Web.

———. *Oblivion*. New York: Little, Brown and Company, 2004. Print.

———. "A Supposedly Fun Thing I'll Never Do Again." In *A Supposedly Fun* 256–353. Print.

———. *A Supposedly Fun Thing I'll Never Do Again: Essays and Arguments*. New York: Little, Brown and Company, 1997. Print.

Wittgenstein, Ludwig. *Tractatus Logico-Philosophicus*. Intr. Bertrand Russell. London: Routledge & Kegan Paul, 1958. Print.

Zenby, Chuck. *The Devil's Details: A History of Footnotes*. Montpelier, VT: Invisible Cities Press, 2002. Print.

MOLLY SCHWARTZBURG

CONCLUSION:
OBSERVATIONS ON THE ARCHIVE
AT THE HARRY RANSOM CENTER

THE PAPERS AND library of David Foster Wallace arrived at the Harry Ransom Center at the University of Texas at Austin in late 2009. As curator of the British and American literature collections at the Ransom Center, I have watched these materials travel through the stages of cataloging and housing required to make them available to researchers and students. Before and since they opened in September 2010, the papers have been the source of extraordinary interest among readers, scholars, journalists, and the center's own staff. Like James Joyce, another writer with extensive holdings at the Ransom Center, Wallace inspires a deep intellectual and personal dedication among those who have read his major works, particularly *Infinite Jest*. (By the time this essay is published, many of those readers will also have read *The Pale King*, which will be published about six months from today.[1]) The Ransom Center's Joyce holdings continue to draw a large number of scholars, and we continue to acquire significant Joyce materials almost seventy years after the writer's death. We cannot foresee Wallace's place in the literary canon circa 2078 or how many more Wallace-related collections we will have acquired by that date. What we do know is that scholarly work in the newly opened papers and library will very soon begin to transform the already significant body of scholarship on both Wallace's work and his biography.

The work of special collections might arguably be boiled down to one word: mediation. With our dual mission of providing access to and extending the lifespan of the precious materials entrusted to us, everything we do is an attempt to best protect not just the artifact but also any surviving evidence of its history and contexts that may be of value to researchers. In order to do so, we surround the artifact (such as, in Wallace's case, a dictionary, essay draft, letter, airplane reservation, Alcoholics Anonymous guide, award certificate, etc.) with materials that identify it and protect it (physical material like archival folders and boxes, and digital metadata like database entries, EAD-encoded archival inventories, and MARC catalog records [2]). These materials are provided to researchers and students wrapped in yet another layer, this time one of specialized social conventions (researcher orientations and reading room handling guidelines) inside a reading room that is itself designed specifically to hold the artifact and its reader. Exhibitions, lectures, performances, symposia, blog posts, and other projects undertaken by the center further mediate these materials.

Readers of Wallace, of all writers, are likely to appreciate the interest that mediation holds for special collections librarians and archivists, in both theory and practice. Wallace, of course, had an enduring interest in the idea of mediation. The essay "Host," the footnote filmography in *Infinite Jest*, and the "Author's Note" chapter in *The Pale King* come to mind as the most explicit examples of his own engagement with the concept in published works. The archive paints a fuller picture of this enduring concern. There, for instance, one can see Wallace's extraordinary instructions to copy editors regarding the smallest details of punctuation and wording. Where most writers will defer to a publisher's or magazine's house style, Wallace insists upon precise and often eccentric variants, resulting in texts that gently but repeatedly nudge the reader into remembering the *fact* of reading while he is reading. So, to be explicit about how we at the Ransom Center have and will continue to mediate researchers' access to Wallace's papers and books seems particularly salient.

Archival institutions are always caught in a challenging mediatory tug-of-war. On the one hand, we seek to avoid imposing our expectations of scholarly use upon our cataloging of a particular collection, knowing from experience that researchers will walk in the door with needs we could never imagine, whether they arrive tomorrow or in fifty years. On the other hand, we must mediate the materials to some degree. Even the simplest fact of how one names a collection mediates it, and naming must be at least somewhat consistent across collections — and among institutions — for the naming to be meaningful and useful. In this essay, I will not interpret the collection contents or forecast its likeliest uses by researchers, for doing so will surely doom me to failure. Rather, my effort will be descriptive: to explain the specific ways that Wallace's materials have been mediated since their arrival at the Ransom Center, making explicit what makes possible the moment in which a researcher first encounters a Wallace artifact in our Reading and Viewing Room.

In many ways, the incorporation of the Wallace archive into the Ransom Center collections has been unexceptional. The collection arrived clean and without special conservation concerns. It contained no unusual or unfamiliar media, and standard special collections cataloging and preservation procedures sufficed to catalog and house it. In other ways, the process has been exceptional. General staff interest in the acquisition has been so high that an *Infinite Jest* reading group was organized; eleven readers (more than ten percent of our full-time staff) completed the novel in the summer of 2010. Internal statistics from the last few months show that information on our Web site about Wallace has been tweeted, Facebooked, and blogged more widely than any other topic. Related to this is the great interest in the collection among young researchers, who have already visited the Reading and Viewing Room to study the collection for dissertation and undergraduate thesis work. Wallace was born a decade later than any other writer whose papers are held at the Ransom Center, and the acquisition of his papers literally begins a new generation of collecting at our institution.

Staff directly involved in processing the archive have all expressed a growing personal investment both in the materials and in David Foster Wallace. Those most deeply involved with the collection have generously shared their reflections with me: Megan Barnard, Deputy to the Director for Acquisitions and Administration, who assisted in the acquisitions process and has spent a significant amount of time studying the collection in preparation for exhibitions[3]; Stephen Cooper, Archivist, who processed the manuscripts; and Jacqueline Muñoz, Rare Book Cataloger, who cataloged the library.

Acquisition

The process of acquiring the David Foster Wallace archive officially began when the center's director, Thomas F. Staley, was contacted on behalf of the Wallace estate by Glenn Horowitz, a manuscript dealer who frequently offers writers' archives to the center. But the Ransom Center had been interested in Wallace for many years. His name appeared on what we call "the post-1950 list," which holds the names of about 600 Anglophone writers — living and dead — whose first book was published after 1950, the first editions of whose works we acquire as a matter of policy. These writers are separated into three lists: writers whose papers we hold, writers whose papers we imagine we may acquire some day, and writers whose papers we do not expect to acquire. Wallace was a key name in the second list and had been added to it early in his career.

A few years before Wallace's death, Staley sent him a letter of interest, prompted in part by the striking letters by Wallace that arrived at the center as part of the recently acquired Don DeLillo papers. The letters contain Wallace's thoughtful reflections on the craft of writing and suggested to Staley that this was a writer whose working documents might have much to offer scholars. The connection to DeLillo was itself important. Staley's collection policy is one of networks: each acquisition prompts the search for related collections (fellow writers, agents, publishers, editors, friends, lovers) that will, in turn, prompt similar acquisitions. While each collection acquired is itself a rich resource for researchers, underlying every acquisition is a broader vision: the production of a set of conditions in which researchers can work among multiple collections, unearthing, reconstructing, and reframing intellectual, social, professional, and other networks implicated in multiple collections in combination with one another.

Though Wallace did not respond to the letter, it was the first step in a process that may well have ended with Wallace placing his papers at the center. After learning of the estate's interest, Staley entered into negotiations, and the purchase was completed in the fall of 2009; a shipment of books and manuscripts containing the vast majority of the collection arrived that December. Also included in the purchase was a significant quantity of material relating to Wallace's unfinished novel *The Pale King*. As part of the purchase agreement, the Ransom Center will receive this material after the paperback edition of *The Pale King* has been published. Once it is no longer required by the volume's editor, Michael Pietsch, it will be cataloged and added to the materials that arrived in 2009.

The archive as a whole has strong affinities with the center's holdings far beyond the immediate association with Don DeLillo. Anglophone fiction has long been one of the institution's great strengths, dating from 1957, when Harry Ransom took over directorship of the Rare Books Collection, which was renamed the Humanities Research Center in 1958.[4] The center went from being a good rare book collection to a world-class institution with the 1958 purchase of T. E. Hanley's massive collection of modernist books and manuscripts, which contained major manuscripts of Joyce, Oscar Wilde, D. H. Lawrence, Samuel Beckett, and more. In the decades that followed, the papers or major collections[5] of many American fiction writers arrived, including Edgar Allan Poe, Sinclair Lewis, William Faulkner, John Steinbeck, Carson McCullers, Henry Miller, and Edward Dahlberg. Since Staley's directorship began in 1988, American fiction archives have flourished. A selection of his acquisitions includes the papers of Bernard Malamud, Peter Matthiessen, Norman Mailer, Russell Banks, Tim O'Brien, Jayne Anne Phillips, and Denis Johnson. The center's strong holdings in the manuscripts of experimental fiction writers offer a particular complement to the Wallace acquisition: they include the papers of John Fowles, Ron Sukenick, and Steve Katz, small but rare holdings of Jorge Luis Borges and Thomas Pynchon, and the technologically motivated experiments of Christine Brooke-Rose and hypertext novelist Michael Joyce. Finally, the Ransom Center has a special strength in the personal libraries, complete or partial, of major literary figures including Thomas Hardy, James Joyce, Evelyn Waugh, Virginia Woolf, Ezra Pound, Anne Sexton, Hugh Kenner, Guy Davenport, and Ron Sukenick. As these lists demonstrate, Wallace fits clearly into a number of literary trajectories already represented in the center's holdings.

The staff's first view of the collection came in the form of preliminary lists that broke the collection into five sections: "The Pale King," "Juvenilia," "College and Graduate School Work," "Manuscripts of Published Books," and "Annotated Books." These categories represent a collection that was, like many archival acquisitions, already "curated" before it arrived in Austin. Bonnie Nadell, Wallace's agent, described for the center's blog the experience of gathering the manuscripts together to send them here:

> David left his work in a dark, cold garage filled with spiders and in no order whatsoever. His wife and I took plastic bins and cardboard boxes and desk drawers and created an order out of chaos, putting manuscripts for each book together and writing labels in magic markers. (Nadell)

The selections sent from Wallace's library were likewise the product of hard, careful work. When interviewed for a 2010 *Boston Globe* article about writers' libraries, Nadell explained that more than thirty boxes of Wallace's books were given away after his death; working under a deadline to clear out Wallace's office at Pomona for its new occupant, she and Wallace's widow set aside all the books they could find with Wallace's markings to include in the archive sent to the Ransom Center (Ferhman).

No archive is ever "complete" when it arrives at a repository — nor was there a time when an archive was *ever* complete. The default condition of a writer's working materials is one of partiality and flux; papers and books are always entering and leaving writers' workplaces, living spaces, and their lives. The great care taken to save materials of value to Wallace scholars is clear, and the relatively small size of the Wallace archive belies its immense research value. When I first began working at the Ransom Center, Staley explained to me one of the rules of thumb he had learned over decades of acquisitions: often, ten percent of a collection contains ninety percent of its value. That is, often you will acquire, catalog, and house in perpetuity a large collection in order to acquire a much smaller number of rich materials within it. This rule does not apply to the Wallace acquisition: everyone who has worked with the Wallace collection so far has noted how consistently high its research value is. I have yet to see an item that does not offer significant insight into Wallace's work or life.

The first stage of mediation at the Ransom Center occurred at the standard collection inspection required for all incoming materials, attended by staff volunteers and managed by Stephen Cooper in his role as manuscript accessioner. These brisk, efficient events take place just next to the loading dock so that insect infestations, mold, and other problems can be diagnosed before a shipment comes any further into the building. They also provide curatorial staff with a first peek at an acquisition known only through printed lists and descriptions. Often, the potential research value of the collection is revealed to be even higher than expected.

Every carton is opened and its contents removed, inspected, and replaced (maintaining the original organization of each carton) by staff who have been trained to look for problems. Conservation staff oversee the inspection, answering questions and inspecting smudges, loose dirt, and other questionable tidbits found by the inspectors. Despite the garage conditions described by Nadell, the cartons were free of problems, and we were able to pause to enjoy Christmas-morning–like discoveries. I happened to inspect a carton made up entirely of annotated books, including a stack of beat-up DeLillo paperbacks. My next carton included large butcher-paper–wrapped stacks of hand-annotated computer typescripts, each representing a stage in the composition process of *Infinite Jest*. After everyone who was present had quickly compared our finds and confirmed the collection's condition, public affairs staff selected items to photograph for the upcoming acquisition announcement, and the boxes were taken up to the manuscripts department, awaiting their turn in Cooper's processing workflow.

Processing the Manuscripts

Cooper's first step was to undertake an archival appraisal of the collection's contents — to gain an overall view of what was actually there, what should be transferred to other departments, and what cataloging problems and challenges were likely to arise. Central to this particular appraisal was determining the fate of the three hundred or so books in the collection. Most of these are heavily annotated and many of the annotations are directly related to the composition of Wallace's works. Megan Barnard noted that she came across more than one volume in which a sentence penned in the margins by Wallace appears almost verbatim in one of his essays, and as I looked through the collection, I found lengthy character and concept sketches for *The Pale King*[6] so substantive that if the notes had appeared on a sheet of paper, they would certainly be considered (small) stages of the book's compositional process. In such cases, one might argue that the book *is* a manuscript; its annotations "trump" the published book. We might place such an item in the manuscript collection with other draft materials to ensure that researchers can track all parts of a work's compositional process. But in Wallace's case, this would have meant placing the majority of the books in manuscript boxes — a terribly inefficient method of storage, and one that might skew researchers' interpretation of the volumes and obscure other potential paths of research within that volume and the library as a whole. On top of these problems, any number of books contain annotations related to multiple projects, and deciding which manuscript the book should be stored with would be far too subjective an endeavor. After discussions with me and other colleagues, Cooper separated out almost all of the books to be sent to the book cataloging division. One published volume by Wallace was cataloged as a manuscript: a copy of the hardcover edition of *Infinite Jest* used by Wallace to mark changes for the paperback edition. Issues of the Amherst humor magazine *Sabrina*, which Wallace coedited, are the only other published copies of Wallace's own works that arrived with the collection and likewise are housed as part of the Wallace papers. A handful of annotated proofs of works by Don DeLillo and other writers are similarly housed with the papers, as they are themselves technically manuscripts.

Also central to the Wallace appraisal was the question of whether there was an "original order" to the materials that needed to be preserved. Many writers' materials arrive arranged much — or exactly —

as they were in the writer's home, office, or storage facility.[7] In some cases, there is no conceptual order to this arrangement, while in others, the writer's organizational scheme is present and must be preserved.[8] Upon its arrival, Wallace's collection contained little evidence of Wallace's organizational scheme, such as it was.[9] Drafts of some works are numbered in his hand and some manila folders contain his descriptions of their contents. But it was clear that no overall filing system or other vision of a "whole" could be found. Various items suggest that Wallace's papers had undergone multiple transformations over the years. Cooper noted to me that the folder containing proofs of the *New Yorker* story "An Interval" (1994) was marked in Wallace's hand: "Mary correspondence — unpleasant." In another instance, Cooper was faced with an empty manila folder that read "Emptiness/Closeness Essay" in Wallace's hand on its tab and also read "Harper's Draft — Cruise Essay" on its front in someone else's handwriting.[10]

Knowing that the collection had already been arranged by Nadell and Wallace's widow, Cooper concluded that it was appropriate to group the manuscripts in a different scheme than the one that appeared in the dealer lists. No contextual information was available for the vast majority of the materials, and, as he put it, "original order was never an issue." The new arrangement broke the manuscript portion of the acquisition into three large series, each containing subseries when necessary: "Works," "Personal and Career Related," and "Copies of Works by Don DeLillo."[11] Drafts and correspondence directly pertaining to one work that appeared to be mistakenly grouped with materials relating to another work were moved to the appropriate section of the collection (exceptions were made if such reorganization would break a significant meaningful connection between any objects). Materials related to *Infinite Jest* arrived neatly arranged and needed little intervention, but many of the nonfiction pieces required quite a bit because so many distinct published versions exist. For instance, materials relating to four published versions of the many-titled essay on John McCain (including an audio book) needed some unraveling before they could be arranged and described accurately. Original folders, whether they were marked in Wallace's or others' hands, were housed with the items they had held upon arrival, but binder clips and other damaging fasteners were removed and replaced with white paper folders to preserve the fact of the fastened unit of material.

I asked Cooper to explain the kinds of research involved in arranging the materials and composing the archival inventory (also known as a "finding aid" and available on the Ransom Center's Web site). In order to identify and properly arrange the materials, he depended on a range of printed and online sources. Editions of Wallace's books were required to identify or confirm the order of drafts, and published interviews and biographical essays, such as David Lipsky's 2008 *Rolling Stone* profile and the recently published *Although of Course You End Up Becoming Yourself*, were valuable sources for the narrative components of the finding aid. The bibliographies and other information on Web sites *TheKnow(e):dfw* and *The Howling Fantods!* were likewise essential to all stages of the cataloging process.

When I asked Cooper what set the Wallace project apart from other collections he had processed, he made three points. First, he noted that along with the lack of any original order, the papers contained very little correspondence and none of the personal materials that often arrive mixed together with a writer's professional papers. The collection is compact rather than voluminous, dense rather than sprawling. Second, he noted that the chaotic conditions described by Nadell stood in stark contrast to Wallace's attention to detail on the page. Though his work spaces were disorderly, Wallace's method was "meticulous": extensive revisions from draft to draft and detailed comments to editors and copy editors (some noted by carefully placed sticky notes) stand apart from those of most writers whose papers Cooper has cataloged. Cooper's third observation was that he became fascinated by the self-conscious humor that peppers the comments Wallace wrote to his editors. When we tried to think of similarly funny manuscript collections at the center, I came up only with George Bernard Shaw, but Shaw's sharp knife shares little with Wallace's anxious, yearning marginal humor. Smiley faces, jokes, and self-deprecatory comments pepper the manuscripts at all stages of the publishing process. Even (or perhaps especially) when Wallace was frustrated with his editors (the instruction "stet" appears with great frequency on copyedited drafts), he maintained his sense of humor. Cooper noted the gallows humor in notes written to editors clearly meant to indicate that they were off the mark and in smiley and angry faces written in the margins alongside or in place of comments to editors. It seemed to Cooper that Wallace "just wanted to be liked" by his editors, and that his jokey tone showed the discomfort he felt with his own resistance to his editors, even as he knew he needed to protect his writing from changes he knew were wrong.[12] At the end of our discussion about cataloging the manuscripts, I asked Cooper what he would ask Wallace if he could have a conversation with him. After laughingly saying he would be "too intimidated!" he changed his answer, saying, "I would pick his brain about how someone so smart feels so insecure about such unbelievable writing."

Fully cataloged, the David Foster Wallace papers fill thirty-four archival boxes and eight flat file folders. An inventory is available to researchers around the world on the Harry Ransom Center's Web site.

Cataloging the Books

Jacqueline Muñoz was visibly excited to talk about cataloging Wallace's books. This came as no surprise to me; the two of us had read *Infinite Jest* together during the winter between the acquisition and its public announcement, and both of us had been profoundly moved by the experience (Megan Barnard joined us, but this was her second read of the novel). It had been a long time since our last Wallace conversation, and I was eager to hear all that Muñoz had experienced in working with the books. Cataloging books is very different from cataloging manuscripts. Most importantly, the subjective perspective of the book cataloger is much less visible in the finished product. An archival inventory is a single document that both describes and interprets a manuscript collection. The relatively objective box and folder listing is accompanied by quite a bit of prose, including a biographical sketch and a description of the "scope and contents" of the collection, in which the archivist summarizes the whole and highlights significant items or well-represented works or subjects. These portions of the inventory are written at the end of the process, after the archivist has touched and arranged every item, and they represent his extensive knowledge of the collection. Books, in contrast, are cataloged as individual units, and no overarching narrative description or summary is linked to a discrete collection such as an author's library. The books in Wallace's library are united in only two ways: they are shelved together in the stacks, and every book's call number is followed by a three-letter collection code, "DFW" (all Ransom Center book collection codes are three letters long, and luckily for us, the combination DFW had not yet been used). Because the books arrived in no particular order, as is common with author libraries, they were cataloged and arranged in Library of Congress call number order.

Unlike Cooper, Muñoz did not need to perform an appraisal of the carts of books wheeled into her workspace from the manuscripts division. Because there was no need to catalog the books in any particular order, she said, she skimmed the carts to find the perfect first book. She selected *The Adult Child's Guide to What Is Normal* (HV 5132 F753 1990 DFW): "I picked it because [the *Infinite Jest* characters] Hal and Avril and James are all adult children." The method with this book would be duplicated over and again for another 301 items (mostly by Muñoz, but a handful were cataloged by two other catalogers): the cataloger matches the book with the existing MARC record for the identical item in the Library of Congress catalog and "copy catalogs" that record. Then she customizes the record, adding information in the record's 790 field, "Local Added Entry — Personal Name": this is a custom field that the Ransom Center uses to note a book's previous owner. In the case of Wallace's library, two or three entries were usually made in this field: an entry indicating that the item is part of the David Foster Wallace library; an entry indicating that David Foster Wallace was a previous owner of the book; and an entry indicating that the book is annotated by David Foster Wallace (these latter two entries may appear in books that are not in the David Foster Wallace library). When relevant, the cataloger adds additional entries in the 790 field; for instance, Wallace's *American Heritage Dictionary* (PE 1625 A54 1976 DFW) also notes that his mother, Sally Wallace, was a previous owner (she signed her name on one of the first pages). If a book was inscribed to Wallace, the name of the inscriber is also included in this field.

There are significant limitations to the 790 field, which requires that data be entered using a strictly controlled vocabulary in order to ensure a high return in certain kinds of catalog searches. As a complement to this, the 590 field, or "Local Note," offers a flexible space for a cataloger to describe the special qualities of the book. For instance, in the case of the dictionary, the exact wording of Wallace's mother's signature is noted ("Sally F. Wallace") and David Foster Wallace's annotations are described: "David Foster Wallace's annotations throughout." This field also might contain detailed information about the printed edition (which numbered printing, whether it's the hardcover or paperback, whether the item has a dust jacket, for instance), descriptions and partial transcriptions of inscriptions to Wallace when a book was given by a friend or colleague, and so on.

Small differences in the description may or may not capture the quantity of annotations: sometimes the cataloger notes simply that annotations appeared (meaning the book was not heavily annotated), or that they appeared "throughout" (heavily annotated), and when very few annotations appeared, she notes their page numbers. Different catalogers' styles can be found in the use of the words "markings" and "annotations," which may or may not distinguish between nonalphabetic and alphabetic notations respectively, depending on the cataloger. It would have been impractical to be any more specific than this in the case of Wallace's library: to begin describing the nature of specific annotations would have led to months of work, and the resulting descriptions would not likely fulfill the needs of researchers, the vast majority of whom would need to look at the actual item regardless.[13] Was Muñoz tempted to add specific information? "Absolutely. I wanted to note certain subjects like *Infinite Jest* annotations, but I had to hold back to avoid a critical slant." She noted later in our conversation that reading the notes about *Infinite Jest* that are scattered throughout Wallace's library changed her view of the novel. But one of her favorite items was a book whose annotations seemed to reveal more about Wallace the person than any specific project: it contained quotes from the film *The Matrix* (including, she recalled, the line "His neurokinetics are way above normal"). These annotations seemed to have nothing to do with the book they were in, and Muñoz knew that there was no appropriate justification for noting these annotations without noting every phone number, word list, and doodle in the remainder of the collection. When I asked her the title of the book, she rolled her eyes and said, "I can't remember, and of course it's not noted in the record." She was able to include more detail when handling brief inscriptions, which are often given more detail in rare book records (due to rare book libraries' traditional strength in recording provenance). She was glad to be able to note that Wallace signed his name "D. Wallace, Pop-Buyer" inside his well-annotated copy of Linda Schierse Leonard's *Witness to the Fire: Creativity and the Veil of Addiction* (RC 533 L47 1989 DFW). Over the course of all 302 entries which are included in the University of Texas Libraries online catalog, many such glimpses of Wallace's marginal voice may be found.

Considering the brevity of the book records, some description of Wallace's interactions with his books seems to be in order. First, he seems to have had no qualms about writing in his books. Wallace's library is made up mostly of cheap paperbacks, many purchased used, plus a number of hardcovers that were presumably purchased in that format only because they were not available in paperback. His preferred tool was a felt-tipped pen: black, red, green, blue, pink, and purple ink appear, and though I haven't done a careful study of the subject, the order in which I have named the colors appears to be his order of preference. Often, multiple inks will appear throughout the same volume, frequently on the same page. Pencil and ballpoint pen occur, but rarely. Drink stains (coffee?) appear irregularly throughout the collection. Dog ears are rare, but broken spines are not. Annotations may appear on all pages of a book and the inside covers are frequently covered with markings of all sorts. Within the text block, markings are generally limited to commentaries on the book itself and on-the-fly notes about Wallace's own works in progress; the top margin appears to have been Wallace's favored location for the latter, followed by the bottom margin.

Almost all of the books are marked with some combination of the following: underlined passages and vertical lines in the margins alongside passages; check marks, asterisks, exclamation points, question marks, and circled page numbers; intertextual comments on the character development, plot, themes, and rhetoric of the book being annotated; quotations transcribed from the book (mostly, Muñoz thinks, examples of what Wallace felt was "masterful writing") and lists of page numbers with accompanying notes in the back or front cover of the volume; lists of unusual or obscure, often Latinate words culled from the book and perhaps other sources; character sketches, sentences, phrases, and plot points for Wallace's own works in progress (sometimes dated, sometimes titled); Wallace's name (often "D. Wallace"); pages of reading assigned (presumably for his students); notes about other books; phone numbers, addresses, and directions (I found myself Google-mapping an address written in the back of John McPhee's *Levels of the Game* [GV 994 A7 M3 1984 DFW]); and lengthy inscriptions from friends like Mark Costello and David Markson. Books used for particular purposes (he was assigned to review the book, he had assigned the book to his students, or he was using the book while doing background research for a novel or essay) contain annotations particular to that project.

It is impossible to summarize the range of markings, but just a handful of examples reveal their potential relevance to researchers interested in Wallace's reading habits, writing habits, teaching methods, and personal life. Devil horns and a hairpiece grace the author photographs of Cormac McCarthy and James Crumley respectively. Wallace wrote the dialogue for an entire scene entitled "A Conversation Between a Dying Father and His Child" on the front endpaper of a Paula Fox novel (PS 3556 O94 D47 1984b DFW). A reader can track his growing frustration with an Alice Munro short story in *The Best American Short Stories* (1990) over several pages, culminating with the words "I quit!" written emphatically next to a line drawn to indicate the stopping point (PS 648 S5 B4 1990 DFW). He marked the initials "DFW" in the margins alongside passages that appeared to strike him as relevant to his own personality, in nonfiction and fiction books alike. Most mysterious to me was the repeated use of what looks like the word "Do" at the beginning of one or more notes written in various books; at first, I assumed it was a sort of "to-do" list, but many of the notes do not seem to indicate a "to-do" item. I began to wonder if it was a personal code for a project (much like the marking "IJ" that appears in volumes annotated during that book's composition).

I could go on with countless further examples. No author library at the Ransom Center even approaches Wallace's in the number and richness of annotations, and the effect overall is a bit dizzying (in many such libraries, a single choice annotation is enough to make an author's copy of a book a showpiece for exhibitions and fodder for a scholarly article). At the end of my discussion with Muñoz, I asked her how she had changed over the process of cataloging this extraordinary collection. One of her answers was that the experience had made her want to undertake scholarly research on Wallace — this was the first time she had the urge to do so in her years as a cataloger at the Ransom Center. And she was ready to give *Infinite Jest* a second read.

DFW Mediating DFW

Although the line between Wallace's library and the papers is fuzzy at best, there is a marked difference in the degree to which Wallace is writing for others and for himself in each. A large percentage of the papers show Wallace composing texts he expected to become public in some form, while many of the library's annotations appear to have been intended only for Wallace himself. But even within these more "private" texts, Wallace was in conversation — sometimes with the book he was reading and sometimes with an earlier version of himself (many books contain annotations in two or more different pens). The line between public and private was, of course, a topic of great interest to Wallace himself, and to study the archive of a master of self-consciousness is to wade into murky waters. Throughout the collection are reminders that even after the researcher has gotten past the Ransom Center's many layers of mediation and is face to face with the materials themselves, there is no such thing as an unmediated archive. The best we can do is to make our own mediations apparent; we leave the rest to you.

Notes

1. I note this essay's inevitable belatedness up front, expecting that some of the observations I make here will be superseded by articles published in the coming months by scholars and journalists currently using the Wallace collections in our Reading and Viewing Room and that, over the longer term, the Wallace collections may grow in size and their arrangement may change. In the time since I submitted my first draft to this anthology's editors, *The Pale King* has been published and the Ransom Center has acquired a number of small Wallace-related collections, including a small but significant collection of agent Bonnie Nadell's professional correspondence with Wallace.

2. "Encoded Archival Description" is the current standard used for marking up manuscript inventories in XML for the web; "MAchine Readable Cataloging" is the standard for book records. Both are used by the Library of Congress and most libraries and archives.

3. Barnard has curated three exhibitions from the Wallace archive: two small selections of highlights placed on view in the Ransom Center lobby to mark the acquisition and the collection opening, and a larger selection included in the Spring 2011 exhibition, "Culture Unbound: Collecting in the Twenty-First Century."

4. A detailed account of the Ransom Center's history may be found in Barnard.

5. For readers unfamiliar with archival terminology, the words used here to describe manuscript collections have specific meanings. The words "collection" and "archives" may refer to a broad range of collection types, from a single page of written or typed text to a large gathering of material including drafts of works, correspondence, personal papers, computer disks, computers, books, and so on. Such materials can come from any source — the person who created the materials, a private collector who has gathered individual items relating to a person or subject for many years, a person who received a gift of manuscripts from their creator, and so on. The term "papers" is used only to refer to collections created by the subject of the collection itself — most often, writers' papers are transported directly from the writer's working space to the repository. The similar term "records" refers to the working materials of organizations.

6. These appear, respectively, in Wallace's copies of James Crumley's *The Last Good Kiss* (PS 3553 R78 L3 1988 DFW) and J. M. Coetzee's *Disgrace* (PR 9369.3 C58 D5 2000 DFW).

7. John Fowles's widow recently sent the novelist's writing desk to the Ransom Center to join his archive. At the collection inspection, staff were

surprised — and delighted — to see that the desk was shipped just as he had left it, its drawers filled with pens, typewriter ribbon boxes, memorabilia from Greece and Lyme Regis, a handful of manuscripts and photographs, and a fossilized TicTac candy.

8. Isaac Bashevis Singer's and Don DeLillo's papers are examples of each type respectively. Singer's is a case in which original order was not maintained (or, more accurately, a case in which only documentation of the *fact* of the original order was important to maintain): Singer stored papers by stacking them on the floor of his apartment. The packers shipped box-sized "chunks" of these stacks. The story of unpacking them is often told at the Ransom Center: in the middle of one box sat a tile that had fallen from the apartment ceiling and landed squarely on a stack; Singer apparently never noticed and continued to add papers atop it. To maintain such an arbitrary order would have been to the detriment of scholars' work and would have contributed little information about Singer's writing process. Don DeLillo, in contrast, used a complex personal filing system for the correspondence he sent to the center. When the papers arrived, catalogers saw four discrete sets of correspondence files: files named alphabetically after the letter writer (including a folder for David Foster Wallace), files containing the letters of miscellaneous senders, files of correspondence regarding specific DeLillo works, and files arranged by year. These meaningful groupings remain intact in the Ransom Center archival inventory.

9. Wallace appears to allude to his lack of a filing system in a passage in *Although of Course You End Up Becoming Yourself*. Explaining the editing of the essay "Tennis and Trigonometry" for *Harper's*, he says, "It's pretty good — but *Harper's* changed it a lot. It's real different than what the original is. The original was about math. He made it this really neat essay about failure. I'm really bad at saving stuff. I'm just poorly organized" (Lipsky, *Although* 52). No drafts of this *Harper's* essay appear in the Wallace papers.

10. In an example of chance archival poetry, this empty folder may be found inside its own archival folder, cataloged into the collection on its own as a discrete item.

11. The coming *The Pale King* materials are not included in this arrangement.

12. Cooper's sense of the uniqueness of Wallace's editorial notations has been confirmed in the informal conversations I have had with two copy editors lucky enough to have worked with Wallace, both of whom described the experience as the highlight of their careers. One of them, Martha Spaulding of the *Atlantic Monthly*, wrote to me describing her experience editing the spectacularly complex essay "Host": "We debated very small points of grammar and punctuation at great length, and my clearest memory is that he would say

'Throw me a bone on that' when it was clear we weren't going to reach agreement. Needless to say, I threw him every bone he requested. When it was all over, he sent me a poinsettia. Collaborating with him was the most fun I ever had in 32 years at the *Atlantic*" (Spaulding).

13. Indeed, even months of work would not be enough, considering that the annotations in the 302 books likely number in the thousands. I hope that an enterprising doctoral student with a forward-thinking dissertation advisor might decide to undertake as a dissertation project an online database that thoroughly catalogs the books and their annotations, noting every possible connection to Wallace's own books, essays, and teaching.

Works Cited

Barnard, Megan, ed. *Collecting the Imagination: The First Fifty Years of the Ransom Center.* Austin: University of Texas Press, 2007. Print.

Ferhman, Craig. "Lost Libraries: The Strange Afterlife of Authors' Book Collections." *Boston Globe* 19 September 2010. Web.

The Howling Fantods!. Ed. Nick Maniatis. Web.

Lipsky, David. *Although of Course You End Up Becoming Yourself: A Road Trip with David Foster Wallace.* New York: Broadway Books, 2010. Print.

———. "The Lost Years & Last Days of David Foster Wallace." *Rolling Stone* October 2008: 100–1. Print.

Nadell, Bonnie. "The archives are a window into his mind." *Cultural Compass* 8 March 2010. Web.

Niman, Ryan. *The Know(e).* Web.

Spaulding, Martha. E-mail to the author. 18 October 2010.

NOTES ON CONTRIBUTORS

SAMUEL COHEN is associate professor and director of graduate studies in the University of Missouri's Department of English. He is author of *After the End of History: American Fiction in the 1990s* (University of Iowa Press, 2009), series editor of the New American Canon: The Iowa Series in Contemporary Literature and Culture, and author of two textbooks, *50 Essays: A Portable Anthology*, and *Literature: The Human Experience* (with Richard Abcarian and Marvin Klotz). He is currently at work on a book project, "What Comes Next: Recent American Fiction and the Question of Canon Formation."

DON DELILLO is the author of fifteen novels, including *Falling Man*, *Libra*, and *White Noise*, and three plays. He has won the National Book Award, the PEN/Faulkner Award for Fiction, and the Jerusalem Prize. In 2006, *Underworld* was named one of the three best novels of the last twenty-five years by the *New York Times Book Review*, and in 2000 it won the William Dean Howells Medal of the American Academy of Arts and Letters for the most distinguished work of fiction of the past five years.

DAVE EGGERS is the author of six previous books, including *Zeitoun* and *What Is the What*, and a finalist for the 2006 National Book Critics Circle Award. Eggers is the founder and editor of McSweeney's, an independent publishing house based in San Francisco that produces a quarterly journal, a monthly magazine (*The Believer*), and *Wholphin*, a quarterly DVD of short films and documentaries. A native of Chicago, Eggers graduated from the University of Illinois with a degree in journalism. He now lives in the San Francisco Bay area with his wife and two children.

ED FINN received his Ph.D. in English and American literature from Stanford University in 2011. His dissertation, "The Social Lives of Books: Literary Networks in Contemporary American Literature," extends the arguments made here as it explores the changing relationship between authorial fame and digital reading practices. He edits the "First Person" thread at the *electronic book review* and is a member of the Electronic Literature Directory Working Group and the Stanford Literature Lab research group. He is a 2011–2012 University Innovation Fellow at Arizona State University.

KATHLEEN FITZPATRICK is director of scholarly communication of the Modern Language Association and professor of media studies at Pomona College. She is the author of *The Anxiety of Obsolescence: The American Novel in the Age of Television* and of *Planned Obsolescence: Publishing, Technology, and the Future of the Academy*. She is cofounder of the digital scholarly network MediaCommons (http://mediacommons.futureofthebook.org) and has published articles and notes in journals including the *Journal of Electronic Publishing*, *PMLA*, *Contemporary Literature*, and *Cinema Journal*.

JONATHAN FRANZEN is the author of four novels — *Freedom*, *The Corrections*, *The Twenty-Seventh City*, and *Strong Motion* — and two works of nonfiction, *How to Be Alone* and *The Discomfort Zone*. He lives in New York City and Santa Cruz, California.

PAUL GILES is the Challis Professor of English at the University of Sydney, Australia, and an associate member of the Faculty of English at Oxford University. His most recent books are *The Global Remapping of American Literature* and *Transnationalism in Practice: Essays on American Studies, Literature and Religion*. His essay on David Foster Wallace, "Sentimental Posthumanism," appeared in *Twentieth-Century Literature*, Fall 2007.

HEATHER HOUSER is assistant professor of English at the University of Texas at Austin. She is completing a book manuscript entitled "Eco-Sickness: Environment, Disease, Emotion." Recent essays appear in *American Literature*, *Contemporary Literature*, and *American Book Review*.

LEE KONSTANTINOU is an ACLS New Faculty Fellow in the English Department at Princeton University. He wrote the novel *Pop Apocalypse: A Possible Satire* and is completing a literary history of irony after World War II. His writing has appeared in the *Believer*, *boundary 2*, *io9*, and the *Los Angeles Review of Books*.

DAVID LIPSKY is a contributing editor at *Rolling Stone*. His fiction and nonfiction have appeared in the *New Yorker*, *Harper's*, *The Best American Short Stories*, *The Best American Magazine Writing*, the *New York Times*, the *New York Times Book Review*, and many others. He contributes to NPR's *All Things Considered* and is the recipient of a Lambert Fellowship, a Media Award from GLAAD, and a National Magazine Award. He's the author of the novel *The Art Fair*; a collection, *Three Thousand Dollars*; and the bestselling nonfiction book *Absolutely American*, which was a *Time* magazine Best Book of the Year.

RICK MOODY was born in New York City. He is the author of eight books, most recently *The Four Fingers of Death*. In 1998, Moody received the Addison

Metcalf Award from the American Academy of Arts and Letters. In 2000, he received a Guggenheim fellowship. He lives in Brooklyn, New York.

IRA B. NADEL, professor of English at the University of British Columbia, has published biographies of Leonard Cohen, Tom Stoppard, David Mamet, and Leon Uris. He has also published on Joyce and Ezra Pound. New work involves Philip Roth and Brecht, although not together.

MICHAEL PIETSCH is executive vice president and publisher of Little, Brown and Company, where he acquires literary novels, thrillers, biography, and narrative nonfiction. Some of the writers he has worked with include Martin Amis, Michael Connelly, R. Crumb, John Feinstein, Janet Fitch, Peter Guralnick, Mark Leyner, Rick Moody, Walter Mosley, James Patterson, George Pelecanos, Alice Sebold, David Sedaris, Anita Shreve, Nick Tosches, David Foster Wallace, and Stephen Wright. In 2011, Pietsch published Wallace's incomplete third novel, *The Pale King.*

JOSH ROILAND received his Ph.D. in American Studies from Saint Louis University in 2011. His dissertation, entitled "Engaging the Public: Toward a Political Theory of Literary Journalism," explores the civic significance of literary journalism through various pieces of war reportage. He is currently a SAGES Teaching Fellow at Case Western Reserve University in Cleveland, where he teaches the course "Literary Journalism in America." A version of his chapter was published in *Literary Journalism Studies* 1.2 (Fall 2009).

GEORGE SAUNDERS's political novella *The Brief and Frightening Reign of Phil* was published in 2005. He is also the author of *Pastoralia* and *CivilWarLand in Bad Decline*, both *New York Times* Notable Books, and *The Very Persistent Gappers of Frip*, a *New York Times* children's bestseller. In 2000, the *New Yorker* named him one of the "Best Writers Under 40." He writes regularly for the *New Yorker* and *Harper's*, as well as *Esquire, GQ*, and the *New York Times Magazine*. He won a National Magazine Award for Fiction in 2004, and his work is included in *The Best American Short Stories 2005*. He teaches at Syracuse University.

MOLLY SCHWARTZBURG is the Cline Curator of Literature at the Harry Ransom Humanities Research Center at the University of Texas at Austin. She received her Ph.D. in English and American literature from Stanford University in 2004 and has worked at the Ransom Center since 2006. Recent projects include exhibitions on the Beat Generation, Omar Khayyám, Edgar Allan Poe, and the Greenwich Village Bookshop in the 1920s. She welcomes any and all inquiries about the David Foster Wallace and other literature collections at the Ransom Center.

PERMISSIONS

"All Swallowed Up: David Foster Wallace and American Literature," by Paul Giles, appears courtesy of Paul Giles.

"Informal Remarks from the David Foster Wallace Memorial Service in New York on October 23, 2008," copyright ©2008 by Don DeLillo, reprinted with permission of the Wallace Literary Agency, Inc.

"Getting Away from It All: The Literary Journalism of David Foster Wallace and Nietzsche's Concept of Oblivion," by Josh Roiland, appears courtesy of Josh Roiland.

"Informal Remarks from the David Foster Wallace Memorial Service in New York on October 23, 2008," by George Saunders, copyright ©2008 by George Saunders, reprinted with permission of the author.

"Tribute Written for Wallace Family Memorial Book, 2008," copyright ©2008 by Rick Moody, reprinted with permission of the author.

"An Interview with David Foster Wallace," by David Lipsky, from *Although of Course You End Up Becoming Yourself: A Road Trip with David Foster Wallace*, copyright ©2010 by David Lipsky, reprinted with permission of Broadway Books, a division of Random House.

"*Infinite Jest*'s Environmental Case for Disgust," by Heather Houser, appears courtesy of Heather Houser.

"Foreword to Tenth Anniversary Edition of *Infinite Jest*," by Dave Eggers, from *Infinite Jest* by David Foster Wallace, copyright ©1996 by David Foster Wallace, appears by permission of Little, Brown and Company.

"Becoming Yourself: The Afterlife of Reception," by Ed Finn, appears courtesy of Ed Finn.

"Informal Remarks from the David Foster Wallace Memorial Service in New York on October 23, 2008," by Jonathan Franzen, copyright ©2008 by Jonathan Franzen, reprinted with permission of the author.

INDEX

221; "Incarnations of Burned Children," 16; *Infinite Jest*, xiv, xviii–xx, 10, 13, 16, 17, 23, 25, 42, 47n9, 47n12, 59–69, 72–4, 76–7, 80, 85–6, 90, 91–2, 98–9, 101–3, 104, 113n10, 118–40, 144–7, 156, 159–60, 161, 163–4, 165–6, 168–72, 174n2, 177, 179, 182–3, 184, 191–8, 201, 204n8, 204n10, 210, 216, 217, 219, 221, 223, 226, 232, 233; "It All Gets Quite Tricky," 38; "Joseph Frank's Dostoevsky," 31, 35, 109n9; "Just Asking," 12, 235; "Mr. Squishy," 219; "My Appearance," 18; "Oblivion," 17; *Oblivion: Stories*, xiv, 46n5, 86, 97, 104, 216, 219; "Octet," 93–8, 103; *The Pale King*, xiii, xiv, 77n1, 107n3, 109n12, 110n13, 138, 161, 174n11, 175n15, 241, 242, 245, 246, 248, 257n1, 258n11; "Philosophy and the Mirror of Nature," 14; "Some Remarks on Kafka's Funniness from Which Probably Not Enough Has Been Removed," 43; "The Suffering Channel," 15; *A Supposedly Fun Thing I'll Never Do Again*, xiv, 25, 46n2, 71, 161, 165, 168, 216, 221; "A Supposedly Fun Thing I'll Never Do Again," 29, 31–2, 37, 39, 42–3, 46n2, 47n9, 47n13, 49n16, 49n19, 220, 237n4; "Tennis Player Michael Joyce's Professional Artistry as a Paradigm of Certain Stuff about Choice, Freedom, Discipline, Joy, Grotesquerie, and Human Completeness," 32, 33, 46n2; *This Is Water*, xxin8, 6–7, 25, 35, 43–4, 45n1, 105, 139, 190; "The View from Mrs. Thompson's," 13, 46n2; "Up Simba: Seven Days on the Trail of an Anticandidate," xxiiin8, 28, 29, 36, 38, 46n2, 249; "Westward the Course of Empire Takes Its Way," 68, 69–72, 91, 210

Waugh, Patricia, *Metafiction*, 73–4, 88–9

Wittgenstein, Ludwig, *Tractatus Logico-Philosophicus*, 222

Wood, James, 86–8, 93, 104, 107n5, 108n8, 175n13